THE SENSE OF THE WORLD

The Sense of the World

Jean-Luc Nancy

Translated and with a Foreword
by Jeffrey S. Librett

University of Minnesota Press
Minneapolis
London

The University of Minnesota Press gratefully acknowledges financial assistance provided by the French Ministry of Culture for the translation of this book.

Published by the University of Minnesota Press
111 Third Avenue South, Suite 290
Minneapolis, MN 55401-2520
http://www.upress.umn.edu

Printed in the United States of America on acid-free paper

Library of Congress Cataloging-in-Publication Data

Nancy, Jean-Luc.
[Sens du monde. English]
The sense of the world / Jean-Luc Nancy ; translated and with a foreword by Jeffrey S. Librett.
p. cm.
Includes bibliographical references and index.
ISBN 0-8166-2610-3 (alk. paper)
ISBN 0-8166-2611-1 (pbk. : alk. paper)
1. Values. 2. Aesthetics. 3. Political science—Philosophy.
I. Title.
B2430.N363S4613 1997
194—dc21 97-11889

Contents

Translator's Foreword
Between Nihilism and Myth: Value, Aesthetics, and Politics in *The Sense of the World*

> That which, for itself, depends on nothing, is an *absolute*. That which nothing completes in itself is a *fragment*. Being or existence is an absolute fragment. To exist: the *happenstance* of an absolute fragment.
>
> JEAN-LUC NANCY, *The Sense of the World*

Aesthetics, Politics, and Value Today

Politicization and *aestheticization* impose themselves today as ferociously competing imperatives indistinctly positioned in a realm of uncertain *values*. Both politics and aesthetics are dimensions of the world that are quasi-universally considered—at least to some degree—important or *valuable*. But there is very little consensus on the sense and value of each dimension relative to the other. Conventionally "left" political agendas tend to be compelled to marginalize aesthetic considerations, seeing them as reflecting diverse forms of complacency, resignation, denial, or false universality—in short, ideology. "Right" agendas tend in turn to see the left politicization of culture—as exemplified for the right by, say, the kind of people who admire the work of Robert Mapplethorpe or the supporters of critical museum politics, and so on—as an avatar of the aestheticist-decadent-nihilist erosion of moral and thus also ultimately of political values. Meanwhile, those who speak affirmatively in terms of the autonomy of art become—as the middle of the road—the objects of the shared derision and/or hostility of both left and right. Is politics an absolute that legitimately relativizes aesthetics or vice versa, and in what senses of all these terms? Evidently, even as we pour endless energy into the attempt to adjudicate this very complicated question, we continue to lack a sufficient account of how art and politics actually relate to the distinction between absolute and relative values.[1] That is, we manifestly lack an adequate account of how both this distinction between absolute and relative values and the general notion of value it determines apply to the question of the relation between politics and art.

Where is the recent work of Jean-Luc Nancy—a French philosopher working in the tradition of deconstruction—to be situated within this mêlée over the relative (or absolute) values of art and politics? And what light does his work shed on the terms in which current debates on the subject rage?

In order to answer these questions in what follows—and in doing so to introduce Nancy's recent work to readers in English—I will try to show how Nancy's text approaches the general question of value, and how he specifies his answer to this question in terms of politics and aesthetics. First, Nancy displaces received notions of value by affirming the interruption of the dialectical interplay between absolute and relative values. (The affirmation of this interruption must be understood more positively, I will suggest, as the affirmation of the *absolute of relativization.*) Further, on the basis of this unsettlement of the dialectical opposition between relative and absolute values, Nancy displaces in turn the principal conventional positions on the relative values of politics and aesthetics. It is no longer possible, on the far side of this displacement, to maintain either that—in accordance with autonomous aesthetics—politics pales in the face of the absolute importance of aesthetics (whether the autonomy of the aesthetic be defined in terms of "feeling," "technique," "form," or otherwise), or that—in accordance with an absolute of politicization, be it of left or right inclination—the aesthetic is either an empty triviality or a mere subordinate means to the authoritative reality of politics. Rather, both politics and aesthetics become diverse sites of an experience of intervention whose predominantly audible imperative is the insistence on the assumption of ontoaxiological responsibility for the infinite finitization and absolute relativization entailed by being-in-relation. As such sites of interventional experience, both politics and aesthetics have the status of relative absolutes configured against a ground of absolute relativity.

The Sense of the World and the Question of Value: Between Nihilism and Myth

The best way to show that Nancy's text is indeed an answer—even if a somewhat oblique answer—to the question of *value* is to retrace the determinations of "sense" and "world" with which Nancy begins. The term *value* enters first as a virtual and provisional synonym for *sense.* From this point of departure, Nancy will gradually determine *sense* more specifically as that—infinitesimal and always deferred—dimension of value that makes up the mere *border* between absolute value (as posited by what Nancy will call "mythical" discourse) and relative value, a relative value that always ends up amounting to an absolute absence of value (and this absence is posited by what Nancy appropriately calls "nihilist" discourse).[2] But let us start at the beginning.

The opening gesture of Nancy's book (comprising its first two brief chapters), in which he takes his first step toward the establishment of what he will call the "tautological" relationship between "sense" and "world," consists in the enunciation of the apparent paradox that the sense of the world today is that there is no such thing as either sense or world. The enunciation of this paradox, the subordinate steps of which we are about to retrace, makes it possible for the reader to be apprised from the outset that *The Sense of the World* will be a book about neither the positive presence of sense and world nor their twin absence. Rather, it will be a book about the twilight border *between* the presence and absence of both sense and world. But in what sense is there no longer any sense or any world?

When Nancy begins by stating that there is no more sense left in the world, one is to understand the sense hereby negated principally (but only provisionally) as "supersensous sense," transcendent "meaning," any essential summation of existence that would somehow provide a teleological orientation in terms of absolute values. The loss of sense or meaning is to be understood from the start also as a loss of absolute values. And Nancy explicitly indicates as much when he warns the reader both against the danger of yielding to the temptation to look for a new sense or any "security, identity, certainty" from philosophy conceived as a "distributor of values, worldviews, and . . . beliefs or myths," and also against the opposite danger of insisting on "a nihilistic nonsense."

In his brief second chapter, titled "The End of the World," Nancy goes on to argue that, as a result of the absence of meaning or sense, no more world remains. Here, we are to understand *world* initially (and again only provisionally, for the book means to displace the senses of both *sense* and *world*) as the "sensuous," referential, or factual reality—traditionally the sphere of merely *relative* values—in which this (no longer extant) meaning would normally be taken to be concretized.

Nancy's opening point, then, is quite simply this: if there is no more meaning, then the term *world* can have no meaning. Where meaning breaks down, reference, too, ceases to have meaning. Or in ontological terms: where all possibility (or essence) is lost, reality (or appearance) withdraws also from our grasp, becoming difficult to locate in its turn.[3] Finally, in axiological terms: where there is no absolute value, relative value also ceases to exist.

As Nancy goes on to point out, however, the fact that both meaning and world (knowledge and its object, or "ought" and "is") have disappeared is itself a kind of *fact*, an *experience* whose *reality* cannot be denied. The lack of meaning and world indeed make up our world and, in turn, as the world in which we live, they must have some kind of meaning, although this meaning must be pursued as the ever-indeterminate meaning of a meaningless worldlessness:

> It is this loss that is happening to us. . . . *it is necessary indeed* that there be something like a sense of the world. . . . "being-*toward*-the-world," if it takes place (and it does take place), is caught up in sense well before all signification. . . . if there is being-toward-the-world in general, that is, if there is world, there is sense. . . . "there is something, and that alone makes sense."

In terms of value, the nonsituatability of relative values (or world), which follows from the absence of absolute value (or sense), is what comprises the sphere of relative value (that is, the world) for us in its very absoluteness (as in its sense).

This diachronic series of steps—by means of which Nancy passes in a kind of interpretation of the contemporary historical situation from the negation of sense and world today to the guarded reaffirmation of both world and sense—must be understood as the allegory of a synchronic, *structural* situation. It describes the *mutually (de)constitutive structural interdependence* of (supersensuous, ideal, or absolutely valuable) sense and (sensuous, material, or only relatively valuable) world, even if it describes this interdependence by means of a two-step sequence of events made up of the initial erasure and subsequent reinscription of sense and world. By constating the disappearance of ideal meaning, a disappearance that leaves as its residue a material world devoid of meaning, Nancy simply reduces ideal meaning to the material world. The meaning of the world—the supersensous sense of the sensuous, or the absolute essence of relative appearances—appears as nothing other than the world of mere sensuous appearances. And conversely, if merely by being found to be devoid of meaning the world can come, in turn, to be unsettled in its very appearance, that is, in its sensuous presence and the experience thereof, this is because, in structural terms, the world itself depends on, in other words, is ultimately reducible to, its meaning: relative appearance resides in absolute essence, or sensuality resides in supersensous sense. As Nancy goes on to summarize, "*world* is not merely the correlative of *sense,* it is structured as *sense,* and reciprocally, *sense* is structured as *world.* Clearly, 'the sense of the world' is a tautological expression." The (present-absent) sense of the world is merely the (present-absent) world, while conversely the (present-absent) world is merely the (present-absent) sense of the world. Or, absolute and relative value (de)constitutively depend on each other.

For Nancy, however, there are three principal ways of understanding this tautologically or chiasmatically structured identity of sense and world, and only one of these ways is ultimately tenable:

> The whole question is whether this tautology reduces to the repetition of the same lack of signification in two distinct signifiers (which would amount to nihilism) or whether, instead, the tautology states the difference of the same, through which sense would make world and world would make sense, but quite otherwise than by the returning of a signification.

> What is at stake here is enormous—indeed, it is incommensurable. But one must view it neither as a problem to be solved nor as a discovery to be made. If viewed in this way, it would be pitifully laughable or dangerously paranoid to propose a book titled *The Sense of the World,* in a gesture that was supposed to mean "here is the solution." Neither a problem nor a solution....

In his attempt to elucidate the tautology of world-sense (or value), Nancy means to avoid both "nihilism"—the doctrine of a pure lack of absolute meaning and value—and the deluded proposal of a "solution," which he elsewhere calls "myth"—the proposal of a pure fulfillment of the desire for such absolute meaning and value. Instead, between nihilistic lack and mythical fullness, which are the twin ideological summations of the relativity of (self-)difference and the absoluteness of (self-) sameness, respectively, he will trace out "the difference of the same, through which sense would make world and world would make sense." If what is at stake is nonetheless "incommensurable," and thus in some sense the "absolute" or "absolute value," Nancy's discourse will posit and explore not the total absence or the total presence of this absolute value, but its infinitely deferred approach (that is, this approach, by way of relativization, as the absolute value still to approach itself).

To grasp the precise relationship that obtains between the "difference of the same" and the nihilistic and mythical extremes it must avoid, one must understand that while Nancy posits the necessity of withdrawal from these extremes, he knows that this withdrawal can only be conceived rigorously insofar as one attends to the consequences of its remaining *bordered* by them on either side. Because of the paradoxical logic of the *border*[4]—whereby the border separates two sides only by being on both sides at once (and on neither)—one will continue marginally to participate in both nihilism and myth, even when one has withdrawn from both into the borderline no-man's-land of the "difference of the same."[5]

Nancy determines this intermediate position of world-sense between myth, or the presupposition of a "sense... [conceived as] purely given," and nihilism, as the abyssal figure of a "sense... purely desired," as follows:

> Sense always already given, deposited there as a comprehensive unity (or trap?), or sense not yet attained, fleeing . . . truth: either disposed in accordance with the power of myth or thrown frozen into the bottom of the abyss.
>
> Myth and the abyss are the two postulations or figurations inscribed by philosophy, from the very beginning, as its own limits. Together they form the double border of the opening that philosophy itself wants to be: stating the truth of both, of myth and the abyss, and getting sense going, in the open space, as the very tension, intensity, and extension of the open.
>
> Just as, to those who devote themselves to the abyss (that is, to nihilism), "sense" makes no sense, so to those who live in myth "sense" would doubtless appear to be deprived of sense. Sense makes sense only in the space of philosophy as it ends by opening up the world.

Myth gives itself here to be the myth of the givenness of sense, where givenness implies the groundedness, absolution, and absoluteness of absolute value. In turn, nihilism is taken here to comprise the pure abyss, the yawning mouth of an absolute desire for which all that is given, except itself, is given as only relatively given, that is, as not given. Furthermore, although nihilism is opposed to myth, it is itself a form of myth, insofar as it posits that the only presence is the presence of the purely relative—the null and void—so that the void ultimately becomes the absolute. But neither myth nor nihilism, its specular double, is to be definitively excluded from (or definitively included within) the borders of the discourse of world-sense that itself comprises the border between these extremes. The discourse of world-sense—"philosophy as it ends by opening up the world"—traces the double border between the discourses of the presence and absence of value (as meaningful reality or as presence itself), between the discourses of myth and nihilism, respectively.

In case his discussion of myth and nihilism has not yet made it sufficiently clear that "the sense of the world" as he conceives it is positioned on the edge of *absolute value,* where it withdraws into the nothingness of its *relativization,* Nancy dissolves the remaining unclarity by going on to specify in this context that the sense that opens up the interval between myth and nihilism is nothing other than (a revision of) the "Good" beyond being itself:

> If sense is contemporaneous with philosophy, . . . one ought to ask oneself how it offers itself at the birth of philosophy. There, it bears the name of *agathon:* Plato's "Good," the good or excellence that is to be sought (desired? appropriated?) *epeikeina tēs ousias,* beyond being or essence.
>
> The excellence of the *agathon* is without content: it concerns merely the position beyond essence. . . . The *agathon* is neither any specific "good" nor a "good" in the sense of a "possession." . . .
>
> On this account, already from the very beginning *agathon* names something of ex-istence. . . .
>
> But the *agathon* thus names also sense, as metaphysics produces it, at the junction (conjunction? collision?) of the given and the desired. The gift that anticipates desire, the desire that is guided toward the gift: mutual fulfillment, onto-theo-erotology achieved. Sense is thus the reciprocal and unreserved being-toward-the-other of desire and gift, the systematic adjustment of lack and fullness: the *jouissance* of truth and the truth of *jouissance.*

Like the sense of the world, the *agathon* is situated on the edge of being, where it meets up with its meaning (as with its nonbeing). Both world-sense and *agathon* are *beyond* being, and yet still, in some sense, *are* (or are *in being,* namely, in the being that one paradoxically posits as being *beyond* being). However,

> here . . . disaster strikes. For in order to be *sense* . . . in Plato's terms, the excellence that is qualified by . . . the tension of the mutual aptness of desire and gift—sense cannot be determined as the effectuation of this aptness, as its fulfillment or discharge. A satisfaction that accomplishes and saturates both desire and gift denatures at once both gift and desire. All of the mad, unappeasable tension . . . of the *epeikeina tēs ousias* falls away and is annulled. And this takes place whenever the *agathon* is determined and understood as "Good," whether this "good" be a matter of axiology or possession or both at once. Sense as "good" annuls sense as being-unto-the-other of desire and gift. And doubtless this annulment is already vertiginously involved in the determinations of "desire" and "gift" insofar as they arise out of the preliminary philosophical assignation of the given (the already-given of myth) and the desired (the still-to-come of the satisfaction of Eros). . . .
>
> To think sense as the in-appropriative encounter of desire and gift, as the excellence of the *coming* of the one *toward* the other, this is the task. Thus, neither desire nor gift but, rather, the following: that the desire of the gift should desire essentially not to appropriate its "object," and that the gift of desire should give that which cannot be given and should give no "subject" of an "object."

As the "tension of the mutual aptness of desire and gift," the Good beyond being is always in danger of being resolved or dissolved, either into the image of a satisfaction in which desire would disappear into gift—this would be the mythical (re)solution—or into the negation of any possible satisfaction, whereby gift would disappear into an endlessly self-undoing desire—which would be the nihilistic (dis)solution. Nancy thus situates world-sense, his reinterpretation of the Good of the "being-beyond-being" (or "presence/absence"), precisely in the interstitial space *between* these two extremes of myth and nihilism, in the space of their mutual and endless approach. The Good here is so excessively Good that *Good* would no longer be the word for its incommensurability. To the degree that the Good—the absolute—is neither present (as gift) nor absent (as desire), its absoluteness is relativized. If one regarded it as present, it would become the objective foundation that myth posits for itself, absoluteness itself. If, alternatively, one saw it as absent, one would effect thereby—nihilistically—the infinite relativization and consequent emptying out of value and meaning from within the world of the given. One would be left with either absolute value or the void of value, where the void is dialectically identical with its other insofar as the void is taken as a *given,* as precisely the *absolute* state of affairs. In contrast, when one sees the Good as marked by the undecidability of its presence or absence, at the interrupted center of this dialectical identity, the Good becomes an absolute infinitely relativized by the nonresolution of its presence or absence.[6] Indeed, as "sense of the world," the Good spells out the absolute of infinite relativization: being-in-relation as an ultraethical gift of desire.[7]

Interrupting the Dialectics of the Aesthetic: Beyond Fragmentation and Wholeness

If world-sense is poised between nihilism (or the reduction of the incommensurable to the void of relative values) and myth (the symmetrical elevation of specific relative values into the status of given absolute), what light does this (non)thesis of world-sense shed on the question of the relative values of aesthetics and politics? Does Nancy privilege, for example, aesthetic considerations over political ones as absolute versus relative values? Or the reverse: politics as absolute over aesthetics as relative value? Does he grant them *equal* importance or value? And in what sense? What, in short, does *The Sense of the World* tell us about the relationship between aesthetics and politics in terms of the deconstruction of the opposition between absolute and relative value?

Nancy launches his considerations on aesthetics the same way he launches his thoughts on sense. As we saw above, our own age presents itself as an age of the radical absence of sense. This absence has in turn become our sense. Nihilism, that is, has become our myth. In the face of this situation, Nancy argues that we have both *more* sense than we think we have (we have the myth of our nihilism) and therefore *less* than we think we have (for the way we have of making sense of our world, this myth of our nihilism, is a distortion, an exaggeration, nothing but a myth). To undo this myth of nihilism (or relativism), we have to move again from myth toward nihilism, to reinstate nihilism (or relativism) against its own myth, by reopening the question of the meaning (or absolute) of relativization, that is, the question of the sense of the world.

In an argument that is analogous to this one, in the main chapter of *The Sense of the World* devoted to the category of the aesthetic, "Art, a Fragment," Nancy begins by considering the loss of aesthetic wholeness in favor of an aesthetics of fragmentation, a loss that here corresponds to the loss of sense experienced by the modern West. With respect to this situation, Nancy momentarily entertains and then proceeds to argue against the notion that the modern (and postmodern) aesthetics of fragmentation, which has predominated since the period of romanticism, might have gone so far as to have exhausted its own possibilities, so that a reversal in favor of a renewed aesthetics of wholeness (like a return to meaning) would be in order. The dialectical tension between wholeness and fragmentation concretizes on the level of the aesthetic the tension between myth and nihilism (or absolute and relative) on the level of values in general. For the becoming-autonomous of art in the modern period has meant also the emancipation of art from its subordination to any religion (including the positivistic religion of the given as a fact to be represented); it has meant the tendentially nihilistic affirmation of a relativity no longer directly attached to or dependent on a mythical absolute.[8] From this point of view, the autonomous artwork has been a mere fragment since the inception of autonomous art, a fragment of the absolute totality from which it broke away. In turn, however, the fact that the fragmentary artwork declares its *autonomy* entails that the fragment takes on in one way or another a wholeness, a completeness, and hence an absoluteness that cancels the relativity it was the purpose of the autonomy of art to affirm. The fragmentary work of art falls short of its idea by becoming an alternative absolute:

> Disruption transforms itself... into the gathering of itself into itself of the broken piece. The latter converts its finitude—its interruption, noncompletion, and in-finitude—into finish. In this finish, dispersion and fracturing absolutize their erratic contingency: they *absolve themselves* of their fractal character.

The nihilistic desire of autonomous art, in short, reverses itself into myth.[9]

It follows from this observation that if we have reason to be dissatisfied today with the aesthetics of fragmentation, this is not because the aesthetics of fragmentation has maintained an excessive distance from an original wholeness, in other words, because its relativization has excessively dissolved all sense of absolutes. Rather, precisely the opposite is the case: the aesthetics of fragmentation has never quite installed the fragmentation it intends. Despite its announced intentions it has remained excessively bound up with an absolute totality of which each fragmentary and relative work has functioned, in its very autonomy, as a synecdochic mirror image.

In response to this noncompletion of the modern project of an aesthetics of fragmentation, Nancy proposes to *exacerbate* fragmentation through *the fragmentation of the aesthetic itself*:

> The "fractality" with which we will have to do from this point on—and which [the aesthetics of] fragmentation also announced—is quite different. Instead of the ambiguous end of the fragment, it is a matter of the fraying of the edges of its trace... the frayed access to a presentation,... the in-finity of a coming into presence, or of an *e-venire*.
>
> The event is... the incommensurability of coming to all taking-place, the incommensurability of spacing and fraying to all space disposed in the present of a presentation.... it is *presentation itself*... as fractal ex-position: presentation as fragmentation.

Beyond the absolutization of the relative, in the sense of the totalization of the fragment, or the reifying reinscription of nihilism as myth, Nancy attempts to develop a discourse of the event of fragmentation that entails a fragmentation of that very event, the endless dispersal of its occurrence. Incommensurability—absolute value—is still what is at stake here, but as the incommensurability of the event to itself, in the sense of the absolute difference between its synchronic and diachronic dimensions. Because the event—being self-incommensurate—is absolutely nonselfrelated and hence nonselfrelative, it is precisely not self-absolving or self-absolute but absolutely relative to that which is other than itself. In place of the absolutization of the relative (the fragmentary work), in the sense of its removal from all relation to what is outside of itself or the cancellation of its relativity, Nancy posits absolute relativization. In place of the mythical recuperation of nihilism, the presentation of its desire as a present (or gift) of desire,[10] he posits the exacerbation of nihilism beyond recognition, the fragmentation of its desire across an endless deferral of the arrival of that desire itself. This fragmentation of the aesthetic takes the form of the attempt to stop construing the fragments as dependent on a prior model of the whole, and instead to insist that the whole depends constitutively on its strewn fragmentation.[11]

Does this endless and always incomplete exacerbation and undoing of the aesthetics of autonomous fragmentation simply amount to a more complete aestheticism and thus to a more thoroughgoing denial of the sphere of political meaning than ever before? Alternatively, does this destruction of autonomous art imply, entail, or require the reinscription of art's figures in the contextualizing ground of the political, as has been undertaken in this century already both by Marxism and, within the history of modernism, by the historical avant-garde?[12] Finally, if neither of these two extreme interpretations seems acceptable, what exactly is the relationship between the value of aesthetics and the value of politics in Nancy's work? In order to put ourselves in a position where we can answer these questions, we must take a detour through Nancy's discussion of politics in *The Sense of the World*, highlighting the role of the dialectics of nihilism and myth in that discussion.

Interrupting Political Dialectics: Beyond Both Citizen and Subject

According to the account that Nancy provides in this text (in the chapter "Politics II" below), the two dominant (and mutually supplementary) models of political organization we inherit from Western modernity both construe politics in terms of "self-sufficiency." Nancy calls these dominant models of a politics of self-sufficiency (or autonomy) the models of political citizenship (a tradition extending from Aristotle to Jean-Jacques Rousseau) and political subjecthood (with variants from Plato to Georg W. F. Hegel).

To begin with the first pole, *citizenship* is a way of organizing political participation that is radically exterior, material, and relative (as dialectically opposed to traditional theological conceptions of the absolute political *subject,* which would ultimately stress that the interiority and spirituality of that subject are the touchstones of its absoluteness):

> The citizen is . . . the one who is defined by . . . the sharing of [the] exteriority [of the city]. Citizenship is one or more roles, one or more procedures, a way of carrying oneself, a gait. . . . the citizen is a mobile complex of rights, obligations, dignities, and virtues. These do not relate to the realization of any foundation or end other than the mere institution of the city. . . . the citizen does nothing other than share with his/her fellow citizens the functions and signs of citizenship, and in this "sharing" his/her being is entirely expressed. . . . the city has no deeper *sense:* it is related to no signified other than its own institution, the minimal signified of the city's mere contour, without other "identity," "mission," or "destiny" to conquer or to expand.

But the city always turns out to be incapable of doing without its dialectical other, the inwardness of subjecthood, which it needs in order to ensure the city's identity as *one* city:

> . . . the city as such pushes religion in principle away to the infra- or supracivic spheres, at the risk of proposing a substitute, a "civic religion," which regularly fails, from Pericles to Robespierre, to take charge of the religious demand, that is to say, of the demand for a subjective appropriation of sense. In doing this, the city perhaps betrays that it is in truth untenable and abstract, characterized by that "abstraction without Idea" with which Hegel reproaches Rousseau as with what "destroys the divinity existing in and for itself, its absolute authority and majesty." . . . Even in Rousseau, the word *people* indeed signals the turning point where the citizen, despite every-

> thing, transforms itself into a subject or enters into a relation with the pole of the subject.

Despite and because of its attempt to render itself autonomous, the exteriority of citizenship cannot do without some mode of interiority. Its dispersion cannot do without some unification, some limit protecting it from total evaporation. Its relativity must absolutize itself, its nihilistic tendency give itself (as) a mythology through a self-internalizing self-reflection. In this way, the politics of citizenship, which begins in nihilism and ends in myth, transforms itself into a supplementary politics of subjecthood, which will in turn enact the passage from myth back into nihilism. But let us look briefly at how Nancy characterizes subjecthood here:

> The Subject, in general, in accordance with its structural and genetic law as stated by Hegel, retains within itself its own negativity. It is this, the appropriation and incorporation of a negativity (for example, a becoming, a relation, a spacing), that constitutes a "self" and a "being-self" as such. Thus, the political subject—or politics in accordance with the Subject—consists in the appropriation of the constitutive exteriority of the city (just as, doubtless, reciprocally the city consists in the projection *partes extra partes* of the interiority of the subject). For the space of the city an identity and substantiality are pre- or postsupposed as its principle or end. This identity or substantiality can take the form of the "people" . . . or . . . the "nation," or . . . property or production. And this pre-supposition of the self . . . comes to crystallize identity in a figure, name, or myth. Politics becomes the conduct of the history of this subject, its destiny, and its mission. It becomes the revelation or the proclamation of a sense and of an absolute sense. From then on, there is religion, the assignation of sense as appropriable knowledge.

While the politics of the citizen is the politics of relative values (and ultimately of nihilism or valuelessness), the politics of the subject is the politics of absolute values (or myth). And as the nihilism of citizenship ends up turning to the myth of the subject in order to preserve itself from dissolution, so the myth of the subject requires the annihilation and/or internalization of all that is outside of itself in order to prove its absolute autonomy. Either way, the subject undoes itself: "The totalitarian subject turns out to be suicidal."

Before we look at Nancy's response to this dilemma, let us pause for a moment to ask the following question: in terms of their respective positions within the dialectical identity of nihilism and myth, how do these models of a *politics* of self-sufficiency relate to the principal models of *aesthetic* organization introduced above? As we have just seen, the model of *citizenship* tends first of all, relativistically and hence nihilistically, toward the erosion of any substantial, mythical absolute, yet it tends secondarily also to cancel this movement by attempting to ground itself in just such an absolute term. Its structured fate is therefore analogous to that of *autonomous aesthetics,* the aesthetics of fragmentation. The model of *subjecthood,* in turn, attempts to establish itself on the basis of a myth of an absolute foundation, but this attempt tends to culminate in the nihilistic dispersion of the desired unity of that foundation. The structure of subjecthood, then, is analogous to that of *the religion of art* (or the art of religion: cultic art), the aesthetics of absolute totality, which ends up giving rise *nolens volens* to the secular dispersions of the aesthetics of fragmentation. Having retraced these analogies, let us now look at how Nancy responds to this double political model of citizenship and subjecthood.

Nancy's response to the impossible alternative of this dialectics of the politics of self-sufficiency is to propose in its place a *praxis* of *non-*selfsufficiency. He understands such praxis as the process of the infinite tying, untying, and retying of the social bond. This tying is always midway between the identity of the individual and the identity of the group, on the site of their coalescent disintegration. Rather than focusing on the social bond as *given* (which would yield either a politics where the subject's identity absorbs the individuals into its overarching and substantial interiority or a politics where the citizens' laws hold the separate individuals together by means of formal, external linkages), Nancy attempts to focus on the *giving* (and giving out) of the social bond, on the processes and practices of its (dis)establishment, of the *tying* of its (k)not. These processes and practices comprise the *liminal* site of the intermingling of exteriorities as of interiorities, the place where inside and outside turn toward each other, yet where atomistic individuality and group identity remain in a state of suspension, remain suspended in the process of their de-finition:

> It is the *tying* of the (k)not that must come to the crucial point, the place of democracy's empty truth and subjectivity's excessive sense.

> The (k)not: that which involves neither interiority nor exteriority but which, in being tied, ceaselessly makes the inside pass outside, each into (or by way of) the other, the outside inside, turning endlessly back on itself without returning *to* itself.... The tying of the (k)not is nothing, no *res,* nothing but the placing-into-relation that presupposes at once proximity and distance, attachment and detachment, intricacy, intrigue, and ambivalence. In truth, it is this heterogeneous *realitas,* this disjunctive conjunction, that the motif of the *contract* at once alludes to and dissimulates....
>
> Such a politics consists, first of all, in testifying that there is singularity only where a singularity ties itself up with other singularities, but that there is no tie except where the tie is taken up again, recast, and retied without end, nowhere purely tied or untied.

As the imperative of the incessant and endless tying and untying of social bonds, Nancy's praxis of nonselfsufficiency is so infinitely coalitional (and so infinitely separatist) that it is not assimilable to either the politics of citizenship or that of subjectivity per se. Insofar as it interrupts and exceeds the dialectical oscillation of the models of self-sufficiency, while these models of self-sufficiency in turn exhaust, at least in one dimension, all of political discourse, the proposal of this notion of praxis exceeds the domain of politics. And yet it is not simply apolitical either. Like Nancy's response to the problem of the aesthetics of fragmentation, which in calling for the fragmentation of the aesthetic remained liminally (but only liminally) aesthetic, this response to the dilemma of the politics of self-sufficiency does emphasize one extreme of political discourse, namely, the self-exteriority of citizenship, even if it does so to the point of exaggerating this extreme almost beyond all recognition. The exteriority, the being-in-relation, of citizenship becomes here so excessive that the phrase "citizenship of the world" no longer even covers its sense, except insofar as one understands *world* with Nancy as the *endless* deferral of the place of identity, that is, as *endless* heteronomy, heteronomy that has no final limit in any governing or central autonomy whatsoever. Here, too, as in the fragmentation of the aesthetic, it is a matter of exceeding the transformation of the relative, or the null product of nihilism, into a mythical absolute pure and simple. In order to exceed this transformation, in a gesture of extraordinary subtlety, Nancy affirms absolute relativization: he pushes the negation of value beyond the point of the ideological erection of this negation as absolute value. This means relativizing not only relativization but, above all, the distinction between relativization and absolutization. In terms of the conventionally recognized translatability of "relativization" into "demystification," it means not demystifying demystification alone (and thereby justifying a return to mystification—which is the intellectually lazy and, at best, self-deluding shortcut of all neoauthoritarianisms from late-romantic conservatism to contemporary neoconservatism), but demystifying the *distinction* between demystification and mystification, demystifying demystification and mystification at once.[13] In this way, the relative comes to appear both absolute in its relativity and absolutely relative, while the absolute comes to appear only relatively absolute, relative in its absoluteness.

Agnosticism in Aesthetics and Politics

If Nancy's politics take the form of the withdrawal from (or the step beyond) the politics of self-sufficiency into the praxis of infinite nonself-sufficiency, while his aesthetics require the fragmentation of the aesthetics of fragmentation, then what relation does he finally establish between aesthetics and politics? Which takes priority? Which has greater *value?* Is one to understand Nancy, despite everything, in the final analysis as privileging aesthetic over political considerations (as absolute over relative values), and thus as aestheticizing the political, reducing the latter to the context of the former? After all, is not his notion of a politics of being-in-relation a bit formalist and/or subjectivist, or at best an aesthetics of textuality, given the emphasis on endless tying and untying of (k)nots? Or is one, alternatively, to see Nancy as privileging politics over aesthetics? Indeed, this interpretation, too, has some plausibility. For example, can Nancy not be seen as translating the aesthetics of fragmentation back into an anarchic politics of constant, coalitional (re)configuration of which the fragmentary work of art would be a merely ephemeral and epiphenomenal product, an imprecise and derivative representation? Can one not see him as destroying aesthetics in favor of an anarchic politics of drifting identities?

Finally, however, the fact that both of these suspicions raise themselves at this point with equal (im)plausibility should help us foresee that neither will be borne out by Nancy's text. Whether one reduces art to politics or politics to art, in terms of *value* what one is doing is elevating one term into an object of belief, adopting it as absolute value, while reducing the opposed term to a mere illusory appearance, relegating it to the status of the ultimate (or absolute) nothingness of relative value. In contrast, with respect to both politics and art, as we have seen, Nancy's text can be called *agnostic,* for it knows neither absolute nor relative value as such but positions itself on the border *between* absolute and relative value, that is, between the presence and absence of value, and this with respect to the realms of both aesthetics and politics. He proposes neither an atheism of the aesthetic nor a theism of the aesthetic but its agnosticism (and thereby an atheism more radical than the atheism that is binarily bound to theism)—its endless fragmentation (which implies also its endless and endlessly transient retotalization). And he posits neither a political atheism nor a political theism but a political agnosticism (again, as the most rigorous atheism thinkable)—a praxis of (un)tying, which is neither a positive nor a negative knowledge (for it is not a knowledge at all, but a praxis). In accordance with this liminal aestheticopolitical agnosticism, Nancy rejects the absolute autonomization of art, or "aestheticism," the logic of whose autonomy moreover always requires that it expand itself into the "aestheticization of politics." And he equally rejects the symmetrical absolute of the autonomization of politics, or (what one might call, for the sake of this symmetry) "politicism," whose logic likewise inevitably forces it to absorb the aesthetic into itself through the "politicization of aesthetics." For example, in a passage where Nancy is insisting on the essentially political character of writing as being-in-relation, and where one might therefore be tempted to understand him as undertaking either the politicization of the aesthetic or the reverse, he explicitly distinguishes his gesture from both of these moves:

> Writing is thus political "in its essence," that is, it is political to the extent that it is the tracing out [*frayage*] of the essencelessness of relation. It is not political as the effect of an "engagement" in the service of a cause, and it is not political—qua "literature"—according to either the principle of the "aestheticization of politics" or its inversion into the "politicization of aesthetics." It is indeed necessary to ask in what way literature and, consequently, aesthetics and fiction become involved here, but only after one has

> affirmed the political nature of writing: *the in-finite resistance of sense in the configuration of the "together."*[14]

For Nancy, then, it can no longer be fundamentally a question, as it still was—at least manifestly—for Walter Benjamin in "The Work of Art in the Age of Mechanical Reproduction,"[15] of a choice between (right-wing) "aestheticization" and (leftist) "politicization," as terms whose values we could somehow *compare* with each other to figure out which we valued most or which was most important or, rather, all-important, absolutely desirable "in the last instance." In Nancy's text, this choice no longer appears possible because aesthetics and politics no longer appear there as either local or absolute values in themselves. Rather, both aesthetics and politics are internally structured as the impossible dialectical oscillation between the absolutization of value and its relativization.

The choice, in sum, *within* both aesthetics and politics is the choice between the perpetuation of this dialectical oscillation of absolutization and relativization (under the domination of the absolutization of the relative), on the one hand, and its deconstructive, liminal interruption, on the other hand. That is, on the one hand, there is the dialectical mirror-play between the absolutization of the relative (the designation of some particular relative term or terms as adequate presentation of the absolute) and its dialectical opposite, the relativization of the absolute (in the sense of a *finite* or *relative* relativization). This dialectical opposite is itself, however, merely one *example* of what it opposes, the absolutization of the relative, because it always relativizes in terms of some absolute point of reference in turn, for example, by reducing religion to psychology or history, by reducing psychology to history or history to psychology, by reducing epistemology to aesthetics or rhetoric, by reducing aesthetics to politics or the reverse, and so on and so forth. On the other hand, marginally outside of this dialectic, on and as the border between its two terms, there is relativization "as such," absolute relativization (or infinite finitization), which does not conclude by arriving at any (relative) term, including the nihilistic term of a given, total absence of value or total presence of pure desire. Formulated in a slightly different and more condensed manner: one must finally decide between the merely relative given, which is the object of the subjective principle of absolutization, and the (neither subjective nor objective) relative absolute: absolutizing relativization.

In broaching the fragmentation of the aesthetic and the politics of nonselfsufficiency, Nancy attempts to affirm this latter option of absolutizing relativization. In so doing, he undertakes an endless project, for the interruption of the dialectic between absolutization and relativization through the absolutization *of* relativization also belongs *within* the dialectic it interrupts as the *border* where each term is transformed into its other. The adoption of the option of absolute relativization, for example, on the edges of what we have come to know as art and politics, has no end in sight.

How, then, are we to understand thought as being, in its *beginnings*, a response?

Response is not merely possible, but necessary, when only one sole thought remains, the thought of the "sense of life," and when one must not understand by such a "sense" anything other than life itself (an ingredient that would be the salt of life, a final judgment in the space of which life would find its orientation), but as the a priori formal constitution of living in its nakedness. For this existential formality is constructed, if one may say so, in the form of a response: it makes of the human being this strange living thing that—whatever it does or doesn't do, experiences or doesn't experience, says or leaves unsaid—responds to the world and is responsible for the world.

—GÉRARD GRANEL, "Le monde et son expression"[1]

TO INTRODUCE A SENSE—this task *still remains* to be accomplished, absolutely, although—granted—there is no sense in doing so.

—FRIEDRICH NIETZSCHE, *The Will to Power*[2]

To write, "to form," in the informal, an absent sense. An absent sense (not an absence of sense, nor a sense that would be lacking, potential or latent). To write is perhaps to bring to the surface something like absent sense, to receive the passive impulse that is not yet thought, being already the disaster of thought. Its patience.

—MAURICE BLANCHOT, *The Writing of the Disaster*[3]

She alone arises breast bared in the sense she consumes.

—MATHIEU BÉNÉZET, *Ode à la poésie*[4]

Not long ago, it was still possible to speak of a "crisis of sense" (this was Jan Patocka's expression and Václav Havel has made use of it). But a crisis can always be analyzed or surmounted. One can rediscover sense that is lost, or one can at least indicate approximately the direction in which it is to be sought. Alternatively, one can still play with the fragmentary remains or bubbles of a sense adrift. Today, we are beyond this: all sense has been abandoned.

This makes us feel a little faint, but still we sense (we have the *sense*) that it is precisely this exposition to the abandonment of sense that makes up our lives.

The women and men of our time have, indeed, a rather sovereign way of losing their footing without anxiety, of walking on the waters of the drowning of sense. A way of knowing precisely that sovereignty is nothing, that it *is* this nothing in which sense always exceeds itself. That which resists everything—and perhaps always, in every epoch—is not a mediocre species instinct or survival instinct, but this very *sense*.

In our time, on the one hand, we are exposed to all the risks of the expectation of, or demand for, sense (as on this banner in Berlin, on a theater in 1993: "*Wir brauchen Leitbilder,*" "we need directive images"), all the fearful traps that such a demand sets (security, identity, certainty, philosophy as distributor of values, worldviews, and—why not?—beliefs or myths). On the other hand, we also have the chance to recognize that we are already beyond this expectation and demand, that we are already *in the world* in an unheard-of sense—that is, perhaps, in that unheard-of sense that eternally returns to make itself heard in sense, an unheard-of sense that precedes all senses, and that precedes us, warning and surprising us at once.

To give way to this excess of sense over all appropriable sense, and to disabuse oneself for once of what Claude Lévi-Strauss called "the exhausting quest for a sense behind the sense that is never good sense,"[5] this is what is at stake here, not at all in a skeptical or resigned sense, but as the stake itself of sense, to be understood beyond all sense, but not as arriving from any "beyond" of the world whatsoever.

Those who give way to the demand for sense (which by itself already seems to make sense and to provide some reassurance . . .) demand of the world that it signify itself as dwelling, haven, habitation, safeguard, intimacy, community, subjectivity: as the signifier of a proper and present signified, the signifier of the proper and the present as such. (Those who signify the world still as the sense of an infinite *quest,* or of a passage toward another world, do not change anything fundamental: the final signified remains essentially the same.) For them, the becoming-worldwide [*mondialisation*] of the world, which comprises our element and event—that is, "cosmopolitanism," teletechnics—disappropriates and de-signifies sense, tearing it to shreds.

I will not oppose them here with either a nihilistic nonsense or a "madness" that would oscillate between debauchery and mysticism. Rather, I will suggest that the only chance for sense and its only possible sense reside either this side of or beyond the appropriation of signifieds and the presentation of signifiers, in the very opening of the abandonment of sense, as the opening of the world.

But the "open" is neither the vague quality of an indeterminate yawning nor that of a halo of sentimental generosity. Tightly woven and narrowly articulated, it constitutes the structure of sense qua sense of the world.

The End of the World

There is no longer any world: no longer a *mundus,* a *cosmos,* a composed and complete order (from) within which one might find a place, a dwelling, and the elements of an orientation. Or, again, there is no longer the "down here" of a world one could pass through toward a beyond or outside of this world. There is no longer any Spirit of the world, nor is there any history before whose tribunal one could stand. In other words, there is no longer any sense of the world.[6]

We know, indeed, that it is *the end of the world,* and there is nothing illusory (nor "fin de siècle" nor "millenarian") about this knowledge. Those who strive to denounce the supposed illusion of the thought of an "end" are correct, as opposed to those who present the "end" as a cataclysm or as the apocalypse of an annihilation. Such thought is still entirely caught up in the regime of a signifying sense, whether it proposes itself in the final analysis as "nonsense" or as "revelation." But the same adversaries of the thought of the "end" are incorrect in that they do not see that the words with which one designates that which is coming to an end (history, philosophy, politics, art, world . . .) are not the names of subsistent realities in themselves, but the names of concepts or ideas, entirely determined within a regime of *sense* that is coming full circle and completing itself before our (thereby blinded) eyes.

Thus, those who proclaim, against a supposed "end of history," that "history goes on" are either saying nothing more than this: "we are still there, children are still being born"—which does not yet make any *sense* in itself and without further ado, or at least no sense we would know how to assign—or else they are implicitly committing themselves to a complete rethinking of the concept or idea of "history." If there is an illusion from which one must protect oneself today more than ever, it is the illusion that consists in getting hung up on *words* (history, philosophy, politics, art . . .) as if they were immediately to be equated with *things*. Those who insist obstinately on this illusion—that is, basically on the realism of the idea—reveal by this type of somnambulistic Platonism that they have not yet joined our time or its ends. This applies to the subject of *the end of the world,* which is, in short, the ground plan of the set of *ends* that we are in the process of *traversing* (for we traverse them through the very gesture by which we bring about their ending).

Consequently, when I say that the end of the world is the end of the *mundus,* this cannot mean that we are confronted merely with the end of a certain "conception" of the world, and that we would have to go off in search of another one or to restore another one (or the same). It means, rather, that there is no longer any assignable signification of "world," or that the "world" is subtracting itself, bit by bit, from the entire regime of signification available to us—except its "cosmic" signification as *universe,* a term that for us, precisely, no longer has (or does not yet have) any assured signification, save that of a pure infinite expansion.

One must attempt to envisage in all of its scope—which may well be infinite, namely, infinite in finitude—this *end of the sense of the world,* which is the *end of the world of sense* in which we had—and still have, day by day—all the points of reference we need in order to continue to manage our significations. For otherwise, one cannot but deceive oneself drastically concerning the sense and the range of the word *end* (and of the words *finite* and *infinite*).[7] Or, rather, one will deceive or blind oneself by continuing to endow the word *end* with a determinable sense (annihilation, liquidation), in the name of which one will then carry on disputes deprived not only of rigor, but of all content.

We must therefore think this: it is the "end of the world," but we do not know in what sense. It is not merely the end of an epoch of the world or the end of an epoch of sense because it is the end of an epoch—an epoch as long as the "Occident" and as long as "history" itself—that has entirely determined both "world" and "sense," and that has extended this determination over the entire *world.* Indeed, we cannot even think of what is happening to us as a modulation of the same world or sense.

One could add, as a kind of counterproof or verification: we cannot understand experiences anterior or exterior to the Occident in terms of "world" or "sense" any more than we can understand our own Occidental experiences in these terms. This means neither that it is easy to trace the confines of the "Occident" (for it did not simply begin in the seventh century B.C. in Greece), nor that we can even characterize something or someone as "exterior" to it without being still enclosed within it (whereas, in becoming the "worldwide" world, the world has already begun to subvert this partition between exterior and interior, that is, this distinction between different "worlds" that seemed to us to configure *the* world). Rather, it means at least that if, on the one hand, we cannot simply posit the "other," we cannot, on the other hand, think of it simply as the "same." To make the point with respect to one of the major paradigms of our entire culture: we cannot say of those who live or have lived in accordance with *myth* that their experience is a modulation or modalization of the "sense of the world." For we do not know in what sense they live a "world" and a "sense." For a long time, we believed we could know this, but we have come to recognize now that we cannot have any access to what *we* have designated as the world of myth. In order to treat myth as a possible variant of a "sense of the world," side by side with the variant "logos," it is necessary to confer on the phrase "sense of the world" an extension so broad that it loses itself completely in the most vague generality. That is, it is a total waste of time to try to rediscover, behind the logos that has governed our twenty-five centuries, something like a "mythical" dimension or sense.

In other words, we cannot take the "sense of the world" (or "sense of existence" or "sense of life," and so on) to be a general category and then admit its particular species or modalities, without thereby losing the very *sense* of the expression.

And yet, it is indeed with this loss that we have to do. It is this loss that is happening to us. There is no longer any sense in a "sense of the world": the significations of each of these words, as well as the signification of their syntagma, is caught up in the circling back on themselves of all "occidental" significations, a circling back that coincides with a "becoming-worldwide" that no longer leaves any "outside" and consequently no longer leaves any "inside"—neither on this earth nor beyond it, neither in this universe nor beyond it—with relation to which a sense could be determined. But there is no sense except in relation to some "outside" or "elsewhere" *in the relation to which sense consists.*

There is no longer this "to" of sense: this "to" of the signifying relay or directional sending, the index of this final and/or referential ideality that is at once the signified term and the ultimate goal of an operation of sense.[8] And thus we are deprived of sense in both of these senses, in all senses.

And yet, one is not wrong either—quite the contrary—to protest that *it is necessary indeed* that there be something like a sense of the world (or *some* sense in the world), in the greatest possible generality of the expression, in its most vague, general, and insignificant generality.

Even if this protestation were coming—and it is necessarily coming, it is already there, as one can read every day in the newspapers—only from what one calls a "sentiment," it would still recall us to *sense* in the greatest semantic generality of *sensing.* That is, it would recall us to sense as relation *to* or as *being-toward-*something, this something evidently always being "something *other*" or "something *else.*" Thus, "being-*toward-*the-world," if it takes place (and it does take place), is caught up in sense well before all signification. It makes, demands, or proposes sense this side of or beyond all signification. If we are *toward* the world, if there is being-toward-the-world in general, that is, if there is world, there is sense. The *there is* makes sense by itself and as such. We no longer have to do with the question, "why is there something in general?" but with the answer, "there is something, and that alone makes sense." (To tell the truth, *answer* is not even the word; for, on the one hand, no one has asked for anything, certainly not to come into the world, and, on the other hand, to say "there is something, and that alone makes sense" is perhaps not to make any kind of statement whatsoever.)

World means at least *being-to* or *being-toward* [*être-à*]; it means rapport, relation, address, sending, donation, presentation *to*—if only of entities or existents *to* each other. We have known how to categorize being-*in*, being-*for*, or being-*by*, but it still remains for us to think being-*to*, or the *to* of being, its ontologically worldly or worldwide trait.

Thus, *world* is not merely the correlative of *sense*, it is structured as *sense*, and reciprocally, *sense* is structured as *world*. Clearly, "the sense of the world" is a tautological expression.

The whole question is whether this tautology reduces to the repetition of the same lack of signification in two distinct signifiers (which would amount to nihilism) or whether, instead, the tautology states the difference of the same, through which sense would make world and world would make sense, but quite otherwise than by the returning of a signification.

What is at stake here is enormous—indeed, it is incommensurable. But one must view it neither as a problem to be solved nor as a discovery to be made. If viewed in this way, it would be pitifully laughable or dangerously paranoid to propose a book titled *The Sense of the World*, in a gesture that was supposed to mean "here is the solution." Neither a problem nor a solution, it is a matter simply of accompanying a clarification that already precedes us in our obscurity, much younger and much older than that obscurity: how our world makes sense. (This implies neither that the clarification is simply luminous nor that it is simply successful or happy. But—some *Enlightenment*, yes, why not? As long as it be not preromantic but truly postromantic.)

One can also put it like this: for as long as the world was essentially in relation to some other (that is, another world or an author of the world), it could *have* a sense. But the end of the world is that there is no longer this essential relation, and that there is no longer essentially (that is, existentially) anything but the world "itself." Thus, the world *no longer has* a sense, but it *is* sense.

In this sense, today anew it is precise to say that it is no longer a matter of interpreting the world, but of transforming it. It is no longer a matter of lending or giving the world one more sense, but of entering into this sense, into this gift of sense the world itself is. Karl Marx's concept of "transformation" was still caught up—if not entirely, at least largely—in an interpretation, the interpretation of the world as the self-production of a Subject of history and of History as subject. Henceforth, "to transform" should mean "to change the sense of sense," that is, once again, to pass from having to being. Which means also that transformation is a *praxis,* not a *poiesis,* an action that effects the agent, not the work. The thought of the sense of the world is a thought that, in the course of its being-thought, itself becomes indiscernable from its *praxis,* a thought that tendentially loses itself as "thought" in its proper exposition to the world, a thought that *exscribes* itself there, that lets sense carry it away, ever one step more, beyond signification and interpretation. Ever one step more, and, in the writing of thought, one stroke more *than* writing itself. This, too—and singularly since Marx and Friedrich Nietzsche—is the "end of philosophy": *how the end of the world of sense opens the* praxis *of the sense of the world.*

I would like here to open up an exploration of the space that is common to all of us, that makes up our community: the space of the most extended generality of sense, at once as a distended, desolate extension—the "desert that grows"—and as a broadly open, available extension, one that we *sense* to be an urgency, necessity, or imperative. This common space is infinitely slight. It is nothing but the limit that separates and mixes at once the insignificance that arises out of the pulverization of significations and the nonsignificance or archi-significance encountered by the need of being-toward-the-world. This limit separates and mixes also the most common, most banal of senses—the evident inconsistency of the justification of our lives—and the most singular, the evident necessity of the least fragment of existence as of the world *toward* which it exists.

In more than one respect, the world of sense is culminating today in the unclean [*l'immonde*] and in nonsense. It is heavy with suffering, disarray, and revolt. All "messages" are exhausted, wherever they may seem to arise. Thus reemerges, more imperiously than ever, the exigency of sense that is nothing other than existence insofar as it *has* no sense. And this exigency alone is already sense, with all of its force of insurrection.

Suspended Step

The dialectical risk leaps into view: the risk of drawing from the annihilation of significations the resource of a superior signification.[9] Dialectics is always the process of an oversignification. But here, it is not a matter of signification. It should be a matter of sense insofar as it does not signify, and not because it consists in a signification so elevated, sublime, ultimate, or rarefied that no signifier could ever manage to present it, but, on the contrary, insofar as sense comes before all significations, pre-vents and over-takes them, even as it makes them possible, forming the opening of the general signifyingness [or significance: *signifiance*][10] (or the opening of the world) in which and according to which it is first of all possible for significations to come to produce themselves.[11]

It is not a matter of signification, but of the sense of the world as its very *concreteness,* that on which our existence *touches* and by which it is *touched,* in all possible senses. In other words . . .

(. . . but it is a matter of nothing but that, *other words* . . .)

. . . it is not a matter of signification because it is a matter of a labor (is it a labor? in what sense?) of thought—of discourse and writing—where thought uses itself to touch (to be touched by) that which is not for it a "content" but its *body:* the space of this extension and opening in which and as which it exscribes itself, that is, lets itself be transformed into the concreteness or *praxis* of sense.[12] But one must understand "concrete" here not as designating the mere exteriority of the impenetrable thing or of its "lived" reality: "concrete" designates that the consistence or resistance of which forms the necessary exteriority of a being-*toward*, hence of a being-according-to-sense. Sense is concrete: that is, it is tangible *and* impenetrable (these two attributes mutually imply each other).

Thus, the step of thought remains suspended over this exscription, which both initiates and terminates it. It does not go on to produce significations. It goes on to suffer a touch of sense that is at once its most proper concern (it is itself the sense, the sensible organ of such a touch) and the very place of its expropriation (it does not exhibit the signification of this touch). In both ways, it is *the thing itself:* the sense of the world. "To accede to the thing itself" can no longer mean "to arrive at the constitution of an originary signification," but *to hold the step of thought suspended over this sense that has already touched us.*

The experience in question is not a mystical experience. Rather, no doubt it is the experience of this, that there is no experience of sense if "experience" is supposed to imply the appropriation of a signification—but that there is *nothing other* than experience of sense (and this is the world) if "experience" says that sense precedes all appropriation or succeeds on and exceeds it.

Sense and Truth

That one speaks of sense does not mean that one abandons or disdains the category of truth. But one does shift registers. Truth is being-*such* [*l'être-tel*], or more exactly it is the quality of the presentation of being *such* as such. Sense, for its part, is the movement of being-*toward* [*l'être-à*], or being as *coming* into presence or again as transitivity, as passage to presence—and therewith as passage *of* presence. Coming does not arise out of presentation any more, indeed, than it arises out of nonpresentation.

(Although the etymology of the word *sense* is not clear, one constant is that the word is attached to a semantic family in which one finds, first of all, in Irish, Gothic, or High German, the values of movement, oriented displacement, voyage, "tending toward." According to a German etymologist, it first signifies "the process of carrying-oneself-toward-something.")[13]

The difference can also be accentuated this way: one could attempt to say, by introducing an infinitely delicate distinction, that truth operates, whether it wants to or not, an untenable separation between being as *such* (which it presents) and being as *being*. The separation is untenable because these two determinations are inseparable from one another. But still, truth proceeds to operate the separation. Being as such is being that is assigned in its essence or in the essence in general (for example, in the phenomenon in the phenomenological sense: being whose essence is—to appear). Its truth consists in the tautology "being is" (or the phenomenon appears, or the substance supports, or the occurrence occurs, and so on) that its void renders immediately equivalent to "being is not."[14] Being *as being* is being as the action of the verb "to be," that is, being that "makes" [things] come into presence (and that, consequently, cannot itself be presented). One could say: being as being is the being that phenomenalizes the phenomenon, substantifies substance, or eventualizes the event. Such being is conceivable only by way of an agrammatical transitivity of its verb (an asemantic syntax or unbound binding): one must understand "being *is* the entity" [l'être *est* l'étant] as if "being" functioned in a manner analogous to "making," "producing," or "grounding," even though it cannot be a matter of any such thing.[15] Since being precisely neither "makes" nor "grounds" nor "receives" the entity, it is in *being the entity* [en étant l'étant] that it becomes "being toward entities,"[16] or more exactly, "being in the direction of the entity," or even more exactly, but with an asignificative exactitude, "being *toward* the entity": being is the sense of the entity, or, rather—and because there is not the entity on one side and sense on the other—being is the structure, property, and sense-event of the entity in general.

Thus, *truth allows us to glimpse sense as its own internal difference:* being as such differs from being as being, or *essentia* differs from *esse,* of which it is, however, the truth. In this way, sense is necessarily presented as deferred by truth: deferred by or according to différ*a*nce as invented by Derrida, that is, coming that keeps on coming without arriving, identity whose presence is a precedence and a prepossessing prevention of itself.

(*Praesum* is not "I am there" in the sense of a simple position occupied, given, installed, immobile, and immanent. It is first of all "I precede": it is being in advance of, at the head of [an army, a fleet, a camp], it is commanding, guiding, leading... and sometimes [in Ovid, for example] protecting. In addition, let it be said in passing, the coming into presence can never itself be submitted to any other "guide." *Praeesse* is being in advance, advancing, forging ahead, but it is being in advance of oneself, of one's own "presence," it is being present simultaneously *to* what follows and *to* what precedes as to the proper "self" of a being-present that, however, is never *to itself* except according to the pre-cedence and the pre-vention of the *to*.)

"Neither a word nor a concept," writes Derrida of différ*a*nce.[17] This is, in short, the definition of sense, or better, the sense of sense: to be neither word nor concept, neither signifier nor signified, but sending and divergence, and nonetheless (or even for that very reason) to be a gesture of writing, the breaking [*frayage*] and forcing of an *a* the entire signification and destination of which (in French the *à* [or in English the *to*] of the *a*) is to *exscribe itself:* to go up and touch the concretion of the world where existence makes sense. To this degree, there is no truth of différ*a*nce, or rather, it is the void of its *a*-semantic truth. But this very (non)truth opens (onto) sense.

Truth can consist only, in the final analysis (if there can be such a thing as a final analysis: but the function of truth is to punctuate and to present an end), in the truth of sense. However, the truth as such, considered for itself, is essentially insufficient, it is inconsistent and inconsequential, for as much as it separates and allows to escape being as being from being as such, or being-*toward* from being-*such*.

At the same time, it is only thus that sense can be determined in its truth: as the *différance of truth itself.* In this way, sense and truth belong to each other as much as they diverge from each other, and this divergence itself gives the measure of their mutual belonging. They are necessary to each other, just as they cannot fail to occult each other or to withdraw themselves from each other.

Truth punctuates, sense enchains. Punctuation is a presentation, full or empty, full of emptiness, a point or a hole, an awl, and perhaps always the hole that is pierced by the sharp point of an accomplished present. It is always without spatial or temporal dimensions. Enchaining, on the contrary, opens up the dimensional, spaces out punctuations. There is thus an originary spatiality of sense that is a spatiality or spaciousness before any distinction between space and time: and this archi-spatiality is the matricial or transcendental form of a *world.* In turn, truth is in principle instantaneous (if one wanted to pursue the parallel, one could say that it is the a priori form of a universe, in the literal sense of the gathering-into-one). An ecstasy of truth, an opening of sense.

One is tempted to say further: truth is semantic, sense is syntactic. But one can do so only if one goes on to specify that syntax enchains, enchains itself, involves itself, and carries itself away *across* semantic punctuations—and that these punctuations in turn have value and validity only insofar as each is swept along toward, involved in, and even carried away beyond, the others.

Thus—and this is the example of examples—the sense of the word *sense* traverses the five senses, the sense of direction, common sense, semantic sense, divinatory sense, sentiment, moral sense, practical sense, aesthetic sense, all the way to that which makes possible all these senses and all these senses of "sense," their community and their disparity, which is not sense in any of these senses, but in the sense of that which comes to sense. From touching, from the "mere" contact between two things (as soon as there is something, there are several things, and there is the being-toward of one thing toward the other), all the way to the general, the absolute signifyingness or significance of a world as world, there is one sole coming, the same, never identical, one sole sense presencing (itself) or pre-sensing (itself), that is, deferring (itself) in its very truth. Differing/deferring signifyingness.

Philosophical Style

In this regard, and from the angle I am adopting at the moment, it is a matter of indifference whether truth is determined as *adequatio* or, with Martin Heidegger, as *alētheia:* in both cases, it is a question of presentation. To be sure, this characterization does not quite do justice—indeed, far from it—to Heidegger's analysis of *alētheia* (which itself involves one, as I have indicated, in what I am attempting to call "sense" here). But it is also only by beginning with a certain reservation in principle of the sort I am evoking here that it will be possible to do justice to this *alētheia.*

This reservation concerns the degree to which truth as *alētheia* ("veiling/unveiling"), like all other types of truth, continues to operate in terms of presentation, placing-in-view, exhibition, and manifestation. If sense is, in a sense, still manifest insofar as it is on the surface of the world and nowhere else, insofar as it is the patency or openness [*apérité*] of the world, it is nonetheless not manifest in the mode of a placing-in-view or placing-in-the-light on a scene, display, or monstrance. The opening that it is or that it makes is not frontal: it is a passage through a narrow pass, *praes-entia.* One would be right to say in French that sense is *obvie,* which is in our language a synonym for "evident" (even more, for example, than the English *obvious*), but this would have to be in the sense of *ob-vius,* that which precedes us on the path, that which comes to meet us and which thus opens the path, but which nonetheless does not interrupt the road by the illumination of a revelation. There is no "road to Damascus" for sense—for when such an ecstasy takes place, it offers merely, instantaneously, the void of truth.

More broadly, it is necessary to say that this reservation concerning *alētheia,* along with all other types of truth, is a reservation with respect to the theme and posture of phenomenology in general, including thus also their Heideggerian and other transformations. Without a doubt, this theme and posture opened up to us a new access to the world. They made possible the modern "transcendence" of the world, delineating it as the absolute horizon of sense that is no longer subordinated either to a beyond-the-world or to mere representation (that is subordinated neither to the heavens nor to nature). But, nonetheless, phenomenology does not open us up to that which—in sense and consequently in the world—infinitely precedes consciousness and the signifying appropriation of sense,[18] that is, to that which precedes and surprises the phenomenon in the phenomenon itself, its coming or its coming up. In a sense, phenomenology speaks of nothing but that: appearing. But it still irresistibly convokes us to the pure presence of appearing, to *seeing.* For this reason, despite everything, it does not yet sufficiently touch on the *being* or the *sense* of appearing. This is why, for any phenomenology, that is, definitively for any philosophy that is articulated (expressly or not) around a "subject" of the vision of *phainein,* there remains a proper, immanent/transcendent point of origin for sense, a point with which, consequently, all sense is confounded.[19] Nonetheless, all types of phenomenology, indeed all types of beyond-phenomenology, do not open sufficiently to the coming of sense, to sense as a coming that is *neither immanent nor transcendent.* This *coming* is infinitely presupposed: one does not let oneself be taken in, carried away, or put out of sorts by it.

Indeed, in a certain way, phenomenology, along with any other philosophy that preserves this presupposition, still functions as a protection against—as the maintenance of a distance from—that (sense) which exceeds the phenomenon in the phenomenon itself. Such a distancing makes itself felt in the very particular style of the Husserlian discourse—a style that functions also as an absolute extreme of philosophical discourse, in the impressive and irrepressible inflation of its constitutive rigor, which finally seems to deny itself the right to turn back on precisely what unleashes it. Or, rather, it is in the incessant will to turn back on itself in order to appropriate its own process, in the reduction to the "immanence" of an origin (subject, consciousness) that contains all "transcendence," that phenomenology (and with it, in this sense, philosophy as such, which it indeed completes with ultimate rigor) ensures that it will miss something of the "transcendence" (if one must still speak in such terms) it wants to bring out. It misses the excess or the initial spacing of this "transcendence," which it nonetheless has in view.

But "to miss" is not the right word. For this excess, this exceeding of the origin—and of sense—is not, in any case, to be seized. It is to be received (or "let be") and enacted simultaneously. And this simultaneity requires a completely different gesture of thought, a gesture different even from the most exacting, different even from those that strain most intensely toward the surging forth or surrection of being in its transitivity (for example, as "call" or "event"). To the most extreme of these gestures some value of scintillating phenomenality remains invincibly attached, something in the final analysis like a "miracle of being" that seals its mystery in its very scintillation.[20] But every mystery is a revelation, every revelation a truth, merely a truth. And in the same way, every scintillation of appearance persists in fascinating with the spectacle of an origin. But—one can put it like this: the world is too old; it will offer us its *big bang* only in a laboratory; if its sense is obvious, there, on the road, it is obvious without scintillation, in a trivial manner, like the *trivium,* the crossing point of routes that extend in all directions. Can we think of a triviality of sense—a quotidianness, a banality, *not* as the dull opposite of a scintillation, but as the grandeur of the simplicity in which sense exceeds itself?

One can put it also this way: there is no *epokhe* of sense, no "suspension" of a "naïve thesis" of sense, no "placing in parentheses." The *epokhe* itself is already caught up in sense and in the world. That sense itself is infinitely suspended or in suspense, that suspension is its state or its very *sense* does not prevent but, rather, imposes the condition that there can be no possible gesture of the suspension of sense by means of which one could gain access to the origin of sense as to its end. A different gesture is necessary.

In many regards, this different gesture is what is at stake in contemporary philosophical labor. It responds to this, that archi-constitution must pass by way of its own deconstitution, or that truth must expose itself to sense. This presupposes a different relation of philosophy to its own presentation. Once the possibility of signifying truth is a thing of the past, another style is necessary. The end of philosophy is, without a doubt, first of all a question of style in this sense. It is not a matter of stylistic effects or ornaments of discourse, but of what sense does to discourse if sense exceeds significations. It is a matter of the *praxis* of thought, its *writing* in the sense of the assumption of a responsibility for and to this excess.

All contemporary philosophical advances arise out of this need for another style, another tracing or marking [*frayage*] of sense.[21] This need produced, at first, its most visible and most "dramatic" effect when, from within phenomenology, Heidegger turned away from the style adopted by *Being and Time* and *Kant and the Problem of Metaphysics.* One reads on the first page of the *Beiträge* that the philosophical project undertaken there "must remain distant from all false pretention to a 'work' of the style hitherto in force," for "thought to come is a *process* of thought (*Gedanken*gang)."[22] Thought as process is no longer thought as it was; it engages otherwise with the *praeesse* of presence and its presentation. *Style* is not an "acoustico-decorative" matter, as Jorge Luis Borges said somewhere, but a matter of *praxis,* and therefore also a matter of the *ethos* of both thought and thinker.

This does not mean, however, that the different styles that take their departure here, in Heidegger and then in so many others, consistently represent this *praxis* or *ethos.* Far from it. One now knows, indeed, all too well how this development in Heidegger also became involved, contrary to the style of phenomenology, with the style of an oracular-poetic proffering that leads equally—and in a much more captivating and dangerous way—to a presentation of truth. But this in turn indicates how the question or necessity of style is to be construed: between a constitutive science and an evocative poetry, beyond this face-to-face encounter between a presentation of truth and its identical double, the stake of style or writing configures the space of a tracing [*frayage*] of sense. A space itself traced out [*tracé*] by the passage to the limit of significations, the exscription of thought *into* the world.

It is not a matter of "style." It is not a matter of literary effects (but herein resides everything at stake in what the modern world seeks obscurely in the name of "literature": a sensibility and a sensuality of sense). It is a matter of the revival of a tension internal to all philosophy, a tension that originates with philosophy, and that is the very tension between sense and truth. At its birth or constitution, philosophy distinguished *myth* from itself as an immediate identity of sense and truth (a road of presented, recited sense)—an immediate identity in which philosophy recognized neither sense nor truth. The dislocation of myth projects the two poles of "sense" and "truth" as the two extremities of an implacable tension that is at once a tension between two extremities of style: that of "poetry" and that of "science." Myth itself is without style, that is, it is on the near side of style: the question of exposition does not pose itself when figure and narrative [*récit*] assure its immediate unity. This is, moreover, why the ideal of both poles is the ideal of an absence of style, of an infinitely sober prose that ultimately effaces itself in presentation.

The partitioning and passing out [*partage*] of style or styles—one could say just as well the partitioning and passing out of *voices*—is nothing less than the task of thought that begins with the interruption of myth. It does not stop straining and agitating the space between sense and truth, the internal difference by which philosophical presentation is affected at its origin—where philosophical presentation is nothing other than the occidental mode of being-in-the-world.

By virtue of certain surface effects, and for a certain amount of time, it appeared possible that philosophy would *end up* presenting itself as a reconstituted identity of sense and truth, now in the style of "science," now in the style of "poetry." But the end of philosophy is quite precisely the end of these effects, and the active repetition of the most ancient and the deepest aspects of the tradition: the division of voices, the tension of style as spacing and unsettlement of truth according to truth's own différ*a*nce. The end of philosophy is consequently not the reconstitution of myth — of which romanticism still dreamed — but, rather, renewed tension, the exigency of writing without any ideal or model of "style," turning style against style, "philosophy" against "literature," sense and truth against each other, both of them being "auseinandergeschrieben," to use Paul Celan's untranslatable word.[23]

How the Desert Is Growing

In and as its end, philosophy—or what Nietzsche and Heidegger called "metaphysics"—manifests itself to itself as this tension that exceeds or eludes on its own (passing out of itself, *auseinanderschreibend*) all the assignations of signification to which it has given rise, including the most powerful ones.

It restores itself thus, in Jean-François Courtine's phrase, to its "principled anonymity" (as one knows, "metaphysics" is in the beginning nothing but a taxonomic index in Aristotle's courses) "in making apparent its essentially aporetic, dialectical, or better, diaporematic character."[24] Metaphysics at its end—and here it is phenomenology that says so—declares to itself its own noncompleteability as the end of its nonbeginning, of its properly nonassignable beginning, or (if you like) its in-auguration.

This "inextricable obstacle and disquietude" (*diaporēma*), this *final* (that is to say, also quasi-teleological) noncompleteability means hence:

1. that "philosophy" is finished, always finished qua construction of a signification (representation, figuration, Idea, system of the world, system of principles and ends);

2. that it is nonfinishable, yet not according to the bad infinity of a perpetual reposing of questions that would remain open quite simply because they are badly posed and/or because they pose excessive de-

mands—but, rather, nonfinishable to the degree that the *excessive* or the *badly posed* character of the question is entailed by the demand of signification as such.

To this degree, logical positivism—that other major witness to the "end of philosophy"—was right to disqualify the questions-demands of metaphysics. And since, at least most of the time, positivists do not infer from this disqualification the simple, senseless inanity of the world, they affirm also in their way that sense is beyond signification, beyond in-different truth. But they abandon this affirmation even before having stated it, letting it fall with all of its weight into pragmatism.

Philosophy *in its end* does not let go of this affirmation: it is thus that philosophy touches ceaselessly on its end, reviving and replaying its non-commencement, opening, and tension, which consist in nothing other than this affirmation—before any question whatsoever.

This affirmation—sense beyond all sense, sense in the absence of sense, the overflowing of sense as element of the world or *world as absolute excess of sense*—can be considered tragic, comical, sublime, and/or grotesque. Indeed, it can and should be considered all of these things at once, and the monumental history of European culture is woven of nothing other than these judgments, the proper names of which are: Sophocles, Plautus, Augustine, Dante, Michel de Montaigne, William Shakespeare, Blaise Pascal, Jean-Jacques Rousseau, Friedrich Hölderlin, Victor Hugo, Franz Kafka, James Joyce, Samuel Beckett. When one thinks of it, one begins to imagine that what has been most genial in Europe, and maybe even its very idea of *genius,* arose above all out of a formidable necessity of putting on stage *the sense of sense,* figuring and agitating its masks, its explosions of light, its trajectories, in an intense dramatization the resource of which is the Occident itself as an original obscuring of sense: an interruption of myth and sacrifice, which become what the Occident can henceforth only mime (this is what it says of itself).

No doubt the cycle of dramatic representations is closed. It is not by chance that theater today is without any new fable [*fable*], without *mythos,* having exhausted the total fable (Richard Wagner or Paul Claudel), the modern fable (Bertolt Brecht), the fable of the end of fables (Samuel Beckett). The curtain has fallen on the metaphysical scene, on metaphysics as scene of (re)presentation.

But that which is *played* henceforth in other ways, and on a theater of the world that, quite mistakenly, certain people take to be a vast screen of simulation, while others (at bottom, the same) take it to be a scenario of "disenchantment," that which is played in the formidable drifting and cracking of all the continents—the becoming-worldwide and becoming worldly of the world itself—is anew the sending of an affirmation of the absolute excess of sense. Again, to be sure, it is sublime and grotesque, atrocious and laughable, but it is also already and anew beyond these judgments, beyond these assignations of the sense of sense. Not that everything simply has to be accepted: but the resistance to the unacceptable itself ought to proceed from another sense, from the nude, denuded affirmation—all the more pointed and exigent—of the sense of the world as world. The end of philosophy, the task of thought.

The task of being-toward-the-world. Maybe it is still true to say that "the desert is growing." However, the curtain has fallen on the luxuriances and fertilities by comparison with which our "desert" could be measured. Often, too, we have learned the extent to which these superb oases of the legend of the centuries have merely covered up enslaved misery and amounted in the end to little more than the fruits of our nostalgia for a golden age. The growing of the desert could indeed unveil for us an unknown space, an unknown, excessive aridity of the sources of sense. The end of sources, the beginning of the dry excess of sense. Maybe nothing will grow but this drought, and it is this drought that will carry us. And maybe it will be overturned by something else: a major economic crisis, a collapse of States, a world conflict—East-West or North-South (or both of them crossed)—great genetic or ecological mutations and manipulations, discoveries in space, sudden progress in one science, or the exhaustion of several cultures. But the unforeseeable matters little. What is not foreseeable but *already* present, it seems, is that there will no longer be any "reason in history" or "salvation of the human race." No more *parousia,* in short, no more present, attested sense (*if there ever was such a thing*), but a completely different eschatology, another extremity, another excess of sense.

If ever things were really different: for of course a different history is at stake and one that will make us reread our entire history. No longer the directional and signifying history of a sense that unfolds and redeems itself, but an intermittent history, conjectural and reticulated, traversed by pulsations rather than by flux. No longer the sense of history, but a history of sense—and yet, at the same time, the recasting of an infinite liberation. And this history, our history, our *coming* of sense, is not coming to conclude a development or extend it further, but, rather, to repeat, to replay the multiple chances of what the other history, occidental history, at once set into motion and dissimulated: a permanent excess or absenting of sense. Metaphysics and ontotheology, whatever their surface effects may have been, have never truly attempted to fill up this excessive absence. Rather, they have acknowledged it—in every case, and against their wills, or, rather, against their discursive bodies—to be the transcendental/factual absolute of the world and of existence.

In fact, it is rigorously possible and necessary to reduce all metaphysics to the integral system that would be delimited by the following three propositions (among so many others one could also choose): "True and essential reason, whose name we steal on false pretenses, dwells in the bosom of God; there is her lair and her retreat"; "nature has no particular goal in view... for if God acts for an object, he necessarily desires something which he lacks"; "God himself presses so to speak in the direction of this world by which he has finally cast all being outside of himself, in which he has a world free with respect to *himself,* a creation truly *beyond* him... *this* world *here,* the world in which we actually find ourselves."[25] The diversity, that is, the disparity and oppositions between these propositions in accordance with their contexts and epochs do not contradict the reduction I am talking about. Rather, the movement of this reduction is in the final analysis nothing other than the very movement of the occidental history of *sense* as the movement of an ontotheology in principle involved with its own deconstruction, the *end* of which, in all senses, is precisely "this world *here,*" this world that is to such an extent "*here*" that it is definitively beyond all gods and all signifying or signified instances of sense: itself alone all in-significant sense.

If the end of this (hi)story—this end that is our event—is an end *in all senses,* it is also the case that its two senses affect each other and disseminate each other. The end-as-termination puts an end to the end-as-goal, and this is why there is no "moral of the story" [*sens de l'histoire*] of the (hi)story of sense. But the end-as-goal opens in its termination a dimension quite different from that of annihilation, without however reconstituting a teleological process. And this is why there is a history, our history, the world in the becoming-worldwide of its sense. In the end that is neither "end" nor "end," it is up to us to "seize" the—once again, infinite—chance and risk of being in the world, although we know full well (is it a knowledge?) that there is nothing to "seize."

The Sense of Being

The question or the issue of the *sense* of being (or of sense taken absolutely):

1. Agrammatical or exscribed transitivity: being is or *entrances* [*transit*][26] the existent.

2. In this transitivity, that which is transmitted from "agent" to "object" or "complement" is the act of being [*l'acte d'être*], the actuality of existence: that the being exists [*que l'étant existe*].

3. The actuality of existence is not a property that can be conferred or not on a thing. It is that there is the thing. The sense of (the) "being" is the transmission of the act that *there is.*

4. The act cannot be transmitted by anything other than itself (it is not a passage from potential to actual): "being is the being," or "there is something," indicates thus an anteriority/posteriority of the there is "in" itself. It transmits/entrances itself. Gift, différ*a*nce: the difference between the being and being is not a difference between terms or substances, but the différ*a*nce of being, or more exactly, *the différance being is.* Différ*a*nce *extrapolates* the ontico-ontological difference: it makes it exist.

5. But "to make exist" makes no sense: that which is neither a property nor a substance—the act or as-act of being-as-act—cannot be produced. Nor does it produce itself, not having the resources of a sub-

ject (for it is an agent, identical with its action, not a subject). It "is produced" in the remarkable sense of "taking place," "happening." The entire aporia of the concept of "creation" is here: insofar as it takes production for its schema and insofar as it presupposes a creating subject that is itself self-engendered, it does not touch on the act/event of existing that nonetheless haunts it. (The *ex nihilo* formulates the aporetic contradiction: in principle, *nihil* suppresses the production that *ex* affirms.) Or, "creation" deconstructed yields the being-as-act of existence, along with its differ*a*nce.

6. In Aristotelian terms, one could put it like this: differ*a*nce of and in *energeia* (being-as-work) or differ*a*nce of and in *entelekheia* (being-completed-in-the-end). (*Différance* as energy of energy, entelechy of entelechy.) That which is not an accomplished work, finished, closed, absolved of all rapport, that which is not *in* its end (deferring itself in its end, deferring its *end* in itself), is *toward* itself: the "*a*" of differ*a*nce reinscribes itself accentuated in the "*à*" [in English, the "toward"] of "l'être-*à*" or "being-*toward*." From being to being, all the accents of the "toward" ["*à*"]: distance, direction, intention, attribution, élan, passage, gift, transport, trance, and touch: *sense* in all senses, sense of the eksistent. But in Aristotle the model of that which is a single act, a single entelechy, even as it differs within itself as one being from another being, is sense as the act of sensing and being sensed: the act of sensing and the act of the sensed are the same.[27] Existence is the act internally differing from its own sense, its self-sensation as its own dehiscence. Nothing else is at stake, in the final analysis, in the *Ego sum, ego existo* of René Descartes, in the obscurity of its self-evidence and in the madness of its self-certainty.

7. In Spinoza, this is called *conatus*,[28] in Kant, *a being of ends* ("man"), in Hegel, the work of the negative, in Heidegger, *Ereignis*. In each case, and taking all differences into account, it signifies at least this: that sense does not add itself to being, does not supervene upon being, but is the opening of its very supervenience, of being-toward-the-world.

Infinite Finitude

If I say: finitude is the truth of which the infinite is the sense, I do more than give an example that would fulfill the formal determinations of punctuation and enchaining, semantics and syntax, instantaneous presentation and spaced-out coming.

In truth, what provides a ground for these formal determinations is the "content" or "signification," the "matter" that is given with the phrase, *finitude is the truth of which the infinite is the sense.*

In other words, there is no "case" or "type" of sense apart from this infinitude related to a finitude further determined as truth. Sense is just that, and all its sense resides there. (Where *there* means also *da,* the *there* of *Dasein,* which is "being-the-there," that is, the *here* as the right-*here* of this world *here.*)

Finitude is not the being-finished-off of an existent deprived within itself of the property of completion, butting up against and stumbling over its own limit (its contingency, error, imperfection, or fault). *Finitude is not privation.* There is perhaps no proposition it is more necessary to articulate today, to scrutinize and test in all ways. Everything at stake at the end of philosophy comes together there: in the need of having to open the thought of finitude, that is, to reopen to itself this thought, which haunts and mesmerizes our entire tradition.

If finitude were privation, it could not be conceived as the structure or "essence" of being or existence. In fact, there can be no thought here of privation pure and simple—of being as pure privation or of an existent in absolute, and absolutely private, privation. (For one must hear also, let it be said in passing, the *private* opposed to the *public*—the two senses of the privative have indeed the same etymology, *privare,* "to place apart from, to distance from"—and one must think there also the being-in-common of finitude as a fundamental theme. Sense is *common,* or it is not.)

If one wanted to conceive of a pure privation, then that of which there is privation would still have to be manifesting itself—and even manifesting itself more than anything else—within the horizon of a process, access, or transmutation that would be supposed to render possible the appropriation of that of which there is privation, entailing thus the annulment of privation. For otherwise, the privation could not even be designated as such. In one way or another, *privation annuls itself,* essentially. In turn, and this is what we have to think through, *finitude affirms itself.*

For if one persisted in positing a privation that would not accede at all to the appropriation of that of which it is deprived (thus, according to the lexicon of the most classical ontotheology, a sensible instance that would not be in any way saved into the intelligible, or a creature that would have no link with its creator), even such a single absolutely "private" (deprived and privatized) existent—if one could still designate it as "private"—would drag the totality of being into a nullity of which one cannot see how it could even *take place.* Or else—and this comes down to the same thing—the uniquely "private" existent would annul in itself its own privation, would constitute itself immediately as an absolute, having absolutely and without remainder arrived at itself, at itself as in itself even before existing, existence not taking place, pure *essentia* without *esse.*

Being-finite as being-deprived or being-private has no consistency. Being-deprived and being-private has no consistency except insofar as it is reappropriated—deprivatized—in an infinite being, its reason, ground, and truth. But this infinite being is in turn posited as pure, absolute, consistency-in-itself, as the pure immanence of a pure transcendence that, itself deprived of *esse,* does not even go so far as to take place. At bottom, this is the summary of the history of God or of Being as supreme being.

Esse, to the contrary, drags *essentia* into existence before it is annulled in its immanence, before it has closed itself in on its nowhere, therefore, "before" it has become "essence." "Before" the not-taking-place of a world, *esse* "constitutes" the taking-place of the world, this world here. *Being,* consequently, is transitively (in the agrammatical "sense" indicated earlier) the essence before the latter even has a chance to be or to constitute the essence it is. Being, therefore, does not deprive the essence of essence: essence simply does not take place. *Being entrances the essence.*

That is what we call *existing.* Existing entrances the essence (its "own" essence): it traverses the essence and transports it beyond itself (but there will not have been a "within"), and first of all, for example, it lifts essence out beyond its generality and ideality into that baroque, paradoxical status of the "singular essence" (or *infima species*) that Gottfried Leibniz wanted to recognize in individuality (conversion or convulsion of the thought of essence into the thought of finitude). The singular as essence is the essence existed, ek-sisted, expelled from essence itself, disencysted of its essentiality, and this, once again, before the cyst has even formed.

The entranced essence is the essence traversed, before itself and in front of itself, the essence passed and passed away (*transir* originally meant, intransitively, "to die"), penetrated and crippled by trembling, fear, respect, admiration, even love or hate, pleasure or pain—the essence transgressed, transcended, and affected. *"Finitude" names the essential affection that ek-sists the essence:* the essence is deprived here of its essentiality, but this privation is privation of nothing. Rather, it is the privilege of existence, the reserved law of existence, the proper law of its singular property of being—each time—singularly exposed to this trance that is the *esse* of being. (Privilege: that there should be a world, which Leibniz still understood as "the best of all possible worlds" . . .)

"Finitude" should therefore be attributed to what carries its *end* as its own, that is, what is affected by its end (limit, cessation, beyond-essence) as by its end (goal, finishing, completion)—and is *affected* by it not as by a limit imposed from elsewhere (from the outside of a supposedly essential, infinite immanence of the essence to itself, from the outside of an *essentia* absolute and null), but as by a trance, transcendence, or passing away so originary that the origin has already come apart there, the origin, too, it first of all entranced and abandoned.

If death comes to punctuate all of philosophy (from Plato to Hegel and Heidegger) as the truth itself, as the phenomenon of truth, this is—in a first sense, a metaphysically restrained sense—because death is the only presentation of essence as essence. For this reason, philosophy is marked as deadly—and the end of philosophy, in the exhaustion of its sense as sense, is a suicide programmed into the Socratic tragedy. But in another sense, in the interminable sense of metaphysics, one has to do here with a death that has always already taken place in existence, as existence itself: death as birth, from Hegel himself, but perhaps also from Plato, up through Heidegger and beyond. Henceforth, *not* as birth to a beyond-the-world, but simply to this world *here.* Less a "being-for-death" or a "being-toward-death" than "death" as the *being-toward-infinity* of what does not have its end *in* itself—does not contain its end—because it is infinitely affected by that end.

Being-*essentia* that has its end in itself—and that, in this sense, is finished, achieved, accomplished, and perfect, infinitely perfect—is at most pure truth, but truth deprived of sense: and it is exactly due to this that God, as such a being, is dead. (One really ought to trace, from the God of Thomas Aquinas to the God of classical rationalism, the slow, deadly accentuation that displaces the index of God from *esse* to *essentia,* from act to truth. But this historical accentuation effectuates also the program of a death-born or stillborn God, which is the ontotheological program in its Christian determination.)

Sense is thus the property of finitude qua existence of the essence. Sense is: that existence *should be* without essence, that it should be toward that which it *essentially* is not, its own existence. Toward death, if you like, but where "death" = the nullity of essence, existence. In other words, *toward* death would mean toward life, if "life" did not refer too simply to the contrary of death (immediacy as opposed to, and in the final analysis as identical with, infinite self-mediation). Hence, *toward* existence.

Existence is exposed—it is this exposition itself—not to a risk that comes from outside (it is already outside, it is being-outside), not to an adventure in the element of the foreign (it is already being-foreign, being-estranged) in the mode of Hegelian consciousness (which, however, has *also* contributed to the modern history of our finitude): it is exposed to and by the *ex* that it is, exposed to and by this swooning of the essence, which is older and more affirmative than any constitution of essence, and which constitutes existence, that is, which throws toward the world, toward itself insofar as it is being-*toward*-the-world, and toward the world insofar as the world is the configuration or constellation of being-toward in its plural singularity.

Différance

It is not to be treated as an acquired concept, since it is "neither word nor concept." And it is not to be turned into the key to, or the fetish or seal of, a sense that has been deposited somewhere. It is—if it "is"—the index of sense as absent sense without any privation of sense.

It is thus—or it is nought but a turn of writing that one must not stop rewriting, transcribing, and that one must prevent from remaining closed in on itself, producing the effects of sense like an ineffable concept or the Idea of a mystery. And so, let us begin again the work, play, and *praxis* of sense onto which this turn opens: the ontico-ontological difference is the difference of *esse* and *ens* (the mere onticoformal, metaphysical difference being the differentiation of *ens* into *existentia* and *essentia* as two species of one genus. Jean-Paul Sartre remains suspended between these two differences, and his formula—"existence precedes essence"—bears witness to this indecisive suspension, whereas what is at stake will turn out to be this: that existence precedes and succeeds on itself).

The ontico-ontological difference puts the transitivity of being into play in the form of being-the-existent. From the heart of this difference, *différance* envisions a dehiscence of *esse* away from *esse* itself, a diastole or fold of the same act (or entelechy): its ek-sisting. In a sense, this very entelechy that differs (from itself) senses itself in accordance with the logic of the entelechy of the sensible that we have recalled above. Being senses itself deferring and differing. It senses itself or knows itself to be differing and different. But différ*a*nce, "the whole differ*a*nce," if one may say so, is precisely that here there is neither "sensing oneself" nor "knowing oneself" in the sense of an appropriation or revelation.[29]

Being senses and knows itself being: one may indeed say that sense consists precisely in this. But this cannot be sensed or known in any mode of sensitive or cognitive appropriation. It does not make sense, does not signify, and does not signify itself. Being happens, but it does not happen on itself and it does not reduce or return to itself—not without remainder. And yet without being deprived of anything at all. Or, being takes place, but its place spaces it out. In every instance of its occurrence, being is an area, and its reality gives itself in areality. It is thus that being is body. Not "embodied," nor "incarnated," not even in a "body of its own": but body, hence possessing its own outside, differing and deferring.[30]

This spacing is not the launching of a delay, like the temporizing necessary to the ultimate effectuation of being. For in this case, finite or infinite, the delay would end in an essentialization of being (and in the fact of death, but death does not consummate existence: one would, rather, have to say that it prevents it from turning itself into essence). Différ*a*nce is not a temporizing, and if it designates also a spacing out of time, such spacing is not—or not only, not merely—the spacing out of successive moments into a distension of linear time. It would be, rather, the interior spacing of the very line of time: that which distances from one another the two edges of this line, which, however, has no thickness whatsoever, in accordance with the coming of being, the coming of a singularity, of an "instant" (or of an "eternity") of existence. The *coming* is infinite: it does not get finished with coming; it is finite: it is offered up in the instant. But that which takes place "in the instant"—in this distancing of time "within" itself—is neither the stasis nor the stance of the present instant, but its instability, the inconclusiveness of its coming—and of the "going" that corresponds to that coming. The coming into presence of being takes place precisely as nonarrival of presence.

No doubt this sketchy summary of an elucidation of différ*a*nce is still a bit too phenomenological-constitutive. The *coming* (but is there "the" coming, and not rather a "to come" that comes without allowing of substantialization?) demands something else, and no doubt, first of all, a letting-come and a letting-overcome, an aptitude (necessarily inapt) for the surprising of sense, and also for its letting-go. This other turn, if there is one, is on the confines of philosophy, but it is not either science or poetry. It is therefore still philosophy. How philosophy is still philosophy in its end, or how it exceeds itself on the edge of the coming, of sense as coming.

How to tell you: "*The philosopher has nothing to tell you that you do not already know and that s/he does not already know by means of all that is not 'philosophy' in him or her, and with a knowledge so neat, so pointed, so exact. . . . A naked, unkempt coming—truth on its way, mad, in truth—of sense common to all of us, like simple good sense. . . . This sense will defer itself and will differ always from all that you will seize, from all philosophy, and yet you will have had a sense of it, and philosophy will have had the sense precisely of this, that we all have a sense of it . . .*"? How to tell you? It has been said, however, and it has not been said. It is not unsayable: it is, rather, that which speaks truly in all that is said and resaid.

Space: Confines

In order to be understood as a world of sense—of "absent sense" or exscribed sense—the world must also be understood in accordance with the *cosmic* opening of space that is coming toward us: this constellation of constellations, this mass or mosaic comprising myriads of celestial bodies, their galaxies, and whirling systems, deflagrations and conflagrations that propagate themselves with the sluggishness of lightning, the almost immobile speed of movements that do not so much traverse space as open it and space it out with their motives and motions, a universe in expansion and/or implosion, a network of attractors and negative masses, a spatial texture of spaces that are fleeing, curved back, invaginated, or exogastrulated, fractal catastrophes, signals with neither message nor destination, a universe of which the unity is nothing but unicity [*unicité*] open, distended, distanced, diffracted, slowed down, differed, and deferred within itself. What is coming toward us is a universe that is unique insofar as it is open on nothing but its own distance from nothing, within nothing, its "something" having been thrown there from nowhere to nowhere, infinitely defying all themes and schemes of "creation"—all representations of production, engenderment, or mere origination—and nonetheless not a mere, self-posited, sempiternal, inert mass but, rather, a coming more extended and distended than the coming of all origins, a coming always pre-vented and pre-venting, devoid of providence and yet not deprived of sense: a coming that is itself the sense (in all senses) of its starring.

We do not yet have any cosmology adequate to this noncosmos, which moreover is also not a chaos, for a chaos succeeds on or precedes a cosmos, while our *a*cosmos is neither preceded nor followed by anything: on its own, it traces—all the way to the confines—the contour of the unlimited, the contour of the absolute limit that nothing else delimits. But it is a cosmology of this sort that we need, an acosmic cosmology that would no longer be caught by the look of a *kosmotheoros,* of that panoptic subject of the knowledge of the world, whose figure shed, in Kant's work, for one last time, its last brief rays.[31]

In order to achieve such an acosmic cosmology, we would have to begin by disengaging ourselves from the remains of the old cosmo-theo-ontology, such as these remains still supported a "conquest of space" conceived, if not in terms of *kosmotheoria,* at least in terms of *kosmopoiesis:* mastery and possession of the universe (*we have walked on the moon*) and thus mastery and possession of its (re)production by and for the subject "man." This representation is already on the decline. More than twenty years ago, Stanley Kubrick's famous film, *2001: A Space Odyssey,* the subtle lesson of which still awaits its commentary and its difficult decision, bore witness to this decline. It can be schematized as follows: man sends himself into space thanks to a technique he ultimately disconnects from itself as will and project (that is, as the paranoia of mastery and work by which the computer Hal is overcome), a technique, at once finite and in-finite, that goes astray [*désoeuvrée*]. Instead of securing for himself an empire in space, this man, touching the limit (of space as of himself), retraverses time, crosses the spatial distances of time all the way back to the origin, in order then to stray, adrift, like a fetus floating in the placenta of the galaxies, a great eye open on disoriented space, on time without direction, and on us, the spectators of this pensive eye, which, however, is nearly devoid of gaze, absorbing all of space, even as it breathes and distends itself within itself.

This film is anything but "science fiction," and even less "*space opera.*" On the contrary, it eludes and discredits these categories. It takes space seriously, with all the seriousness of thought: as dis-orientation and as spacing of sense (of humanity, history, and technical progress). If the film proposes something like an instance or indication of sense, it is the black monolith. Absolutely compact and impenetrable, the monolith does emit some signal, call, or intimation, and it does give a chance—this is the beginning of the film—to all of technology and to the (in)humanity it contains. But the monolith is not God, and it is not present except by virtue of its smooth, hard surface, as the presence of an absence. (It is indeed true that at this point Kubrick leaves room for an interpretation in terms of negative theology, but what can elude this interpretation is that the monolith, by means of its impeccable parallelepiped form, presents itself rather as if it were itself already a product of technology, a factory-made product. . . .) *Odyssey:* straying and return, but here—in this we are different from Ulysses—we see the return to straying, the return of technology to technology, the deconstruction of Ithaca, Penelope, and Telemachus, that is, sense that does not close itself off and round itself out.

To take space seriously in this way is precisely no longer to take it seriously in accordance with the vision of an inspection of the universe by the light of reason (the film marks this vision with a sign of irony by accompanying by the "Beautiful Blue Danube" the round of space ships). It is to accompany as closely as possible the *praxis* of a technoscience that is in the process of detaching itself, by its very movement, from Promethean ideologies. Here, the twentieth and twenty-first centuries take their leave of the nineteenth. And *sense* cuts itself adrift from all conceptions of the world and worldviews—from all significations of the world.

The exorbitant eye of the fetus, the eye of the coming, of self-preceding existence, does not operate the *synopsis* of a world-cosmos. Its gaze comes before the gaze, it pre-views in an inverted sense of pro-vidence. No doubt it receives and even gathers within itself the obscure immensity over which it is suspended (and it is first of all we, the spectators, whom this eye gazes on and regards), but it gathers only insofar as it is open. For it is itself also immensely, immeasurably open onto this space into which it is thrown, this space that it does not organize first into a representation but that it adjoins from all directions and in all senses.

Today, if something like a "philosophy of nature" is possible in a new way, it is as a philosophy of confines. We are at the confines of the multidirectional, plurilocal, reticulated, spacious space in which we take place. We do not occupy the originary point of a perspective, or the overhanging point of an axonometry, but we touch our limits on all sides, our gaze touches its limits on all sides. That is, it touches also—indistinctly and undecidably—the finitude of the universe thereby exposed and the infinite intangibility of the external border of the limit. It is henceforth a matter of the *vision* of the limit, that is, vision *at* the limit—according to the logic of the limit in general: to touch it is to pass it, to pass it is never to touch the other border. The limit unlimits the passage to the limit. A thought of the limit is a thought of excess. Such a thought will have to be articulated not in terms of schemes of transcendence or transgression, but in terms of the beyond-scheme of the passage to the limit, in which the *to* combines the values of *on the edge of, beyond, across,* and *along,* the values of touching and detachment, of penetration and escape, transitive and intransitive at once. Whereas the world was reputed to have its sense either outside or only inside itself, it has or is this sense henceforth on its confines and as a network of confines.

At the confines: neither *kosmotheoroi* nor *kosmopoietes,* but cosmonauts, or better still, as they prefer to say, significantly, *spationauts.*

Sense as navigation to (or on) the confines of space—rather than as return to Ithaca.

Of course, more than anything else, it is technology that is at stake here. (It is not by chance that a film serves here as exposition, and a film that mobilized all of the "technological sophistication" of its time.) The "question of technology" is nothing other than the question of sense at the confines. Technology is quite precisely that which is neither *theoria* nor *poiesis:* that which assigns sense neither as knowledge nor as work. This is why, in addition, science can be called *technoscience* today without it being a matter of "degrading" its knowledge to the status of a "mere" instrumentality: science no longer designates, in a metaphysical manner, the virtually final punctuation of a knowledge of truth, but on the contrary—increasingly—the enchaining and entailing of truths along the edge of *teknē,* neither as knowledge nor as work, but as the incessant passage to the confines of *phusis. Phusis* and nature were figures of self-presentation. *Teknē* makes coming get going, so to speak, where "coming" refers to the différ*a*nce of presentation. *Teknē* thus withdraws from presentation the values of "self" (on the side of the origin) and "presence" (on the side of the end).[32]

The world of technology, that is, the "technologized" world, is not nature delivered up to rape and pillage—although barbarity and madness are indeed unleashed there as much as rationality and culture, according to the scale of the technological gesture itself. It is the world becoming *world,* that is, neither "nature" nor "universe" nor "earth." "Nature," "universe," and "earth" (and "sky") are names of given sets or totalities, names of significations that have been surveyed, tamed, and appropriated. *World* is the name of a gathering or being-together that arises from an *art*—a *teknē*—and the sense of which is identical with the very exercise of this *art* (as when one speaks of the "world" of an artist, but also of "the world of the elite [*grand monde*]"). It is thus that a world is always a "creation": a *teknē* with neither principle nor end nor material other than itself. And in this way, a world is always sense outside of knowledge, outside of the work, outside the habitation of presence, *but* the *désoeuvrement* of sense, sense in *excess* of all sense—one would like to say the *artifical intelligence of sense,* sense seized and sensed by *art* and as *art,* that is, *teknē,* that which spaces out and defers *phusis* all the way to the confines of the world. There is no point in protesting—and it is even dangerous to protest—against the putting-to-work of technology on nature, or in wanting to subordinate technology to the ends of a mythical "nature" (as the "totalitarianisms" have done). But it is necessary to come to appreciate "technology" as the infinite of art that supplements a nature that never took place and will never take place. An ecology properly understood can be nothing other than a technology.

No doubt it is exact to say that the endlessness of technology contains within itself a terrible ambivalence, quite foreign to nature, the universe, or the earth (sky). *The* world, *as such, has by definition the power to reduce itself to nothing just as it has the power to be infinitely its own sense, indecipherable outside of the* praxis *of its art.*

But without this ambivalence, there would be no being-toward-the-world.

Space: Constellations

The cosmography of our technical navigation on the confines of space ought to begin by retracing its own provenance: the long history, the entire history of the Occident—and beyond, perhaps, assuming that we can even know where the Occident begins—the history of a relation to space and to the sublimity of Kant's "starry heavens" (which themselves limit space). The Kantian stars occupy an ambiguous position and function as a kind of hinge. They still present, in some respects, the order of a *cosmos*. But at the same time, and because the imminence of a chaos haunts without respite the modern thought Kant inaugurates (a sensible chaos, a chaos of senses and of sense), they expose an immensity of dispersion that is none other than that of the heavens from which the Unconditioned Being has disappeared—leaving its place to the unconditioned of a "law" whose freedom is the response "within me" to the "starry heavens above me."[33] This reference from one world to the other remains formal: the law does not govern nature, as nature does not constitute the law. The sense of each, the directedness of each *toward* the other, is suspended. Sublimity: from one end of the world to the other, there is nothing but the formless form of infinitude.

Thus, the cosmic con-stellation, the immediately sensible order, detaches itself from the signification of "heaven" and "earth" (and "man"), as it had detached itself already earlier on from the crystal spheres and their musical harmony. Another message has come from the stars, with Galileo's *Sidereus nuncius,* with Descartes's *Meteors,* with the *Plurality of Worlds,* and the first ear opened up by this message was Pascal's, who heard "the eternal silence of these infinite spaces."

Hence, the history of *disaster*—from Hugo's "frightful black sun" to Stéphane Mallarmé's "obscure disaster" and Maurice Blanchot's "writing of the disaster." (But this history began in Plato's cave.) The disaster is the disaster of sense: unanchored from the stars, the stars themselves unanchored from the vault and its riveting, its scintillating punctuation of truth(s), sense escapes in order to make acosmic sense. Sense makes itself a constellation with neither name nor function, deprived of all astrology, dispersing as well the points of reference of all navigation, sending them off to the confines.

Thus—and this is the event of the entire epoch, the *occidental* event par excellence[34]—we are confronted with the end of *consideration,* that is, with the end of the observation and observance of the sidereal order, an order regulated to the point where it was necessary to reestablish its truth against the appearance of aberrant motion presented by certain stars. That was called "saving the phenomena," and the stars in question were named *planets* ("wandering ones"). Henceforth, the entire world will have become *planetary:* wandering from one end to the other. But the word *wandering* [*errance*] is still too narrow, for it presupposes a rectitude with respect to which one can then measure the deviation or the divagation of what wanders. But the *planetary,* the planetary disaster, is something other than a wandering, something other than a phenomenon one would have to save from its appearance: it exhausts being in its phenomenon, and its phenomenon exhausts itself in the nonappearance of the intersidereal spaces, a universal occident, without directions or cardinal points. Neither simply wandering about nor in error, the universe drifts along by its own momentum [*l'univers court sur son erre*]. That is all. It is as if all of sense were proposed to us by means of a monstrous physics of inertia, where a single motive were propagating itself in all senses and directions at once . . .

Henceforth, this entire matter of sense, our entire concern with sense, has to do with the fact that it is proposed to us in this way. Not given, precisely, but pro-posed, *offered,* reached out toward us from afar, from a distance that may be infinite. But if one is even to discern what this proposition proposes, what this monstrosity demonstrates, if one is even to receive the signal (devoid of message) sent from the planetary confines, it is necessary to become thoroughly clear about the suspension of consideration: it amounts to nothing less than the suspension of an allegiance to the sidereal order that no doubt configures all of the great cultures beyond the Occident. Consideration configured the world, and the *constellations* presented the figures and names of the heaven of sense in its very presence. (In this respect, if Plato's cave is the first place and milieu of a de-sideration, the Jewish god and his Christian son are the first agents of the deconsideration into which they have been drawn.)

Desiderium: desideration engenders desire.[35] With the motif of desire, philosophy—and psychoanalysis as well—has most often and most manifestly mobilized the motif of privation. *Desire* is our word for an infinite loss of sense. *Desire* does not cease to advertise the philosophical truth: either the true, as object of desire, is constituted as structural lack, as abyss, as an empty place; or else desire is itself the true that it essentially hollows or empties out. One ought to say even: hyperessentially. In desire as thus understood, there is a secret exacerbation of the essence, which resembles existence in that it may appear to carry off and to entrance the essence, but which, in fact, takes essence beyond its ordinary traits of stability, plenitude, and presence, in order to reinvest these very traits in the figures of movement, lack, and tension. Thus desire becomes, in an ontoerotology, now that in which sense consists, now that which functions as a norm for the relation to sense. In short, as the opposite and symmetrical extreme of a submission to the objectivity of *consideration,* this submission to desire amounts to submission to desideral subjectivity (the subject is lacking from the very start, and it is the subject of its lack: appropriation of negativity as resource of presence). This submission to *desiring* subjectivity is a trap set for every movement of our thought (including those whereby we attempt to think history, intention, and project, as well as those whereby we attempt to think exposition, alterity, community, and so on).

Consideration, desideration: the very thing that leads to the disaster. The stars are deposed, other lights announced. But the Enlightenment of the eighteenth century also delivered sense—which it had wanted to illuminate from the earth up—to desire, that is, to romanticism. It did so by placing sense simultaneously beneath the double light—or by placing sense in the double truth—of a *reason* and a *skepticism* that blinded each other with the glare of their mutual illumination. It comes down to us to arrange the lights in some other way. Without giving up on either reason or skepticism, we must arrange them in such a way that their clarities, instead of annulling each other, diffract and multiply each other into other constellations, other gatherings of sense. But in one way or another, it should be a matter neither of consideration nor of desideration, but of the end of sideration in general. *Praxis.*

Schema:

Cosmos—myth—given sense.

Heaven and earth—creation—announced/desired sense.

World—spacing—sense as existence and *teknē.*

(But worldliness does not merely succeed, it precedes as well. The world before humanity and beyond humanity is also *our* world, and we are also *toward* it.)

Psychoanalysis

What psychoanalysis represents—not what it actually does, or what is thought in its name or beneath its heading—above all what it marks in our landscape, with the prevalence of desire, is a severe punctuation of pure truth, that is, a pure privation of sense. No doubt we will one day understand that it will have been the necessary catharsis of an excess of sense, of an excessive demand for sense, and that, once it has fulfilled this function, it involves us on its own with something other than what it still represents.[36]

The singularity of psychoanalysis—which confers on it all of its disruptive force and epoch-making scope—consists in having inaugurated a mode of thought that, in principle, dissolves all sense, that not only situates sense outside of truth and rigor (as other Viennese were doing also in Sigmund Freud's day), but in principle renders sense destitute by reducing it to a mere demand of sense, and by exposing truth as the disappointment of that demand.

The "unconscious" that Freud brought to light does not unveil another sense. It is the business of the *doxa* to come up with vulgar versions of psychoanalytic sense: sense as drive, sexual sense, phantasmatic sense, archetypal sense, and so forth. But the "unconscious" designates—and this is what Jacques Lacan understood—the inexhaustible, interminable swarming of significations that are not organized around a sense but, rather, proceed from a significance or signifyingness [*signifiance*] that whirls with a quasi-Brownian motion around a void point of dispersion, circulating in a condition of simultaneous, concurrent, and contradictory affirmation, and having no point of perspective other than the void of truth at their core, a void itself quite superficially and provisionally masked by the thin skin of an "ego."

Thus, what Freud, as the inheritor of a romantic tradition, maladroitly named the "unconscious" is not at all another consciousness or a negative consciousness, but merely the world itself. The unconscious is the world as totality of signifiability, organized around nothing other that its own opening. For psychoanalysis, this opening opens on nothing, and this is what, from the standpoint of psychoanalysis, it is necessary for the subject to come to be able to sustain or to bear. And in this, indeed, the testimony of psychoanalysis concerning the "end of philosophy" is impeccable, irrefutable. And I do not have the slightest intention of suggesting that it would be necessary at present to substitute a new truth for the "nothing" of this yawning abyss. The question is, rather, how to understand the "nothing" itself. Either it is the void of truth or it is nothing other than the world itself, and the sense of being-toward-the-world. How is there *world* for psychoanalysis?

Insofar as it places itself principally beneath the sign of a therapy—whatever one wishes to understand by this word and even if it were at the greatest distance from any normalization and "comforting of the ego"—but insofar as it precisely does not determine anything in the world as a normal or healthy state in terms of which it could regulate its procedures, psychoanalysis cannot be conceived merely as a therapy within the world, but must ineluctably envisage the therapy of the world itself, of *everyone in the world.* To this necessity, *Group Psychology and the Analysis of the Ego* and *Civilization and Its Discontents* may seem to respond with an admission of powerlessness. But this is what we ought perhaps to understand differently today: the world is not incurable, nor is it to be cured, for it is the space in which *sense engages itself* or *invents itself,* beyond truth, and as a consequence of the "responsibility for the truth" to which analysis is supposed to lead.[37]

An engagement or invention of sense, the "introduction of sense," as Nietzsche said, is the opening of a world, the world of some*one* (a "subject," according to the Lacanian conception). For someone—every *one*—makes up a world insofar as s/he is in the world. It is a matter of "the subject appropriating its world and creating it as 'world' by exteriorizing it."[38] But in order for that to be possible, some*one* must have access to the *world.* A "subject" cannot make up a world—make sense—if they cannot expose themselves to the world of all the monadic worlds, to worldness as such. This access cannot take place by means of truth alone. One more step is necessary here—the step beyond analysis, the step of analysis beyond itself.

Psychoanalysis stops at the border of the world: the world is not its concern, but the concern of some*one.* This is why it envisages the world with a *cold eye,* and in terms of the punctuation of truth. And no doubt, this *cold eye,* this insensitivity to sense, is a liminal and necessary condition for access to the world. But what this coolness denies it also admits: truth can be what it is only by spacing itself out into a world. Here the step of analysis is suspended, the step through which it lifts itself out beyond medicine and exposes itself to writing or *praxis.* For this world is common, it is before "someone," it supports the *one* of every*one* only on condition of being before and after them, of pre-venting and succeeding on them. Perhaps it is necessary to say: *before even the tie of the Law, there is the network of the world.* Before the symbolic, there is this spacing out without which no symbol could symbolize: there is being-in-common, the world.

This being-in-common is very much the concern of psychoanalysis (it is the "unconscious"), and this is why psychoanalysis is a privileged witness or symptom of the end of the world-cosmos and the birth of the *world.* The *world* is not the "Other," and it is not the "Law." It is an alteration older than the Other and a legislation older than the Law, even if it does not become a "world" without both the Other and the Law. It arises out of an invention more archaic than these, the invention of *sense*—which is the name of the symbolic in its inaugural deflagration. For what Lacan called "the symbolic" is obviously not first of all a structure in the sense of a construction, but at most in the sense of a differential spacing and play (where "play" is to be taken in its mechanical more than in its ludic sense). If the symbolic imposes or supplies structure, it is itself not structured. It is passage, passing, and partitioning of this, that there is or that there could be passage, passing, partitioning (signs, significations, signals, gestures, silences, affects, defects, contacts, separations . . .). Passage and partitioning of nothing, if you like, but this *nothing* does not only have the *consistency of nothing* that often appears—and in more than one analytic discourse—to circumscribe it under the tense guard of *truth.* Just as much, this "nothing" has the inconsistency of sense, of the signifyingness or significance of sense. The symbolic of the symbolic, and the truth of truth, is that sense is not already all tied up in knots, but still to be tied, every time, by every *one,* in all senses.[39] *That which is sane* [sensé] *in sense*—and psychoanalysis is certainly well placed to know it—*is that sense arises this side of an opposition between insane and sane* [de l'insensé et du sensé].

> . . . you will survive me by years, and over mine [death] I hope you will quickly console yourself and let me live on in your friendly memory—the only form of limited immortality I recognise.
>
> The moment a man questions the meaning and value of life, he is sick, since objectively neither has any existence; by asking this question one is merely admitting to a store of unsatisfied libido to which something else must have happened, a kind of fermentation leading to sadness and depression. I am afraid these explanations of mine are not very wonderful. Perhaps because I am too pessimistic. I have an advertisement floating about in my head which I consider the boldest and most successful piece of American publicity: "Why live, if you can be buried for ten dollars?"[40]

Such is Freud's *truth:* the mere question of sense constitutes a pathological symptom. But what this letter at once admits and denies, by means of its mere existence, is that psychoanalysis itself *makes sense,* simply by making it possible to designate the sickness of sense.

But it is not a question of contenting oneself with catching Freud in a trap. It is also true that raising the question of sense is an "illness." Sense can make sense only insofar as it is not being asked to. *The most sane and sensible thing about sense is that it is not possible to say what sense we are talking about.* Which means also—but now we are no longer talking about an illness—that there is a madness of sense, before all reason and without which no reason would be possible.

Gift. Desire. "Agathon"

Consideration/desideration: that is, sense either purely given or purely desired. Sense always already given, deposited there as a comprehensive unity (or trap?), or sense not yet attained, fleeing, like spilled blood. In both cases, it is a pure sideration of truth: either disposed in accordance with the power of myth or thrown frozen into the bottom of the abyss.

Myth and the abyss are the two postulations or figurations inscribed by philosophy, from the very beginning, as its own limits. Together they form the double border of the opening that philosophy itself wants to be: stating the truth of both, of myth and the abyss, and getting sense going, in the open space, as the very tension, intensity, and extension of the open.

Just as, to those who devote themselves to the abyss (that is, to nihilism), "sense" makes no sense, so to those who live in myth "sense" would doubtless appear to be deprived of sense. Sense makes sense only in the space of philosophy as it ends by opening up the world.

But if sense is contemporaneous with philosophy, if sense constitutes what is essentially at stake there, one ought to ask oneself how it offers itself at the birth of philosophy. There, it bears the name of *agathon:* Plato's "Good," the good or excellence that is to be sought (desired? appropriated?) *epeikeina tēs ousias,* beyond being or essence.[41]

The excellence of the *agathon* is without content: it concerns merely the position beyond essence, in this (non)region where it is no longer a matter of presenting being (to oneself), but of being toward being-as-act (to put it in Aristotelian terms *avant la lettre*), of touching on the emergence—or being touched by the coming—of being-as-act.[42] The *agathon* is neither any specific "good" nor a "good" in the sense of a "possession." After all, its name is not attached to a semantics of "goodness," but to a semantics of greatness (cf. *mega,* great, *agan,* much, too much), intensity, and excess. Being touched by and touching the excess of excellence.

On this account, already from the very beginning *agathon* names something of ex-istence. *Avant la lettre,* there already, without a doubt. (All of philosophy is written uninterruptedly *avant la lettre,* before its letter, then long afterward: is deconstructed, takes the step of its end, its necessary event, at once dated and permanent, which opens it to its sense, before/after all of its significations.)

But the *agathon* thus names also sense, as metaphysics produces it, at the junction (conjunction? collision?) of the given and the desired. The gift that anticipates desire, the desire that is guided toward the gift: mutual fulfillment, ontotheoerotology achieved. Sense is thus the reciprocal and unreserved being-toward-the-other of desire and gift, the systematic adjustment of lack and fullness: the *jouissance* of truth and the truth of *jouissance.*

It is quite precisely here that disaster strikes. For in order to be *sense*—in order to be being-*toward,* that is to say,[43] in Plato's terms, the excellence that is qualified by nothing if not by the tension of the mutual aptness of desire and gift—sense cannot be determined as the effectuation of this aptness, as its fulfillment or discharge. A satisfaction that accomplishes and saturates both desire and gift denatures at once both gift and desire. All of the mad, unappeasable tension (which does not necessarily mean the tormented or anguished tension, but simply, calmly: the intensity—literally, *epeikeina* would be rendered by "beyond the most distant things") of the *epeikeina tēs ousias* falls away and is annulled. And this takes place whenever the *agathon* is determined and understood as "Good," whether this "good" be a matter of axiology or possession or both at once. Sense as "good" annuls sense as being-unto-the-other of desire and gift. And doubtless this annulment is already vertiginously involved in the determinations of "desire" and "gift," insofar as they arise out of the preliminary philosophical assignation of the given (the already-given of myth) and the desired (the still-to-come of the satisfaction of Eros). Indeed, the overcoming of myth is deeply ambiguous: it is overcome as a lying fiction, but it is secretly retained as the instance of the already-given. To which desire then adds (1) that there is lack and desire precisely of this already-given; and (2) that the already-given has been marked by the law of its inaccessibility.

In other words, the pure desire of the gift can only be a desire without object, incapable of "envisaging" in any way whatsoever that which, of the gift and in the gift, must remain foreign not only to the giver[44] but also—absolutely surprising—to the receiver of the gift. The desire of the gift programs an appropriation from which the gift as gift escapes—and desire as well. How could one appropriate a gift?[45] Reciprocally, the gift given to desire, in order to be a gift given to what desires in desire, cannot give anything that would fulfill desire. It has to be a gift of desire itself. *The appropriation of giving and the giving of the inappropriable configure the originary chiasmus of philosophy—and of sense.*

The Good names from the very beginning—and right up to the end of philosophy—the appropriation of the giving and the giving of the inappropriable.[46] This is the very disposition of sense, but also the resource of the enormous amphiboly that makes of sense at once the original theme of philosophy and a minor concept, belated, hesitant, and subordinate to truth. Truth is the Good *presented*—in accordance with the abyssal structure of its chiasmus. Sense is the *agathon offered,* in accordance with the excess of its excellence.

To think sense as the in-appropriative encounter of desire and gift, as the excellence of the *coming* of the one *toward* the other, this is the task. Thus, neither desire nor gift but, rather, the following: that the desire of the gift should desire essentially not to appropriate its "object," and that the gift of desire should give that which cannot be given and should give no "subject" of an "object."

The one *offered* to the other. Which means, in a language that we no longer speak and that no longer makes sense, "sacrificed," or, in our stuttering language, not presented but extended toward, left to the discretion of a chance and/or decision whose agent or actor neither desires nor gives but merely *exists.*

Sense, World, Matter

This sense dispersed across the entire earth
JEAN-CHRISTOPHE BAILLY, *Le paradis du sens*[47]

"The sense of the world" does not designate the world as a factual given on which one would come to confer a sense. If that were the case, the sense of the world would indeed be beyond the world, as Ludwig Wittgenstein thinks in the *Tractatus*.[48] The "beyond the world" was occupied not long ago by the God of ontotheology. This God, whom Wittgenstein is still capable of naming in his way, is the concept of a place without place, if the "beyond the world" cannot but be beyond the totality of places. It could not therefore take place "outside." Only the God of Spinoza, through his strict equivalance to "Nature," escapes this contradiction (before Kant ruins its very possibility). *Deus sive natura* does not say simply, through the *sive,* two names for one thing but, rather, this, that this very thing *has its outside on the inside.* In saying this, Spinoza becomes the first thinker of the *world.*

In truth, if one understands by *world* a "totality of signifyingness or significance [*signifiance*],"[49] no doubt there is no philosophy that has thought a beyond of the world. The appearance of such a thought and of the contradiction it entails comes from the Christian sense of *world* as that which precisely lacks all sense or has its sense beyond itself. In this sense, moreover, sense itself is a specifically Christian determination or postulation that supposes a step beyond the *cosmos* to which *agathon* still belongs. To this very degree, that which we have to think henceforth under the title of sense can consist only in the abandonment of Christian sense or in an abandoned sense. Which one can also put like this: sense—if it is still or finally necessary to do justice to the obstinate request of this word—can proceed only from a deconstruction of Christianity.[50]

As soon as the appearance of a beyond of the world has been dissipated, the out-of-place instance of sense opens itself up *within* the world (to the extent that it would still make sense to speak of a "within"). Sense belongs to the structure of the world, hollows out therein what it would be necessary to name better than by calling it the "transcendence" of its "immanence"—its *transimmanence,* or more simply and strongly, its existence and exposition. The out-of-place term of sense can thus be determined neither as a property brought from elsewhere into relation with the world, nor as a supplementary (and problematic or hypothetical) predicate, nor as an evanescent character "floating somewhere,"[51] but as the constitutive "signifyingness" or "significance" of the world itself. That is, as the constitutive *sense* of the fact that there is world.

There is something, there are some things, there is some there is—and that itself makes sense, and moreover nothing else does. It does not make sense only for, through, or in *Dasein.*[52] One really ought to carry out here a very long debate with Heidegger, and in particular on the subject of what *Dasein* ought or ought not to retain of the characteristics of a subject, a human being, a center or end of nature and "creation." . . . In this respect, the categories used in *The Fundamental Concepts of Metaphysics* (the lecture course of 1929–30) appear quite fragile: "The stone is without world"; "the animal is poor in world"; "humanity is world forming." These statements do not do justice, at least, to this: that the world beyond humanity—animals, plants, and stones, oceans, atmospheres, sidereal spaces and bodies—is quite a bit more than the phenomenal correlative of a human taking-in-hand, taking-into-account, or taking-care-of: it is the effective exteriority without which the very disposition of or to sense would not make . . . any sense. One could say that this world beyond humanity is the effective exteriority *of humanity itself,* if the formula is understood in such a way as to avoid construing the relation between humanity and world as a relation between subject and object. For it is a question of understanding the world not as man's object or field of action, but as the spatial totality of the sense of existence, a totality that is itself *existent,* even if not in the mode of *Dasein.*

Dasein—that ordinary German noun for existence, which Heidegger gives as a "title" to humanity and beneath which, for him, humanity and only humanity ex-ists—is the *being-the-there* of being itself.[53] It is transitively the there, that is to say, it entrances—traverses and partitions—the taking-place of the sense of being as the event of a being-*there,* the spacing of an arrival. In turn, the world in the sense of "external" or "circumambient" world is the *here* of this *there* (the *Hiersein* of *Dasein*). The taking-place or the existing takes place *here,* in this world here—or, rather, because the world is not the container of a content, *the totality of existences qua totality of signifyingness constitutes the being-here of being-there.* This may seem uselessly refined. But it says that the there of being, its taking-place, insofar as it is also a ravishment and a distancing[54] (a coming and going of sense), takes place neither anywhere other nor toward anywhere other than the here of this world here. And this world here is not to be distinguished from another world there: to the contrary, it is the same, or much more precisely, *the world here is the totality and the sameness of beings-there.* The distancing and ravishment that sense presupposes do not take place otherwise than as the spacing of this world here.

(*Here is the greatest difficulty: the difficulty of the "transimmanence" of sense. Quite simply, that the sense of the world is this world here as the place of existence. This "quite simply" contains the most formidable stake, the one that requires of us, in order to say this* absolutely simple *thing, a completely different style or, rather, an interminable alteration of style.*)

Even if one supposes that it is necessary to take sense to be exclusively a property of the existent that is *Dasein* (which at least seems to be true of sense as "articulated comprehension,"[55] although it is not certain that sense can be reduced to this), and even if one supposes correlatively that ex-istence belongs exclusively to *Dasein* or humanity (although this, too, is precisely less than certain), it nonetheless remains the case that, in the absence of the factual totality of fragments, this existent cannot exist, assuming (as Heidegger does) that its existence is indeed *factual* and that this factuality is indeed that of a "part of the world."[56] Far from being a mere impoverished and inert objectivity offered up to the purposes and the manipulations of humanity, this factuality, or the world as being-here of all the *beings-there,* is itself also, qua simple being-thrown-here-of-things, an *existentiale* of *Dasein:* that is, in the Heideggerian lexicon, a transcendental/factual condition of possibility of ex-istence. In other words, the insurmountable fact of its *sense.* But it is therefore necessary that it be so without reservations, *materially.*

Once again, with Heidegger, philosophy has turned away from what was nonetheless—and not by chance—one of its very first "intuitions" in the atomism of Democritus, Epicurus, and Lucretius. For this atomism is quite far from formulating a "materialist" thesis as opposed to an "idealist" thesis, and it is quite far, by that very fact, from positing the thesis of a pure and simple privation of sense as opposed to the thesis of a transcendent sense. Rather, "atomism" (whether well or poorly named) represents what one would have to call the other archi-thesis of philosophy (the first being Plato's *agathon*): originary spacing qua materiality, and this spacing itself as *existentiale* of the relation to the *agathon.*[57]

"Matter" is not above all an immanent density that is absolutely closed on itself. On the contrary, it is first the very difference through which *something* is possible, as *thing* and as *some:* that is, other than as the indistinct inherence or hardening of a one that would not be *some one.*

If *Dasein* must be characterized by its *Jemeinigkeit* (the "being-each-time-my-own" of its event), by the singularity of a someone having or making sense of "mineness" (or ipseity), this *someone* would be unthinkable without the material-transcendental (existential) resource of some oneness of the thing in general, without the *reality* of the *res* as material difference. Matter means here: the reality of the difference—and différance—that is necessary in order for *there to be something and some things* and not merely the identity of a pure inherence (which to tell the truth—neither differing from anything other than itself nor even differing from and within itself—could not even be characterized as identical . . .).[58] Matter is a matter of real difference, the difference of the *res:* if there is something, there are several things; otherwise, there is nothing, no "there is." Reality is the reality *of the several things* there are; reality is necessarily a numerous reality.

This circularity of reality and materiality, which is itself the condition of possibility of the distinction of something like a "form" or "articulation" in general—this circularity does not allow of being touched and presented as a material thing. Rather, it is the very condition of all *touching,* all *contact,* that is to say, of all composition of a world (neither pure continuity nor pure discontinuity: touching). If one can put it like this: the ideality of difference/*différance* is indissociable (if not indiscernible) from its materiality. And hence, *the ideality of sense is indissociable from its materiality.*[59]

Matter belongs just as much as *agathon* to the structure of the sense of the world. It is thus that it is necessary to reread, in the work of the Democriteans, the *fall* of the atoms into the void and the *clinamen*: as the distance, contact, assembling, separation, tangency, interval, and interference of the singular, diffracted *there is.* Singularity *is* material, whether one understands it as event or as unicity of existence, or as both at once, and still as sense. Reciprocally, matter is always singular or singularized. It is always *materia signata, signed* matter, that is, matter that is not signified but shown—or showing itself—to be singular.[60]

The *there is is* signed or signs (itself): signature is not signification, but sense as singular coming.[61] This signature is indissociable from a being-*there,* that is to say, a being-*here,* first of all, in and according to the general texture of being qua being-something-somewhere, being a "fragment" of a world whose matter is the very fraying [*frayage*] or fractality of fragments, places, and takings-place. The outline of this signature is also always a *body,* a *res extensa* in the sense of an extension—areality, tension, exposition—of its singularity. But such an exposed body is not the result of the placing-in-view of what, at first, had been hidden or shut away. Rather, exposition is here being itself. This is what we mean by existing. *Unhiding* [*expeausition*]:[62] signature along the surface of the hide, the hide of being. Existence tans its own hide.[63]

Touching

I.

Heidegger declares:

> The stone is without world. The stone is lying on the path, for example. We can say that the stone is exerting a certain pressure upon the surface of the earth. It is "touching" the earth. But what we call "touching" here is not a form of touching at all in the stronger sense of the word. It is not at all like *that* relationship which the lizard has to the stone on which it lies basking in the sun. And the touching implied in both cases is above all not the same as *that* touch which we experience when we rest our hand upon the head of another human being. . . . Because in its being a stone it has no possible access to anything else around it, anything that it might attain or possess as such.[64]

Why, then, is "access" determined here *a priori* as the identification and appropriation of the "other thing"? When I touch another thing, another skin or hide, and when it is a question of this contact or touch and not of an instrumental use, is it a matter of identification and appropriation? At least, is it a matter of this first of all and only? Or again: why does one have to determine "access to" *a priori* as the only way of making-up-a-world and of being-toward-the-world? Why could the world not also *a priori* consist in being-among, being-between, and being-against? In remoteness and contact without "access"? Or on the threshold of access? (And this *a priori* would be identically the *a posteriori* of the material world, the indefinite grouping of threshold with threshold, one thing with another, each on the border of the other, at the entrance yet not entering, before and against the singular signature exposed on the threshold.)

Is it not necessary that there should be nonaccess, impenetrability, in order for there to be also access, penetration? That there should be, therefore, nonsense or, rather, beyond-sense in order for there to be sense? And that *in this sense* the stone and the lizard, too, should be in the circuit of sense, just as I—supposed *Dasein*—am also stone and lizard, not in some subaltern part or aspect, but in accordance with the *there* (*here*) of my being?

Or again, Heidegger determines only negatively here the "touch" of the stone on the earth. This "touch," he writes, is not the relation of the lizard warming itself, and it is even less that of a hand placed—not on a stone but—on a human head. Still, quite remarkably, Heidegger introduces thus first the sun and a communication of heat that, however, does not wait for the arrival of the lizard in order to take place, and then—and above all—a completely different order of "touching," not merely human but at once solemn and consecrated. The truth of the "touch" establishes itself by a sort of solar ascension or assumption. This triple scene is absolutely Platonic in the most unilateral and "metaphysical" sense of the term. There is definitely no question here of a human touch. Rather, a hieratic and paternal pose fraudulently substitutes a knighting for a touch.

Everything is betrayed by the expression "the earth is not *given* for the stone." The *gift* is thought here only as a gift for, finalized and significant—and significant precisely of the *earth,* with all its connotations of support and, beyond this, of proximity, rootedness, habitation, and propriety. But what if the "gift *for*" [don *pour*] were here taken wrongly for a "pure gift" [don pur]? What if it in fact compromised an earlier liberality, generosity—"spaciousness"—of the "gift"? What if the initial "gift"—a "gift" subtracted from "giving" itself insofar as the latter is taken to be intentional—would be more felicitously formulated like this: stone on the earth, and earth as "route" (*via* rupta, rupture, fraying [*frayage*]—and also, already, all the *teknē* of circulation and exchange), as a route already distributing the earth into places, places already receiving the stone, in an indifferent mode, in the mode, to be sure, of the wound for a foot and the barrier for an insect or for a stream, but also in the mode of a mere occupied place on the earth, of shadows cast, or of an ornamental cut incised in space, an unassignable gift, a gift lost as gift, a gift without corresponding desire, neither to be perceived nor to be received as "gift" . . . ?

Heidegger apparently fails to weigh precisely the weight of the stone that rolls or surges forth onto the earth, the weight of the *contact* of the stone with the other surface, and through it with the world as the network of all surfaces. He misses the surface in general, which perhaps does not come "before" the face, but which all faces necessarily also are. Concerning the head on which he would like to place a patriarchal hand,[65] Heidegger forgets, first of all, that it has *also* the consistency and, in part, the mineral nature of a stone. He misses the exposition of surfaces through which, inexhaustibly, delayed arrival singularly exhausts itself.

The stone, no doubt, does not "handle" things (*betasten*), as Heidegger writes in what is, in the final analysis, a rather vulgar manner, evoking the indiscreet, exploratory connotation of a "fingering"). But it does *touch*—or it *touches on*—with a passive transitivity. It is touched, same difference. The brute entelechy of sense: it is in contact, an absolute difference and an absolute diffé*r*a*n*ce. There is difference of places—that is to say, place—dis-location, without appropriation of one place by another. There is not "subject" and "object," but, rather, there are sites and places, distances: a possible *world* that is already a world.

Without that—without this impalpable reticulation of contiguities and tangential contacts, without the play (interstice, interval, and escape) of a geared down *being-toward,* where *toward* has less the connotation of a mere opposition to *in* than the connotation of sense disengaged and delivered from the *in*—there would be no world. "In itself," the thing is "toward" the *other things* that are close, proximate, and also very distant because there are several of them.

The principle that, taken absolutely, the *in-itself* is "abstract," merely and unilaterally present, is the generative principle of the entire Hegelian logic—that is, of the first logic that unfolds as a logic of sense and not merely of truth (insofar as it resists its own process of annulment in infinite truth). Thus, Heidegger's "stone" is still merely abstract. It is not the concrete stone, the concreteness of the stone, which does not come about only when the stone is encountered, thrown, or manipulated by or for a subject. Precisely, the *concrete* comes before or after object and subject. To be sure, the concrete stone does not "have" a world (but Heidegger's formula is ambiguous: "the stone is without world" can be understood as "it has no world," or as "it is not in the world")—but it is nonetheless toward or in the world [*au monde*] in a mode of *toward* or *in* that is at least that of *areality:* extension of the area, spacing, distance, "atomistic" constitution. Let us say not that it is "toward" or "in" the world, but that it is world.

One will say, however, that the world of the stone, or the stone-world, cannot be the "totality of significance." But significance—which I would call the *liability* [*passibilité*] *to sense*—has its own (perhaps existential) condition in the distancing through which world first comes to be. The world is liable to sense, it *is* this liability because it first comes to be in accordance with this—let us say again "atomistic"—distancing. No doubt, this implies, in principle, that the opening of a "comprehension" of sense would have some relation to the opening of concrete areality. Am I in the process of suggesting that something of "comprehension" can be attributed to the stone itself? One need not fear that I am proposing here an animism or a panpsychism. It is not a matter of endowing the stone with an interiority. But the very compactness of its impenetrable hardness (impenetrable to itself) can be defined (or can de-fine itself, precisely) only through the distance, the distinction of its being this here ("The stone is, that is to say, it is this and that, and as such it is here or there," Heidegger goes on to say, as if he reduced "being" to a mere copula of attribution). This discreteness that one could call a *quantum* discreteness, borrowing from physics the discreteness of material *quanta,* makes up the world as such, the "finite" world liable to sense.

Thus, no animism—indeed, quite the contrary. Instead, a "quantum philosophy of nature" (or an "atomistic" or "discrete" one) remains to be thought. For the differ*a*nce of the toward-itself, in accordance with which sense opens, is inscribed *along the edge of* the "in itself." *Corpus:*

all bodies, each outside the others, make up the inorganic body of sense.

The stone does not "have" any sense. But sense touches the stone: it even collides with it, and this is what we are doing here.

II.

In a sense—but what sense—sense *is* touching. The being-*here,* side by side, of all these beings-*there* (beings-thrown, beings-sent, beings-abandoned to the there).

Sense, matter forming itself, form making itself firm: exaction and separation of a tact.

With sense, one must have the tact not to touch it too much. One must have the sense or the tact: same thing.

Spanne

"Time is intrinsically spanned and stretched. . . . No now, no time-moment can be punctualized. Every time-moment is spanned intrinsically, the span's breadth being variable."[66]

If there were, in fact, a punctuality of the now or the present, then the void dimensions of the point would not permit the time of this present to be filled with its own temporal quality, in other words, to *take place.* Everything would pass, no doubt, but nothing would come to pass. Everything would thus proceed along the line of void points, but this "proceeding" would itself be void, immobile like the entirety of the line.

One thus undertakes in vain the representation of time as a succession of punctual presents, and moreover one contradicts oneself in so doing: for it is the *succession* as such that is abolished by such a representation. There can be no *passage* from one present *to* another, if neither the one nor the other takes place.

Thus, there is separation, space. *Spanne,* Heidegger says. Extension, tension, traction, attraction (*gespannt:* tense, excited, seduced, captivated). Agitation, spasm, expansion.

This is indeed why Kantian time, where "everything passes, except time itself," is a time wherein nothing takes place—except for time, which itself takes place as an immobile taking-place, the surging forth, once and for all, of the very substance of the world. But as a result, this surging forth has always already taken place and no longer takes place in time. There is no "once and for all," or, rather, this "once" is the unique "once," which is therefore not a "once" but the spacing of all "onces." (By virtue of its origin, *vix*, the French word for "once" in this sense, "fois," is first of all the *place*, and then the *turn*—"in its turn"—of *displacement* and *replacement.*) The giving of a place for the world by the world.

But "in" the phenomenon of time, there are nothing "but *changes*... of the substance that endures," and never "a birth and an annihilation of substance itself."[67]

Pure time, the time of the pure present, is the time of the indefinite modification of a unique uncreated substance, not produced, not occurring unexpectedly, a substance of which time itself is the unexpected occurrence without beginning or end, and which modifies itself in accordance with the endless enchaining of causes and effects.

And so it is with good reason that the line representing it represents the static, unidimensional, nonspatial copresence of its points (a limit of space, not a space: the limit where space becomes pure time, but where pure time annuls the event).

No passage, no coming, no departure, no birth or death, no surging forth, breaking in, or creation of a new substance, no attraction or excitation of a new subject, and consequently no disappearance of the new, no abolition of its novelty in this other absolute novelty that is its empty place or its tomb. No *not* [*Pas de* pas].

Nothing, however, *is* except in accordance with a *not:* the crossing from nonbeing to being, that is, from being itself insofar as it is nothing to being itself again insofar as it is (entrances) the existent—and the crossing from being to nonbeing.

Being crosses over itself thus in every instant: birth, death, liberty, fraying [*frayage*], encounter, leap. Nothing existent is posited, deposited, or composed to support this crossing that every existent thing presupposes, and that the whole of the existent, the world, presupposes.

Not a bridge for the not of being by which existence comes about.

A tomb is always open, like a woman lying in childbed. It is the spacing of the present that *takes place,* as present, when a "substance" or a "subject" is coming along or going away. The present as present is *praesens,* it precedes (itself), that is, it succeeds (itself) also: it separates itself, it keeps at a distance the presence it carries.

There lies the present that is *given* by being to being when a "subject" is coming or going.

A "subject" is that very thing: a singular present given from being to being (an existence). This is why the word *subject* names it rather badly. For this present of some *one* does not belong to itself in an interiority and does not deliver itself up on the basis of such a reserve. On the contrary, it takes place as the opening or exposition of that which never will have taken place "within itself" before this present and outside of this exposition—the exposition of this existence, this masculine or feminine one. No doubt, a *self* indeed takes place (which does not mean that it would necessarily be a "human" self). But this being-self is *coextensive* with the extension wherein it is made into a present. It is not outside of this outside.

There is no outside of the outside where every present spaces itself out. There is no return into itself of time, no cyclical or sempiternal annulment. There is only eternity as the spacing out of every present of time. The very gesture of the present, the gesture of presenting, the place of the diffraction of the present. Much more remote, much more open than a big-bang, to which it alone can give rise.

Eternity is the other of time that gives rise to time, or for which time gives rise to itself, in the spacing of its present. It is the simultaneity (*tota simul*) by means of which succession takes place as passage, the unique place as displacement and replacement, as the effective step from one existence to another, as singularity of event. The world, in this sense, is eternal or simultaneous, but the simultaneity of the world (and not in the world) is not the "at the same time." It is the *altered sameness* of time—the untimeliness of time—and it is thus that it is spacing, or that it is *insofar as* it spaces itself out.

If it is no longer God who is eternity,[68] it is the spacing of the present of time, its separation and excitation: *Spanne, Spannweite.* Separation as tension—time stretched like a bow of which it would also be itself the arrow. But for that, precisely, in order that there should be separation of the stretching or being-stretched out, no punctuality, no instantaneous instant, but the instant as spacing out, and spacing out as the *simul* of the several things that make up a world.

> space has remained a street-urchin, and it is difficult to enumerate what it engenders. It is as discontinuous as a swindler, to the great despair of its philosopher-papa. . . . beneath our chastely averted eyes, space breaks continuity without a stop. Although we cannot say why, it does not seem that a monkey dressed up like a lady would be but a division of space. In reality, the dignity of space is so firmly established and associated with the dignity of the stars that it is incongruous to affirm that space can become a fish eating another one.[69]

There is not merely one thing in the world, and only thus can there be something (or rather some things). If there were only one, there would be only pure time, immobile duration [*durée*]. But there is more than one thing, and this means not so much that there are several times one but, rather, more than one—the plural of a singular that is itself always and from the very first plural (*singuli,* for "singulus" does not exist)—*more than one* is the more than oneness in the very present of the one, its excess that separates it from itself within itself. Its *sense.*

In an instant, from the very beginning of the game, world, public space, body, being-in-common, extension of the soul—distance of the most proximal, and step (not) across. From the cup to the lips, from the Tarpeian Rock to the Capitol, from Charybdis to Scylla, from one border to the other, from one wall to the other, from one lip to the other, from you to me, from one time to the other.

Someone

My name is someone and no one. . . . I have borne witness to the world: I have confessed the strangeness of the world.

JORGE LUIS BORGES, "Luna de Enfrente"[70]

There are some things, there are *some ones,* there are numerous *ones, singularities.* Sense is the singularity of all the singular ones, in all senses simultaneously. It is singularity first of all in the distributive or disseminative sense of the nonsubstitutable unicity of each singular one (be it, for example, a rock or a man named Peter [*pierre ou Pierre*]).[71] But sense is also the singularity of the singular ones in the transitive or transitional sense of what shares them out and what they all share among themselves (their finitude, common to all, proper to none, as a common impropriety, communicating yet neither communicated nor communion). And finally, sense is singularity in the collective or worldly sense of what makes of the totality of the existent the singular absolute of being (its infinite spacing).

The sense of the world is thus in each one as totality and unicity at once. In this sense, the world of Leibnizian monads is the first thought of the world.[72]

The *some one* is not the "subject" in its metaphysical position. The metaphysical position is indeed always that of a *supposition,* in one or another of its forms: as a supposed substantial support for determinations and qualities, as a point of presence supposed to be the source of representations, as a negation that supposes itself to be the power of its own suspension and overcoming, as a relation to the self (where the *to* is supposed to be the very presence of the *self*), as a power of realization supposed to engender reality, or as the supposed being of the existent. In the synthesis of all these forms, *subjecthood* is called "God," which is thus the name for the supposition of the synthesis itself.

Constantly, the subject of philosophy (or the subject, philosophy) will have supposed itself in both senses of the term: it will have posited itself on its own as its own foundation, and it will have been the hypothesis of its own hypostasis, fiction, or illusion. The point these two senses of the term share in common — a point of paradox or of infinite abyss — is the truth of the subject.

The *sub-* of *sub-jecthood* represents in a way the inverted form of the *prae-* of *pres-ence*: the present that precedes itself and thus also remains behind itself. In fact, it is a matter of both possible positions with respect to that which is "before": one can look back on the anterior, preliminary, and primordial, or one can look forward to that which is posterior, succeeding on, and final. Both positions on that which is "before" us are the same, just as also the *presence* in question here resolves itself into an *absence* in the very instant of its — supposed — presentation. In pre-sup-position, presence annuls all of its possible senses. At the point of the pure subject, all predicates are negated (and so it goes with the God of negative theologies and mysticisms: he is all the more archi-essentially divine as he is deprived of all quality or property). The true subject is being-the-self without qualities, subsuming beneath this absence merely the presence of its presupposition as the presupposition of its presence.

But in this very point, at the tip of supposition, the extremity of *sub-* or *hypo-*, in place of the foundation itself, there will always have been also the *singular one* of the point itself — no longer a "subject" in this sense, but something completely different, or else the *same-thing-completely-different:* an *existence.* Existence, an existence that is each time singular, is the supposition of all supposition, the simple and absolute position that cuts short all supposition, all *sub-* or *pre-*. Existence: that which pre-vents supposition itself, or that which over-comes it by surprise. The same-thing-completely-different: no longer privation of all predicates, but predicates without support, holding each other together mutually, singularly.

This singular existence *is* (= entrances) the first and last position of the Aristotelian *hypokeimenon* (= *subjectum*) as well as the first and last position of the Cartesian *ego sum,* in addition to those of Rousseauist sentimentality. That is to say that its *esse* makes of it the pure supposition as well as the absolute act or the entelechy. But in being-as-act pure supposition dissipates itself in its own purity. There is no longer anything supposed (carried back by hypothesis into the position of the before or underneath); there is no longer anything supposing (the supporting actor of the qualities and attributes is nothing other than their being-as-act: in the end, there is no "*suppositum*"). But there is someone.[73]

Someone: a certain someone, anyone at all, each and every one, but also this one and none other, of whom one says, "she (or he) is really someone!" Someone inimitable and unique, someone identical to all, an outline, a configuration, a point without dimensions, a limit, (not) a step. The imprint of (the absence of) a step—the vestige—that no essence other than the fugitive existence of its singularity configures.

What then *is* someone? This is precisely what one cannot ask—even though this is *the whole question*—because if there is someone, there has already been a response to the question (*s/he* has already responded). But there is someone, there are numerous someones, indeed, there is nothing else. *They* are unto the world. This is what "makes" up the world and "makes sense." *Someone, some ones, the numerous one,* that is to say, the *plural singular* "is" the response that answers the question of the "sense of the world."

"Someone" ought to be approached from the angle of this response. But this response responds to nothing. No one asked, "is anyone there?"[74] It has not been possible to pose this question because something is there. The "response," here, does not contain the presupposition of the question. A response that does not respond to a question is a response that is not the solution to a problem or the appeasement of an interrogation or the conclusion of a search. Instead, as we can see by the etymology of the word *response,* it is a given guarantee, a promise, an engagement.[75] A given guarantee, a promise, an engaged *responsibility.* Some*one* is, first of all, less a being-present than an engaged presence—engaged perhaps first in nothing other than being-*here,* exposed *there.* In this sense, for example, a mere rock "responds" just as much as a man named Peter: there is being-exposed in a crowded world.

Every one is the first and the last moment of its engagement with presence. The Aristotelian *hypokeimenon,* the *subjectum* in action, is the "everyone" (*hekaston*), the singular existent present in sensible experience. The *hekaston* is *eskhaton:* final, ultimate. Every one is eschatological.[76] Each is the end of the coming without end of sense. As such, it offers three distinctive traits: it is "unique," it is "whatever," it is "exposed."

1. *Unique:* the unicity of the singular consists quite exactly in its multiplicity. This is the essential determination—that is, the *existentiell* and existential determination—that ought to open any consideration of any type of "individuality" or "autonomy." The unconditioned existentiality of each *one* is this: it cannot *exist* through *consisting* by itself and in itself alone. Pure auto-nomy destroys itself of itself.[77] But this must be understood in an absolutely originary mode. It is not a matter of adding to a postulation of individuality or autonomy a certain number of relations and interdependencies, no matter what importance one may accord to such addenda. The "someone" does not enter into a relation with other "someones," nor is there a "community" that precedes interrelated individuals: the singular is not the particular, not a *part* of a group (species, gender, class, order). The relation is contemporaneous with the singularities. "One" means: some ones *and* some other ones, or some ones *with* other ones.

What this "and" and this "with" are about involves nothing less than the very texture of the world, the world as the being-exposed-of-the-ones-to-the-others, Paul Celan's "*auseinandergeschrieben*": being inscribes/excribes the one of/in the other as the unique being of every one. All of sense passes this way—and this is still saying too little: all of sense is along the edge of the being "with." For the one-alone, there is not sense, but merely truth. That solitude should be, "in the final analysis," the truth, this is the *commonplace* of a disenchanted romanticism, that is to say, of a thought of subjective supposition that touches its own abyssal character, incapable as it is of even perceiving that it still states its *topos* precisely *in common.*

No doubt, the singular is *per se:* it singularizes itself only by or through its singularity. But this does not mean that its singularity is its own: singular unicity is what shares it out and what it shares [*ce qui le partage et ce qu'il partage*] with the totality of singular multiplicity. Therefore, it does not constitute its singularity on the basis of its own resources—on the contrary, it does so on the basis of the most common resource, the one that comes (down) to each and every one as to none. But this also does not mean that there is a "resource" here in the sense of primary matter waiting to be fashioned and singularized. Not primary matter, but merely the final matter—*ultima materia*—of the existent, merely its "signature." Nor is there the absolutely primary presupposition of a *creatio ex nihilo.* Neither is the singular created, nor does it create itself. It is neither product nor production. It is being-as-act or being-in-action, the entelechy that no power precedes. Actuality *tout court:* nothing more and nothing less.

2. *Whatever:* every one is just as singular as every other one. In a sense, they are indefinitely substitutable, each for all the others, in-different and anonymous.[78] All are substitutable, indeed, up to the point of this so-called "final" decomposition of organic bodies into other, inorganic bodies, through which Peter borders also (otherwise) on rock, a decomposition that is nothing other than the texture of the world insofar as the text of sense exscribes itself therein.

This does not amount to giving sense up either to a "materialist" dissolution or to any sort of "panpsychic" effusion. . . . It amounts to considering that what is common to one and all, their communication with each other, is what singularizes them and consequently what shares them out and divides them up. What is commensurable in them is their incommensurability. Thus, the death of the other is not only that to which I cannot have access, that which I cannot take on myself or appropriate—as little as I can appropriate my "own" death.[79] The death of the others represents also being-with-the-others as being-with-no-body. It is not an empty relation or a relation with emptiness: it is the relation with the singularity of the singular as such. The grave is not a commemorative superstructure posited in an empty place: the grave is itself a place, a space that is valid as such, through its spacing. Before being a sign, it is a passage and a partitioning of sense. We die *into* the world as we are born into it: singular, whatever, substitutable—always capable of coming *in the place* of the other—nonsubstitutable—the place of the other being nothing but the spacing out of the place of the one.

Birth/death, each *as* the other, a singular going-coming, represents this intersection of substitution and nonsubstitution, of the replaceable and the irreplaceable, the whatever, and the unique. The relation takes place through this intersection. Here, there is neither communication and continuity of substance nor discontinuous reproduction of particular examples of a species. There is relation as relation of *example:*[80] every one, being born, dying, being-there, exemplifies singularity. Each proposes itself as *an* example, if you like, but it exposes this example, every time, as exemplary, in the sense of a remarkable model. That which is exemplary each time, that which sets an example, is singularity itself, insofar as it is never anything but *this* or *that* singularity, inimitable at the very heart of its being-whatever.

Eximo (*exemptum, exemplum*) is to place apart, to remove, and also to privilege. The example is chosen and placed apart to present an exceptional thing of greatness. Here what is exemplified is the exception of singularity—insofar as it is also the banal rule of multiplicity. But such a rule, of course, has no instance other than its cases of exception and exemplarity. The example, here, does not refer us back to a generality or universality—to some "ideal existent"—it refers us back only to itself, to the world as a world of examples, as a world of the withdrawal of singularities in their very exposition.

In order to have a relation with the example, one must be interested in it, one must be curious about what it exposes, about its sense as example. Singularities relate to each other first of all through this curiosity. They intrigue each other. A "transcendental" curiosity institutes the relation. It falls short of a confrontation of subjects as well as of a communal idyll, falls short of both benevolence and malevolence. It can open up fear and desire, love and hate, pity or terror. It can be indiscreet and discreet. It can be rejecting or caring: *curiosus* has the same root as *cura,* care or concern; "to care or be concerned about the other" contains all the ambivalence of the relation. That about which there is "care" is the sense of the example in that it is entirely within the example: the exceptional existence of each existent, of any existent whatsoever, the exception-*there* of all this world *here.*

3. *Exposed:* each one is presence itself—final, achieved, eschatological. Each is *parousia,* the end of the world as exteriority, as a rendering extraneous or alienation of presence. Along with each one, the whole is exposed. But what is exposed is exposition itself. What is presented is coming-into-presence, and thus, the diffé*ra*nce of its being-present. The withdrawal and retracing of the example is the originary spacing of its substance or consistence.

The singular exposes every time that it is exposed, and that all of its sense resides therein. There is nothing to be expected from a someone other than—exemplarily—its being-someone. Nothing more but also nothing less: every time, one can expect the act of self-exception, and this act, as act, is not a property that can be preserved, but an existence that exists and that is thus "eximious," every time, in every *hic et nunc.* By comparison with what is it thus "eximious"? With nothing. With nothing or with pure inexposition, with being that would be intransitive, or with a mass that would be indistinct within itself.

What is exposed in this way is thus a singular transitivity of being, and what every one engages in is an attestation of existence. Rather than signifying the signified of being, it attests that sense is to be singularly every time. Or, rather, that sense is every time—singularly—*toward (and in) the world.* What is exposed, if one wants to give it the form of a sensible statement, is something like: "*I am well grounded in my existence.*" But first of all it is not certain that attestation always and only takes the form of a statement: for every thing attests also, each time in its own way, in speech or in silence, that is, every one in the *world* attests. Further, I do not produce in this way any foundation for my existence, neither as cause nor as legitimation. *Here, attestation replaces foundation.*

In its way, this formula contains all sense. At least it does so on condition of being uttered without the least connotation or intonation of an appeal to a hidden sense or revelation—but, to the contrary, abandoned as it is uttered, left, deposited, exscribed as formula. On condition of being *already,* when it is still barely on the page or in the mouth, a *praxis* of whatever sort.

The "Sense" of the "World"

What if there were no sense . . . other than the sense that is lost, the pre-sense that is found always already before us? . . . it is always too late for the question of sense, too late or too soon, it comes down to the same.

MARC FROMENT-MEURICE, *Tombeau de Trakl*[81]

The word *sense* has no unity of sense, no original matrix of sense, not even a univocal etymological derivation: the Germanic root *sinno* ("direction"), is attached only conjecturally, if at all, to the Latin *sensus* ("sensation"). As for the sense of "signification," it appears to have been formed, in Old French and then in Middle French, on the basis of several connotations of two different origins (*sensus* in the sense of "thought" as in "the author's thought," *sen* and then *sinn* in the sense of "right direction, clear-sighted understanding, reason": the one who is pushed beyond good sense is *forsené* (*forcené*).

In this regard, the sense of "sense" does not have any exceptional formal property. On the contrary, this is the general property of sense, except if one exhausts "meaning" [*vouloir dire*] in a gesture of referential indication (which one can very easily do, of course, in the case of "sense," for example, by indicating "the path to be followed" [*le sens de la marche*]. In "truth," there is doubtless no other case in which "sense" can thus function according to mere indication or reference. But in this one case, there is precisely no "sense" other than the "sense" of an orientation, which presupposes the determination of an Orient (hence of an Occident). The "path to be followed" rests on presupposition, presupposing itself in order to be susceptible to indication. In this sense, referential sense makes no more sense than the circular sense of the hands of a clock. Unless, of course, one becomes uncertain about "the path to be followed" and asks oneself if this "way" is a function of the reason for, or the end toward, which one is walking. To recover this sense through some precedent is to presuppose the reason or the goal, for example, of the course of the world. This seems to happen periodically to religions and philosophies: the presupposition of an Orient, and the reduction of *sense* to that of the hands of a cosmic clock. This was the effect produced in the name of a *sense of history.*

But precisely, the historicity or historiality of history, that is, its event-character, the fact that it happens, that it succeeds on itself, or that it *proceeds*—and consequently, along with this fact, that of its worldliness or becoming-worldwide—puts an end to these effects and gives a sense anew to sense. (Of course, and as I have already said, there is not a single thought worthy of the name that can be reduced to such ideological effects, as is amply demonstrated by the uncompleteable achievement of Hegel's thought, whatever one does to try to interpret it otherwise. Every form of thought measures itself against the incommensurable term of sense.)

The whole sense of sense is thus at least the unassignable unity of sensate sense and directional sense. This unity is itself a significance, a possibility of making sense—for example, of making sense of the way things are going in the world where an Orient was presupposed as sensed, perceived, reasoned out, even if under the auspices of mystery. There is no longer any mystery of the Orient, and this is what gives all sorts of unheard-of orients a chance, whether they come from the Far East or the Middle East, from the South or from the bared heart of the Occident itself.

The unity of the senses of sense implies thus the original difference or heterogeneity of at least two senses. But this is not all. For one of these two senses, directional sense, if it does not refer to a direction already given (or "sensed"), presupposes a preliminary orientation, which is only possible, once all references have become confused, by means of a *sense of orientation.* The latter will necessarily arise out of some sort of "sensing." Sensing, as we have seen, is realized through the common being-as-act of sensing and sensed. This common actuality, however, has its unity only in the dehiscence of its two aspects. The *unity* of the act is here identically the *duality* of the actors (who are both reciprocally *patients* as well: they "suffer" each other and this is their act). In addition, there is no possible (phenomenological) "constitution" of sense in this sense.[82]

From which we can draw the following conclusion: in order to orient oneself in the world as well as to "orient the world" (they are the same thing), one must be there first. And in the same way, to orient oneself in sense or to give sense to an Orient, one must first be *in* sense—and to give one or more senses to the word *sense,* one must be in the significance of these words.

The word *world* has no unity of sense other than this one: a world (*the* world, *my* world, the *business* world, the *Moslem* world, and so on) is always a differential articulation of singularities that make sense in articulating themselves, along the edges of their articulation (where *articulation* should be taken at once in the mechanical sense of a joint and its play, in the sense of the spoken offering, and in the sense of the distribution into distinct "articles"). A world joins, plays, speaks, and shares: this is its sense, which is not different from the sense of "making sense."

But what "makes sense" in this way—and perhaps the infinity of possible "worlds," along with the infinity of finite senses—is nothing other than "the world *tout court,*" this world here whose "*here*" is not opposed to a "*there*" but *articulates* all possible beings-there.

One could say: sense is coextensive with the confines of the world, it "goes no further"—*but* only on condition of adding immediately: the world extends to the extremities of sense, absolutely.

It would not be inexact to observe that, under these conditions, the world, that is, the conjunction or the homothesis of this world here and of all the sense of the world, strangely resembles Leibniz's "best of worlds." Of course, this is immediately a painful, insupportable irony for us—who have so many reasons for being convinced that this world here is indeed the worst of worlds. But this is indeed the task: to comprehend how the only world—neither "possible" nor "necessary" but "*here*"—is also the world that can keep us confined to the worst, in fact, by dissolving any sense of world, *cosmos* or *mundus,* in its own becoming-worldly, and to comprehend how this happens . . . (to become sensible) . . . as the nudity in the process of being born that sense itself is.

This situation is the same as that which sends us from the nondetermined cardinal points (from a dis-oriented world) to a sense of orientation that is supposed to sense in the absence of any sensible Orient, and then onward from this sense to an active dehiscence of the act of sensing: that is to say, to *ek-sisting* in general.

But this means *neither* that we have to orient ourselves in a state of complete blindness, *nor* that it is a matter of indifference that we are disoriented, and that there is no difference between the best and the worst. On the contrary, it means that there is no sense given anywhere that could make us tolerate the intolerable, *no more than there is nonsense in virtue of which we could disqualify or annul existence.* In other words, this means that "nihilism" dissolves every bit as much as any "idealism" (or "metaphysics" in this sense) because it, too, remains in the final analysis submitted to the regime of supposition. It dissolves at the touch of the absolute point of existence.

In a sense, there is no longer anything here to be said. The infinite regress of supposition is cut off, and the *praxis* of significance is opened up on this clean cut. At every instant, here and now while I write and while you read, it could be absolutely necessary and pressing to abandon these thoughts and to give oneself up in haste to the event. In fact, this takes place every day. It can take place in a less quotidian manner, and in accordance with the events of the end of the world that we are experiencing. Every discourse on the sense and significance of the world can be suspended, tipping over into insignificance, through a conflagration of misery or sovereignty, through a major technological mutation, through an unheard-of genetic manipulation, through a catastrophe inextricably mixing "nature" and "society," as well as by an accident, a suffering, a joy in my immediate surroundings, of my "own." What one might call "the urgency of the situation" will make me "throw away my pen" (as Friedrich Hölderlin expected to have to do for a Revolution), delivering my discourse up to the derision of "all talk, no action." But *this in itself* bears witness to sense.

At this point, it is true, the insistent perpetuation of theoretical discourse, of the will to a signifying appropriation of sense, can reveal itself to be sick—and to prove Freud right. There is a kind of mania, or whatever one wants to call it (paranoia, melancholy, obsession), of sense that haunts philosophy. Or more exactly: for structural rather than accidental reasons, philosophy will not have been able not to be mad about sense. But *this in itself* is the chance whose double is the risk: the risk of madness/the chance of a folly of sense. "I know of a Greek labyrinth that is a single straight line. Along this line so many philosophers have lost themselves."[83]

Painting

> Friday I looked for you but I didn't know where to look. Your mother wouldn't tell.
>
> I felt so alone and depressed. Like I was a void. And it didn't lessen any. I had lost the only thing of real value I'd ever had or known. My life had lost meaning, it had become a gulf, empty and void but for the shadows and the ever-present ghosts who have followed me for so long.
>
> ... We were together for only two months but it is the fullest two months I've known in this life. I wouldn't trade it for anything. Just two months but I believe that I have known you, that we've known each other, for so much longer—a thousand, two thousand years?—I don't know what we were to each other before, I will know, as you will also when it becomes ultimately clear one day—but I feel we were always lovers.[84]

Sense never becomes clear, and for this reason it is always rending and heartrending. It is not, however, an obscurity that is having difficulty dissipating itself or that is failing to do so, even if the expectation of, and hope for, clarity would like to think it is. Rather, sense is an obscurity that leads to its obscurity. It is to enter, to let oneself enter and come, into obscurity. However, "obscurity" means nothing and might evoke obscurantism or blindness, whereas sense is clear as a thousand suns, clear as a thousand years of love. Sense—this "sense" that one characterizes so often with respect to a text as "clear" or "obscure"—is a clear obscurity, and the clearer it is, the more it is exposed as, and seen for, what it is in its obscurity. Since the beginning of the Occident, it has been a question only of this: entering with eyes wide open into the night and/or into the sun itself. Or declaring that one cannot enter into it without dying (instead of affirming that "dying" is entering into it). Into the night, the sun of sense.

This clarity of the obscure is completely different from chiaroscuro. Chiaroscuro would like to present sense as a mystery, in accordance with the "occidental haunting of half-light (chiaroscuro), which is exactly the same thing as the quest for intimacy (or mystery) in love."[85] It wants to attain to the sense of sense as to the truth of a mysterious intimacy. At least, this is the case for the chiaroscuro of philosophy, for which "pure light and pure darkness are two voids which are the same thing. Something can be distinguished only in determinate light or darkness (light is determined by darkness and so is darkened light, and darkness is determined by light, is illumined darkness)."[86]

But perhaps the chiaroscuro does not refer *in painting* to mystery except for a certain period in the history of painting, the period in which it participates in metaphysical revelations or celebrations. In truth, painting does this: it equalizes and exposes light and darkness, without dialectically mediating them through each other, and in this way it presents, equally exposed and apportioned, the whole of visible presentation, so that the thing should come into view, so that it should come along with its shadow, with its hidden face thus shown. So that the view should come to itself and that it should see this, too: that it does not see.

So that the view should touch the limit, that it should touch its limit, that it should touch itself intact. Painting is always on the threshold. It makes up the threshold between intactness and touching—between the intactness and touching *of* light and shadow.[87] It offers access: sense itself, which is not the access that accedes to nothing, but the access that infinitely accedes, ever further forward into the night/the day, into the trace that divides and joins them. Access is no longer of the order of vision, but of the touch. The clear and the obscure no longer present things (significations), but themselves come to the eye, to its contact, while nonetheless remaining infinitely intact. On this limit, always attained and always withdrawn, sense is suspended, not as a sense more or less clearly deciphered, but as the obscure tact of clarity itself.

"This is perhaps what painting has been good for. Not to freeze or to represent . . . a world withdrawn from the wind and inclement weather—but, rather, a world characterized by an indefinite prolongation of the visible itself: its infinite opening."[88]

But this is also in one way or another the concern of "art" in general: there is no art that is not the art of a clear touch on the obscure threshold of sense.

However, there is no "art" in general: each one indicates the threshold by being itself also the threshold of another art. Each one touches the other without passing into it, and there is properly speaking no art of touching (not even a "minor" art such as those for taste and smell), for touching is sense qua threshold, the sensing/sensed apportioning of the aisthetic entelechy. Touching is the light/darkness of all the senses, and of sense, absolutely. In touching, in all the touches of touching that do not touch each other—touches of color, traced, melodic, harmonic, gestural, rhythmic, spatial, significative touches, and so on—the two sides of the one sense do not cease to come each toward the other, acceding without access, touching on the untouchable, intact, spacing of sense.

Barely to touch: to skim the surface. Sense levels off, the senses skim its surface (all the senses, including those of words). The French word *fleur* [flower] can take on the sense of "surface" because it designates the extreme and the finest part of the plant. There is sense only on the (flowering) surface of sense [*Il n'y a de sens qu'à fleur de sens*]. Never fruit to be harvested—but the *painting* of fruits as their coming ceaselessly resumed, ceaselessly put back into the world, superficially, as on the rosy surface of the skin [*à fleur de peau*].

Music

Teknē mousikē, the term for the technique or *savoir-faire* of the Muses, was at first a term of generic breadth, including all types of execution, recitation, or putting-to-work of a harmony larger and more general than the harmony of sounds. And in the end or in the beginning, it was a matter of the harmony of the entire world-cosmos. Music in our sense, nonetheless, has its own specific way of belonging to the Muses (each one having for an attribute an instrument or a mode of song; none in turn patronizing the "plastic arts").

It is only slowly and late that the sense of the "art of sounds" becomes autonomous, and more precisely still, in the modern mode, the art of instrumental sounds (in the Renaissance). Since then, it seems, music has received a vocation for the universal, a privilege of the essential, at least in a vein of thought that, beyond Nietzsche, runs all the way up through Theodor Adorno. This destiny of music is not without a very intimate and complex relationship with the destiny of sense. Indeed, regulated, rhythmical sonority can take on, at least to our Occidental *sense*, the value of a threshold between sensibility and signification. One could say that music has signified for us significance itself, and even beyond significance the sublime access (say, in the mode of negative theology) to a pure presentation of sense. But in order for this to be the case, it was necessary that it be understood as "an art beyond signification."[89] The threshold of such a "beyond" is the critical point par excellence of any approach to sense: one can always pass on anew to an ineffable (but sonorous, audible, vocal, evocative) "oversignification," but one can also keep to the threshold as to the in-significant opening of sense.

Why does music occupy this site? The answer exceeds my competencies. But to the extent that this point of passage is unavoidable, I will sketch some disjointed traits.

The Muses themselves indicate that the general harmony is not presented as such. Insofar as the *cosmos* is a *harmony,* it is already distributed among the various functions of the Muses. In fact, the law of a harmony in general is its internal apportionment quite as much as its resultant accord. The sonorous register, to which the word *aisthesis* originally referred,[90] is perhaps a witness or elective site of this division. This register is like the line of contact between the most interior and the most exterior: a pure *line of sense,* which would also be the cleanest *cut.* The most interior: the body in a state of sensory deprivation continues or comes to hear itself, to hear its blood, its noise, its heart. The most exterior: sound is, as it were, the least incorporated matter. After having been heard, it still remains somewhere out there, and not merely like color and line in a vis-à-vis. Rather, it resonates elsewhere, at a distance, in an exteriority that is spaced out in all the other directions and that the ear *hears* along with the sound, as the opening of the world. Sound has no hidden surface. It is like a totality of space, on the confines from the very start.

Sonorous coming into presence is thus the most close and the most distant, turned the most fragile by its own coming. The coming of touch withdraws into intact concentration, while the coming of sound disseminates itself into extension (not less intact, having escaped into the distances). Something is lost essentially in the sonorous gift: resonance *itself.* Also, when one considers the proximity (or mutual belonging) of the sonorous and the linguistic, the doubled approach—each toward the other—of voice and speech, it is necessary to consider that the voice will not fail to dissipate into the distances something of all speech. *Verba volant:* the tradition puts it like a loss, regretfully—but what if it were the condition of sense, its vocal différ*a*nce?

Musical fragility (fractality, discretion) resides in the inarticulateness of a sense always both extended—offered—and withheld.

(Here is where all the problems of the relations between text and music are suspended in the history of song, such as one rediscovers them, in a way intact, all the way up through rock 'n' roll.) A signification is proposed, but it must be deciphered or understood—if one can put it this way—in accordance with the execution of its presentation, the way in which its statement is stated. Thus, the musical score (text?) including the words, whenever there are words, is inseparable from what we call, remarkably, its *interpretation*: the sense of this word oscillating then between a hermeneutics of sense and a technique of "rendering" [*rendu*]. The musical interpretation, or *execution,* the putting-into-action, or entelechy, cannot be simply "significant": what it concerns is not or not merely sense in this sense. And reciprocally, the execution cannot itself be signified without remainder: one cannot *say* what it *made* the "text" *say.*[91] The execution can only be executed: it can *be* only as executed.

Further, music can only be *played,* including by those who only listen. The entire body is involved in this play—tensions, distances, heights, movements, rhythmical schemes, grains, and timbres—without which there is no music. The "least" song demonstrates it—and even more, no doubt, it is demonstrated by the existence of the song itself, as a permanent, polymorphic, and *worldwide* execution of musicality. That which is propagated, apportioned, and dispersed with the song, in its innumerable forms, is at the very least—and stubbornly—a playful execution of sense, a being-as-act through cadence, attack, inflection, echo, syncopation . . .

Rather than saying "the impossible beyond of signification" (cf. note 89 above), or better, by means of saying just this, music (and along with music, "art," the entire company of the Muses) becomes the knowledge in action of the sense "beyond," as the play of pronunciation in the absence of any word or name to be pronounced, the pronunciation *not* of an "unpronounceable" name but of what is not at all to be pronounced. This is finally perhaps nothing other than pronunciation itself, the articulation—"harmonia"—and thus the modulation and execution of sense as sense itself.

Beyond . . . not even the silent attestation of the being-placed-there of stones remains truly beyond music: still, already, there is the rustling of the world, the grating, crackling, "background" noise, the noise without noise, or, rather, even simply, the mineral stupor that is still the surprise of the world.

OLGA: [. . .] How cheerfully and jauntily that band's playing—really I feel as if I wanted to live! Merciful God! The years will pass, and we shall all be gone for good and quite forgotten. . . . Our faces and our voices will be forgotten and people won't even know that there were once three of us here. . . . But our sufferings may mean happiness for the people who come after us. . . . There'll be a time when peace and happiness reign in the world, and then we shall be remembered kindly and blessed. No, my dear sisters, life isn't finished for us yet! We're going to live! The band is playing so cheerfully and joyfully—maybe, if we wait a little longer, we shall find out why we live, why we suffer. . . . Oh, if we only knew, if only we knew! . . .

CHEBUTYKIN [*sings quietly to himself*]: Tarara-boom-di-ay. . . . I'm sitting on a tomb-di-ay. . . . [*Reads the paper.*] What does it matter? Nothing matters!

OLGA: If only we knew, if only we knew! . . .[92]

Politics I

All space of sense is common space (hence all space is common space . . .). Sense does not take place for one alone. Because sense is "being-toward," it is also "being-toward-more-than-one," and this obtains even at the heart of solitude. Sense is a tensor of multiplicity. A sense-for-one-alone, if one could even speak of it, would reduce to a truth closed in on itself, in-different and immediately imploded, not even "true." Sense is the fact that sense begins or begins again with each singularity and completes itself neither in any singularity nor in the totality, which is itself nothing but the enchaining of renewed beginnings.

The political is the place of the in-common as such. Or again, the political is the place of being-*together*. In order to discern being-together more clearly, one could distinguish it from love as the place of being-with: the "with" makes up the common concern of a contrast, even a contrariety, that is, a contradiction, posited as such (before the visible division of the sexes, but nonetheless exemplarily represented, if not constituted, by sex), played out between two punctualities, two truths, two names (*two,* not in a contingent way, but precisely because in "one-*and*-the-other" a "one-*or*-the-other" is at stake). From this point of view, love appears to be at the limit of sense, on the side of truth—but of the play of truth between two truths. In other words, its hasty formula would be: everyone for him- or herself, none being reducible either to the self or to a third term.[93] In the *together*, on the contrary, the common concern, beyond "two," is the numerous as such and even in principle the innumerable: it is a matter of the tendentially indistinct anonymity whose grouping is given, while its tie [*lien*] properly so-called is not.

One could say: love begins in pure truth (punctuality, myth) and must, in order to last, come to make sense (assuming that it ought to last), whereas the political begins in pure sense (undifferentiated and vague being-toward) and must punctuate itself into truth (the first punctuation having the form of *power*). For this reason, they have been set up, in our tradition, as two interconnected and antagonistic paradigms, each exposed, in a sense, to the other, each attracting and repelling the other.

Just as the becoming-sense of love can go so far as to deprive love of truth (and thus, at the same time, of sense—of "erotic" sense, at least, converting it into "political" or "social" sense: the family), so the becoming-truth of the political can go so far as to absorb sense into itself. What one calls "totalitarianism" is the complete presentation of a sense in truth: myth, that is, but myth as reality, without the différ*a*nce of its narrative. It is the immediate being-there or immanence of myth. In the fascist version, truth is the life of the community, in the Nazi version, truth is the conflagration of the people, and in the communist version, truth is humanity creating itself as humanity. Life, fire, creation: three figures of completed sense, signifying itself and absorbing itself without remainder in its signified, that is, in its referent—for *truth* here is a concrete punctuation. On this account, politics *must* be destiny, must have history as its career, sovereignty as its emblem, and sacrifice as its access.

One really should retrace the striking history of political sacrifice, of sacrificial politics—politics *in truth,* that is to say, the "theologicopolitical": from expressly religious sacrifice to the diverse Reigns of Terror, and to all the national, militant, and partisan sacrifices. The politics of the *Cause* to which sacrifice is due. In this sense, all theologicopolitics, including its "secularization," is and can be nothing other than sacrificial. And the sacrifice represents the access to truth, in the appropriating negation of the *finite* negativity of sense. To have to do with the *world,* which is not a "Cause"—and which is itself without any Cause—is to have to do with sacrifice no longer.[94]

But what we have hitherto called "democracy" represents merely indeterminate sense, a sense that would remain indeterminate — possessing precisely therein its (resolutely empty) truth — and that would thus not go beyond a kind of last sacrifice, the sacrifice of truth or of the Cause itself, thereby continuing to adhere to sacrificial logic. There is nothing astonishing about the fact that the "crisis of sense" is, first of all and most visibly, a crisis of and in "democracy" (this is precisely what "the thirties" meant). Truth without figure or sense, truth of the absence of sense: law in its absence of foundation, ecotechnics in the guise of Cause . . .

The political question is therefore not how to reconstitute the conditions of sacrifice, but how to induce the *group* comprised of indeterminate *ties* — ties that have come untied or are not yet tied — to configure itself as a space of sense that would not be reabsorbed into its own truth.

This sort of *configuration* of space would not be the equivalent of a political figuration (fiction, myth). It would trace the form of being-toward in being-together without identifying the traits of the toward-*what* or toward-*whom,* without identifying or verifying the "to what end" of the sense of being-in-common — or else, by identifying these traits as those of *each one:* a different "totality," a different unicity of truth. Of being-in-common, it would operate a transitivity, not a substantiality. But still, there would remain something of the "figure," something of the outline.[95]

But how? This question forms the contour, if not of the aporia, at least of the paradox of political sense today: without figuration or configuration, is there still any sense? But as soon as it takes on a figure, is it not "totalitarian" truth?[96] What outline would retain the unexpectedness of sense, its way of continuing to come and to be on its way, without confounding them with an indeterminacy that lacks all consistency? What name could open up [*frayer*] an access for the anonymity of being-in-common? There can be no doubt that Sovereignty, as an identification of the "common" with the *decision* of being in common, has exhausted its resources of sense to become a pure *effect of truth,* the effects of which, in turn, of course, cannot fail to be effects of "purification," for example, the "ethnic purification" that is occurring in the Balkans as I write these lines. . . . But this does not suffice simply to annul all indications and questions of "sovereignty"—that is to say, of a being-in-action of being-together such that nothing precedes or exceeds it. Sovereignty has no doubt lost the sense it had, reducing itself to a kind of "black hole" of the political. But this does not mean that the sense of being-in-common, inasmuch as sense itself is in common, does not have to make itself sovereign in a new way.

In order to begin to get one's bearings within the dis-orientation of the political, it is necessary, first of all, to be clear about what has been called, since Carl Schmitt, the "theologicopolitical." We have too facilely repeated—in particular on the occasion of the bicentenary of the execution of Louis XVI—that Sovereignty, having (sacrificially) deprived itself of theologicopolitical transcendence, wandered off in search of a "secular" substitute. In taking our leave of the theologicopolitical, we have not *lost* something, and we have not entered into a politics of mourning and melancholia that, easily enough, can be transformed into a mourning for the political.[97] What we persistently retain, in the form of this interminable mourning (in its extreme form, as reactionary politics, and in its mild form, as administrative rationality), is doubtless the loss of a truth—but this is the opening of a sense. This is, at least, the sense whose sense we still have to discover. The political task and responsibility are to understand "democracy" in some way other than through a negative theology of the political (as the unnameable, ungroundable instances of justice and law).

On this account, Carl Schmitt's thesis is no longer tenable, if it was in its own time. First of all, one must ask oneself how and up to what point there was *politics,* for the greater number of people, in the epoch of the theologicopolitical. There may well have been no politics, or only very little, in the sense of a *being-together* into which one could *enter,* in the sense of a *knot to be tied* [*lien à nouer*]. In this respect, for the majority there was only religion (in a domestic, ecclesiastical, corporatist, or other variety). And the "end of the political" is thus, like the "end of art," only the end of religion: the end of an order of given, tied-up sense.

To speak here of "the majority of people" is not to speak in a quantitative sense: the coming of all to the public relation—"citizenship"—

is what constitutes the political as a sense to come but, consequently, also as a sense that cannot be subsumed under the signification of a "State," at least not without implying at the same time the multiplicity and plurilocality of relations within "the" relation that is not "one."[98]

The "secularization" of the theologicopolitical of which one has spoken in the wake of Carl Schmitt is a deceptive motif. For if it is exact that "all significant concepts of the modern theory of the state are secularized theological concepts,"[99] it is not less exact that it is *also,* at the same time, in order to exit from the State, and in any case from the State according to its merely secularized theory, that, in principle, the exit from the theologicopolitical has been employed. Once again, this exit is nothing other than the "end of philosophy," qua end—completion and step beyond itself—of the assignation of being in the truth of essence. If Schmitt was right to affirm that "the metaphysical image that a definite epoch forges of the world has the same structure as what the world immediately understands to be appropriate as a form of its political organization. . . . metaphysics is the most intensive and the clearest expression of an epoch,"[100] nonetheless, he was not in a position to appreciate the extent to which *the metaphysics of our age,* that is, the beginning of the twenty-first century—at least if we actually deal with it rather than replaying "the thirties"—is what one can call *the metaphysics of the deconstruction of the essence, and of existence qua sense.* A formula as hasty as this is too simple, of course, and it is nothing more than a summary of problems, as well as an index pointing toward another gesture, "style," and *praxis.* But we are already in the midst of this *praxis* and "style"—as "life style" and "style of existence"—even though they do not yet form on their own a "theoretical vision" disengaged from the metaphysics of the essence and cannot do so in principle: because what is coming shows itself only once it has come and become the past.[101]

However, just as the alternative between the permanence of the old and pure innovation is false (and itself "theological"), so the "end" of the "theologicopolitical" comes to it from out of its own interior and from out of its own past. It would be necessary to go through this entire past, beginning with that which deconstructs itself *of itself* in Christian theology. For the moment, I will make do with the following indication: Rousseau represents at once a "remarkable" example, as Schmitt puts it, of the "politicization of theological concepts,"[102] and an index pointing, beyond even its own knowledge and theory, toward something completely different: not toward principles of the political, but toward the political *in statu nascendi,* the tying of the social knot qua archi-constitution of the "political animal." The model of the contract remains insufficient—that is, impoverished—in this respect, in that it presupposes subject-parties who enter into the contract. Meanwhile, its only sense is to constitute these "parties" themselves. Its only sense is to think the (k)not *to be tied,* and not already tied. In other words, to think the sense of the *in-common* neither as the truth of a common subject nor as a "general" sense superimposed on "particular" senses, but, to the contrary, as the absence of any "general" sense outside of the internally numerous singularity of each of the "subjects of sense." As much as Rousseau "secularizes" Sovereignty, he gears down its truth by deferring its sense, by opening up for it an unheard-of history that is still our own. This is no longer "becoming-secular" but "becoming-worldly," that is to say, the resituation of sovereignty within existence, naked existence.

On this account, Schmittian "decision" is not simply disqualified either. In terms of "becoming-secular," the necessity of decision—that is, the impossibility of assigning a Subject of law and the State that would not be first of all an existent in action—can have recourse only to dictatorship. In terms of "becoming-worldly," this recourse turns around against itself. Decision *is* existence as such, and existence, inasmuch as it does not take place for one alone or for two but for many, decides itself as a certain *in* of the in-common. Which one? Decision consists precisely in that *we* have to decide on it, in and for our world, and thus, first of all, to decide on the "we," on who "we" are, on how *we* can say "we" and can call ourselves *we.*

Labor

The sense of a world reduced to labor, or the sense of labor in the world? In a certain way, this is the question that traverses us from one end to the other, at least once the possibility of labor is effectively present, and presupposing that its absence ("unemployment," on the one hand, and "underemployment," on the other) is not in turn an effect of the general reduction to labor, combined with its unequal distribution.

One could recast this question through a sketch of the history of rock 'n' roll: as is generally known, the birth of rock corresponds to a moment of socioeconomic difficulties accompanied by a (first?) destabilization or fissuring of representations constructed in terms of the "working class," and along with these, of certain forms of popular music. Rock corresponds at its inception to a transformation of the relation to exploitation, in which a desire to evade the working world (by succeeding in what will become showbiz) is mixed with a will to create new popular forms (cf. "pop music" and "pop art"). The middle-class conformism into which a good part of rock and its extensions have ended up flowing does not saturate, even today, the totality of the phenomenon: in its multiple, moving identity, both from the social and from the musical point of view, it continues to be traversed and "worked" over by shocks and ruptures (*hard rock, punk rock, metal, destroy, grunge,* and so on, and inversely, the *understatement* of a new sobriety) that retain a relation to the origin of rock and that accompany its singular worldliness.[103]

Marx always ultimately wanted to liberate, or to "equaliberate,"[104] ends, and not to end a Cause. For him, the name of sense—of the sense of liberation and the deliverance of sense—was "labor" (for him, and for an entire epoque that remains still in several respects our own). It remains thus for us to figure out what "labor" means.

What Marx had in view was not simply the free, equal, and socialized administration of the necessity of "organic exchanges with nature." For it is only "beyond this empire of necessity that the blossoming of human force that is its own end begins, the true reign of liberty, which however cannot flourish except insofar as it founds itself on the reign of necessity."[105] Further, this reign of liberty represents, for Marx, an exit neither from the sphere nor from the category of "labor." Indeed, he elsewhere designates the "human force" of which he speaks here as "labor": "When labor will have become not merely the means of life but also the first need of life."[106]

It is thus a question of labor as the *first need of life.* How are we to understand this?

It should be noted that this phrase is preceded by the following: "When the enslaving subordination of individuals to the division of labor and hence the opposition between intellectual and physical labor will have disappeared." This should be noted because it is not necessary to be either a Maoist or otherwise inclined to subject intellectuals and artists to forced labor to affirm that we cannot consider ourselves to have dispensed with the question posed by this opposition: it exposes at least one determinate figure, and precisely a sociopolitically concrete figure, of the general problem of the "reign of liberty." No doubt, the terms of the opposition need to be carefully analyzed in a situation in which computerized labor, the third sector, so-called "social" work, and so forth, disturb the surface of a "mind/body" distinction, which for Marx was still relatively simple, indeed, phenomenally simple. But the cortex and nerves are part of the body, like the eyes, the ears, the hands. . . . Reciprocally, the entire body, including muscle and bone, plays a role in what we call "intellectual" work. The sensing and the sensed are of the body. *Ergo:* the opposition in question is a figure—even if only one figure—of the distinction between labor as "means" and labor as "end."

It is doubless in this distinction that the essentials of the problematic, the expectation, and perhaps what has until now functioned as the aporia of Marxism lie. ("Until now" because revolt, if not revolution, is once again not unforeseeable, and because it will not take place without reference to Marx, regardless of what it actually is.)

In order to pass from labor as means (everything resides in this: *means,* mediator, operator of/through negativity, or . . . ?) to labor as end, from necessitated labor to free labor, a complete change of sphere is necessary, accompanied by the conservation of something whose identity would be indicated by the name of "labor." Is this dialectic possible? Is it possible to tear from "labor" the secret of a transmutation of necessity into freedom? Is it a matter of dialectics? Or of a dialectics that would no longer itself be "labor of the negative," and in what sense? I do not know the answers to these questions. But it is certainly necessary to explore their conditions.

And, first of all, it is necessary to denounce that which, in the current order of things in the developed countries, no doubt comes down to slyly introducing the (ideological) belief that this dialectic is at work. Because many of the external forms of labor have changed, because the pregnant image of the physical laborer has become blurred (as if there were not *still* steelworks, assembly lines, heavy tools and hard materials, dust, gases . . . , and as if computerized labor did not have its own difficulties and risks . . . to say nothing here of the division of tasks between immigrants and others, between North and South), because the patent distinction between profits on investments and wages for labor has disappeared, because the recent expansion of finance capital supports the lure of little speculative satisfactions, and for still other reasons as well that ought to be brought to light, it seems as if the category of "labor" were extending and distending itself to the point of dilution, as if it were about to "impregnate all spheres of existence" (as Marx wanted politics to do). And this appearance persists in spite of, or perhaps even *in conjunction with,* an opposition more stark than ever before between "leisure" (as epitomized by the brilliant images of Club

Med) and "labor." Insidiously, without truly being proposed as such, the thesis of labor as having its end in itself is gaining ground across what is in reality a generalized becoming-laborious of social existence.

Once one has sidestepped the traps of this illusion, one finds oneself confronted with the fundamental question: the question of how to pass from necessity to freedom *while holding onto labor,* which is to pass from production to creation, or in terms that are more rigorous (more Aristotelian and more Marxist) to pass from *poiesis* to *praxis,* from the activity that produces something to the activity through which the agent of the action "produces" or "realizes" him/herself.

One can put it also this way: it is a question of the passage from "surplus value" determinable as extortion of added value, "surplus value" measurable in terms of labor force and/or labor time, to "surplus value" no longer determinable as "value," and thus to a beyond of value, to the absolute value—not measurable in terms of any other thing (as Kant said of "dignity")—of an end-in-itself or a pure autoteleology (which is, moreover, each time singular and incomparable). All of economics and all of "political economy," *including* its critique, are at stake here.

In still other words: what is at stake is the passage from labor to art, from the one "teknē" to the other. Or from technique to "itself," if that is possible.... One would find for such a program, itself perhaps impossible to program, quite a few pointers in Marx himself.

(As one example of the node of the question in Marx: "No longer diminishing for the sake of excessive labor, the reduction of the necessary labor time will make possible the free unfolding of the individual. In fact, thanks to leisure and to the means placed at everyone's disposal, the reduction of socially necessary labor time to the minimum will favor everyone's development in artistic, scientific, etc., terms."[107] The nodosity of the question has to do with the entanglement of the notions of *surplus labor* [which, in this context, is "stolen" labor in the sense of stolen "labor time"], *social labor*—what would nonsocial or asocial labor be?—*socially necessary labor,* and its implicit correlate [?], *socially free labor,* or *surplus labor*—art or science—in the sense of labor that would work itself out beyond alienation.)

Three large questions follow:

1. Do the first and second "labors" share the same essence or not? Does labor labor on labor? This is perhaps the great hypothesis and/or question posed by Marx. He inherits it from Hegel, of course, but he cuts short what remained understood from Kant to Hegel, that is, that work works on work and liberates it from itself by passing *from one class to another* and simultaneously from one register ("corporal") to another ("intellectual").

2. Is the passage from the one to the other effected by "labor"—and in what sense—or not? (It seems to me that these are questions that have not been answered even by those thinkers of Marxism who have disengaged it from the exclusive sway of the production model and from the model of the "communist" completion of capitalism, for example, Maximilian Rubel and Michel Henry.)

3. Can *technology* be seen as playing a crucial role in this hypothetical passage (in conformity, to some extent, with the views of Marx) if its essence is no longer considered in Heideggerian terms (at least in the way in which these terms are most generally understood), that is to say, as an extortion operated on nature, itself "inspected" as "stock," but in a completely different way, as in-finitization of "production" and the "work," as "inoperation" [*désoeuvrement*]?

These questions underlie the enormous ambiguity that has been emblematized for a long time now by the maxim or slogan that "labor makes us free." Originally the sanctimonious bourgeois ideologeme of a soft dialectics leading from necessity to freedom, this formula ended up, as is well known, inscribed in frightful derision above the gate of Auschwitz (*Arbeit macht frei*).

But even if one supposes that the formula could be understood differently, if one supposes that "labor" accedes to freedom, the formula itself makes visible what it lacks: for it does not state that *labor makes itself free*. But the latter is Marx's problem.

Without claiming to go any further, I will add merely this to the description of the problem.

(a) Would work that was set free to contain its own end in itself amount to setting up the *worker* as ultimate end? One will recall that Ernst Jünger set up this figure as the annunciative figure of a new world, and that Heidegger made use of it in the *Rektoratsrede*. Can the agent, subject, human, *Dasein*, or singularity of *praxis* be "the worker"? And should they be? Should or can it be a question of *work* here? (Of course, the whole theme of revolution as work is at stake here: revolution as work or play...)

(b) At the very least, one thing remains unthought when one attempts to conceptualize work as (self-)emancipating: the difficulty of work, its *painful* dimension (which in French, for example, appears in the etymology of the word *travail*). Is emancipated work and/or is the work through which work would liberate itself (from itself) still painful? What would labor without pain mean? It is not merely a question of words. Much more radically, to be sure, it is an ontological question: it is a matter here of the ontology of necessity, of the necessity of the "body," "nature," and "needs." To put it in Heideggerian terms, perhaps we are lacking an existential analytic of pain, an *existentiale* of painfulness, but one that would not supply pain with a sacrificial justification of any sort.

Is the passage from necessity to freedom a passage from pain to pleasure? Does the passage itself involve no pain? And pleasure itself? What is the role of the (historically proximate) category of the "sublime" here, as a mixture of pain and pleasure? Is there such a thing as sublime labor?

In truth, I am merely trying to state these questions because they are inevitably present. I have not presupposed their answers.

I by no means intend to suggest that one should transform a conquering dialectic into its own dialecticization through an ontological dolorousness—and moralism—such as is already present, no doubt, in the ideology of the "labor that sets you free" ("*Work, take pains: those are the funds we lack the least.*" ... The entire ambiguity of the fable is summarized in this last verse: "*That work is a treasure.*" Is this treasure value or the beyond of value? How are we to construe the *funds* here?) But I would point out that neither Marx nor Heidegger, neither Michel Henry nor Ernst Jünger takes into consideration, directly *and for itself*, the *pain* of work. At most, this pain appears in their texts in the mediated, dialecticized, transubstantiated form of the *effort* that is requisite, as we all know, to all great conquests, above all, to the conquest over "oneself"...

And it is in this vein that one finds in Marx, beyond the pain connected with *alienated* labor, remarks like the following, the more detailed contextual analysis of which remains to be carried out: "*Truly free kinds of labor, for example musical composition, are devilishly serious, requiring the most intense effort.*"[108] In a general way, is there or is there not in Marx nonalienated labor? Is it equivalent to "labor without pain"? Or again, what does "alienation" mean? It is not by chance that some thirty years ago this question split the communist monolith in two. It can be transcribed as follows: what does "self-production" mean? Does it mean *poiesis, praxis,* or some other, unheard-of thing? Could it be that one has to surmount (?) the distinction and to manage a *poiepraxic* or *praxipoietic* thought?

A minimal propaedeutic to questions such as these: it is from the theme of *force* that one must remove oneself here, from the motifs of effort, force, and power, of the *Macht* of *machen* (and can one do this in the name of "labor"?) For pain and the passivity, passion, and passibility attached to pain are not of this register. Nor, indeed, are they of the moral register of Christian condemnation, to which labor has been attached (although it has also been attached to redemption, which perhaps left some traces in Marx).

Can one think "the sweat of the brow" at a distance from both force and sin?

Marx: " 'You will work by the sweat of your brow!' This curse Adam received from the mouth of Jehovah, and it is in just this way that Adam Smith understands labor; as for 'repose,' it would be identical to 'freedom' and to 'happiness.' It is Smith's least concern that 'in his normal state of health, force, activity, talent, and dexterity,' the individual needs also a normal quantity of labor that puts an end to his repose."[109]

Labor as a need? As a need of a normal quantity of this need? Derisive and detestable questions for those leaving the camps, whether of Stakhanovism or of Fordism (supposing that anyone ever actually *leaves* or that we know what it would mean here "to leave"). And yet, one must pose them: they demand, in fact, that we ask about the sense of labor, and up to what point and how this sense needs to be liberated in order to be sense.

> The new conception of labor amounts to the exploitation of nature, which with naïve complacency is contrasted with the exploitation of the proletariat. Compared with this positivistic conception, Fourier's fantasies, which have so often been ridiculed, prove to be surprisingly sound. According to Fourier, as a result of efficient cooperative labor, four moons would illuminate the earthly night, the ice would recede from the poles, sea water would no longer taste salty, and beasts of prey would do man's bidding. All this illustrates a kind of labor which, far from exploiting nature, is capable of delivering her of the creations which lie dormant in her womb as potentials.[110]

In a way, we are closer to Charles Fourier's imaginings than Walter Benjamin thought. But what is happening does not fall under the sign of labor placed in turn under the sign of technology. For does not *teknē* effectively supplement *phusis?* Labor is coming to be eclipsed as production by technology. And technology seems to tend to resemble a *praxis* more than a *poiesis.* It transforms its agent—itself and the technician—more than it fashions a product. Labor indeed subsists, yet it is now deprived not merely of a surplus value but of the very sense of a "production." Nevertheless, this slow drifting of *teknē* away from production is itself ambivalent. It can respond to the "watchword": "Effectuate for the sake of effectuating,"[111] or else it can render *(itself) in-operative* [elle peut (se) *dés-oeuvrer*]: it can have as its end not to make an end of sense. But it is not merely a matter of a choice (which always comes down to the ideology of a choice between "blind technology" and "mastered technology"): it is a matter of deciding on the limit without thickness that separates (and does not separate) an in-finity from another in-finity. Such is the line that divides up the word *labor* between "work" and "*praxis.*"

But this line itself divides itself, of course, along its two borders: work, between an existential painfulness and an extortion of output; *praxis,* between the act of existence and the act of autoteleology one calls "capitalism" or the world economy. The economy can no longer be represented as an "infrastructure." There is no longer an economy. Rather, there is *ecotechnics,* the global structuration of the world as the reticulated space[112] of an essentially capitalist, globalist, and monopolist organization that is monopolizing the world.[113] The more the monopolization of the world makes the phantom of another "economy" disappear—and this is why "real socialism" dissolved of itself, not by failure, but by inconsistency—the more clearly *ecotechnics* displays what is henceforth possible: either ecotechnics takes on the sense of the autism of a "great monad" in a process of indefinite self-expansion, and/or it takes on the sense of the disruption of all closures of signification, a disruption that opens them up to the coming of (necessarily unprecedented) sense. That is, either ecotechnics is the entire sense of labor—of a labor henceforth infinite, dazed by its own infinitude and by its indefinitely growing totalization—or else ecotechnics opens labor up to sense, inoperates labor unto the infinity of sense.[114]

Politics II

How to attempt to discern at least the terms of the political necessities of today? In a first step, I will say how the combination of four terms—*subject, citizen, sovereignty, community*—organizes, saturates, and exhausts the political space closing itself today, a space I will characterize as the space of self-sufficient *sense.* In a second step, I will ask myself how the "social tie" can be conceived in terms of something other than self-sufficiency, which perhaps amounts always to failing *to tie* this tie because one has always supposed it to be *already* tied, given, as a tie of love or hate, force or law (it is always the logic of presupposition that one must confront). How to think the tie as always still *to be tied?* How, that is, instead of conferring sense on the presupposed knot, to make the tying of the (k)not into sense itself?[115]

Subject, Citizen, Sovereignty, Community

The subject is not the citizen (if at least one understands "subject" according to its philosophical or metaphysical concept). Subject and citizen represent two postures of the claim to sovereignty and the institution of community. These two terms, in turn, considered as pure formal notions propose nothing other, together or separately, than an absolute emergence or constitution of sense. In what way is sense postulated when it is viewed from the standpoint of the subject or the citizen, which forms the double polarity of our entire political space? (I underline here once and for all that it is a question only of a double polarity: there is never a pure example of either the politics of the subject or the politics of the citizen.)

The citizen is, first of all, *one, some*one, *everyone,* while the subject is, first of all, *self,* that is, the circling back through which a *one* raises its unicity to the power of unity. The citizenship comprises numerous unicities, subjecthood comprises an identificatory unity. This is why the city (which, as it is necessary to emphasize, doubtless has never taken place as such but figures the projection of one of our two poles) is represented, first of all, as a public space, or as the public qua space, and as a space of citizens, that is, neither as a territory nor as a domain nor as a *no-man's-land,* but as a circulation, a reticulation, an exchange, a sharing, a localization that is at once multiple, overdetermined, and mobile. In this space, the citizen takes (its) place and circulates.

The citizen is, above all, the one who occupies and traverses this space, the one who is defined by it, by the sharing of its exteriority. Citizenship is one or more roles, one or more procedures, a way of carrying oneself, a gait. In this way, the citizen is a mobile complex of rights, obligations, dignities, and virtues. These do not relate to the realization of any foundation or end other than the mere institution of the city. In a sense, the citizen does nothing other than share with his/her fellow citizens the functions and signs of citizenship, and in this "sharing" his/her being is entirely expressed. It is thus that the "Greek" city (and to a certain extent also the "Roman" city) appears to us to be perfectly *autoteleological,* where the *autos* would be utterly deprived of all interiority, without relation either to what we designate as the "private sphere" or to what we call "the nation." In this regard, the city has no deeper *sense:* it is related to no signified other than its own institution, the minimal signified of the city's mere contour, without other "identity," "mission," or "destiny" to conquer or to expand. The in-common of the city has no identity other than the space in which the citizens cross each other's paths, and it has no unity other than the exteriority of their relations. In a certain sense, citizenship in accordance with its pure concept is always virtually citizenship of the "world."

(I would point out in passing that the Greek philosophical reference for this city would be Aristotle and then the Stoics rather than

Plato, whereas Plato would be the reference for the other pole, the subject.)

Thus, the "citizen" of the French Revolution had good reason to think of himself—and to think of "France" or "the Republic"—as having an international, European, that is, cosmopolitan, dimension. This was, up to a certain point, the heritage of Rousseau, and behind him of the entire tradition of the "contract." For, beyond all of the important differences between the various theories on the questions of the causes and effects of the contract, one must see in this tradition the thought of the *res publica* as of a *res* whose entire *realitas* (or substantiality) resides in its formal institution and in the absence of any sense other than this institution itself. As for the themes of "nation" and "fatherland," they come, in turn, from the great European monarchies.

A corollary of this is that the city as such pushes religion in principle away to the infra- or supracivic spheres, at the risk of proposing a substitute, a "civic religion," which regularly fails, from Pericles to Robespierre, to take charge of the religious demand, that is to say, of the demand for a subjective appropriation of sense. In doing this, the city perhaps betrays that it is in truth untenable and abstract, characterized by that "abstraction without Idea" with which Hegel reproaches Rousseau as with what "destroys the divinity existing in and for itself, its absolute authority and majesty."[116]

Inversely—and we will come back to this—a politics of the subject is always a religious politics. This is why one must be very precise when one makes of 1789 the break with the "theologicopolitical." For there are in fact two breaks that are intertwined here (and perhaps inextricably so): the one that leads to the city (to democracy) as to a space that would no longer be theological at all (given a supplementary condition I will discuss below), and the one that leads to the politics of the modern subject (to the Nation-State), where a laicized theology, or if one prefers a romanticized theology, of the "people," "history," and "humanity" substitutes itself for "sacred" theology.

Even in Rousseau, the word *people* indeed signals the turning point where the citizen, despite everything, transforms itself into a subject or enters into a relation with the pole of the subject. The Subject, in general, in accordance with its structural and genetic law as stated by Hegel, retains within itself its own negativity. It is this, the appropriation and incorporation of a negativity (for example, a becoming, a relation, a spacing), that constitutes a "self" and a "being-self" as such. Thus, the political subject—or politics in accordance with the Subject—consists in the appropriation of the constitutive exteriority of the city (just as, doubtless, reciprocally the city consists in the projection *partes extra partes* of the interiority of the subject). For the space of the city an identity and substantiality are pre- or postsupposed as its principle or end. This identity and substantiality can take the form of the "people" in an organic configuration, or the form of the "nation," or those of property or production. And this pre-supposition of the self (one ought to say: this presupposition that *constitutes* the *self*) comes to crystallize identity in a figure, name, or myth. Politics becomes the conduct of the history of this subject, its destiny, and its mission. It becomes the revelation or the proclamation of a sense and of an absolute sense. From then on, there is religion, the assignation of sense as appropriable knowledge.[117]

Thus, the citizen makes itself into the subject at the point of sense, at the point of the (re)presentation of sense. The citizen becomes subject at the point where the *community* gives itself (as) an interiority, and at the point where *sovereignty* no longer contents itself with residing in the formal autoteleology of a "contract," or in its autojurisdiction, but expresses also an essence (and it is indeed thus that, in the context of theologicopolitical essentiality, history has produced the concept of sovereignty). Reciprocally, the subject makes itself into a citizen at the point where the expressed essence tends to express itself in and as a civic space and, if one can put it like this, to "display" subjective essentiality. The very idea of the *Republic* represents this point of reciprocity, in its more than infinitely delicate equilibrium.

Community and sovereignty are thus at the crossroads that is also doubtless the cross of all forms of Western politics (if one considers that the form of "empire" is here nothing other than the most manifest state of the combination of two heterogeneous determinations: a "citizenship" and a "subjectivity"—or multiple "subjectivities"—each of which buttresses the other). In this crucial position, these two terms, *sovereignty* and *community,* doubtless represent quite well all that is at stake in the West with regard to sense between appropriative interiority and inappropriable exteriority.

On the one hand, community can be the division of the very spacing in accordance with which there are singularities, where this division itself, as such, is not appropriable. As division or spacing it is itself the origin or the principle. On the other hand, community can be the interiority in which division appropriates its negativity, becomes the subject that founds and subsumes within itself this division, endowing it thus with a substance of its own (let us say, to put it quickly, the substance of father and mother or the substance of brothers: I will come back to the theme of "fraternity" elsewhere).

Accordingly, sovereignty can either be nothing other than the empiricotranscendental (or aleatory-necessary) circumscription that determines the law of such and such a city as the *ne plus ultra* of the "civity" of this city, the first and last point of its institution and decision, or else this *ne plus ultra* can appropriate to itself the negativity that constitutes it, and it can thus present itself as the self-engendered substance of the supremacy it states.

In other words, sovereignty and community can be the mere outline of an area of shared jurisdiction, or else they can identify themselves as the subject of a fundamental legitimacy. In the first case, sovereignty and community tend to be nothing—to repeat once again the formula that Georges Bataille exhausted himself in thinking through, "*Sovereignty is* NOTHING." They are and have the being of the *res publica* as the absolute "nothing-properly-speaking." In the second case, they are not merely something but the *res cogitans* of a subject effecting in person the autoteleology of its substance (whether this person be the people, the leader, the fatherland, the class, or the individual, as long as it is "consciousness" or "spirit").

But it is not certain that political decision is a choice between this "nothing" and this "everything": rather, one has good reason to ask oneself if these two options are not in an intimate solidarity or connivance.

Indeed, can one avoid identifying the "pure" outline of the city? Consequently, can one actually avoid turning the citizen into a subject—even if insubstantial and nonfigured (but perhaps, therefore, only all the more subtly appropriative of its own negativity)? And can one avoid making of the *res publica* the "thing," the identificatory substance of a community? Our entire history seems to answer that this is not possible—or that to attempt to maintain in its purity either one demand or the other is immediately to precipitate oneself into the inverse purity: the totalitarian subject turns out to be suicidal, but democracy without identification turns out also to be without any *demos* or *kratein* of its own.

At this very moment, when political subjectivity is doubtless to a great degree coming undone, and when substantial sovereignty is splitting up, are we not in the process of learning that the virtual advent, or in any case the almost universally desired advent, of a world citizenship (beginning with that of Europe) nonetheless risks corresponding to the triumph (itself without sharing or division) of what has been called "market democracy"?

This signifies at least, as far as one can see, that citizenship cannot remain without interiority, without the redoubtable constraint of an interiority and its figure, except *to the extent that* precisely remaining in exteriority it remains "formal" (that old word from Marxist critique...) and tolerates extreme inequality and injustice. In all the emptiness of its autoteleology, the absence of appropriation of a "law" [*droit*] admitted to be without foundation (without subject) opens on the infinite appropriation or devouring of a "capital" that is, moreover, no more a subject than is the law, and that would be the empty subject of the pure appropriation of pure negativity (the dialectical process become a butcher's shop: the so-called "end of history"). At the very least, the question designated above as the question of labor and *teknē*—the question of sense—is not posed here.

In saying this, I am not unaware that these questions had already emerged in the first quarter of this century, and that in more than one respect the totalitarianisms wanted to answer them. For this very reason, many intellectuals found themselves led astray. I do not want to stop to consider this point here in detail. But it is important to affirm that these erroneous or false answers do not invalidate the questions to which they were directed.

Is democracy—as the "nothing" of the subject, as pure citizenship—condemned to exhaust itself in the dream of a "politics-without-or-against-the-State" (assuming that the State is simply assimilable to subjectivity, which is no doubt not possible without further ado), on the one hand, while on the other hand, identification (State, nation, people, figure in general) would be unilaterally given over to the devouring of totalitarian and religious appropriation? Or will we pass on, more subtly, into the unraveling of this antinomy, the nothing-of-the-subject becoming the absolute subject of an appropriation as powerful as it is empty, an appropriation whose logic and global figure would be "capital" itself?

Can the world cut a *figure*, can it be fashioned and presented as *its own* identity? "The world"—is it not precisely an in-finity of presentation? But how does one distinguish presence from pres-ence? How *to hold fast* to the *coming* of what is coming?

This tension constitutes the extreme tension between citizen and subject, between the community of the one and the community of the other, between sovereignty and itself. It extends across all of the *Social Contract* and all of our Revolutions, as well as across all of our attempts to put an end to these things. It extends across the entire political apparatus of sense in the West: but sense in the West cannot not be at least *also* political. It makes up the very dialectics or distension of this sense—the dialectics in the course of coming unraveled into distension, that is to say, into an extreme tension that resolves itself as well into an extreme relaxation. No longer any subject, but no citizen either. No longer any infinite return into oneself, but no shared finitude either. Nothing but bad infinitude or bad finitude: it is the same thing, the same simultaneous absence of ties and spacing.

No longer any project, but no law either. People make a lot of noise about the one and then about the other, about the one as about the other, but these invocations remain theological: they invoke the Nothing or the All—and the "thirties" remain still possible, otherwise.

(K)not. Tying. Seizure of Speech

It is not possible to pose the problem in terms of the choice between subject and citizen if this choice only balances between the appropriative violence of the subject and the abstract spatiality of citizenship. Or between supraidentity and subidentity (the Aryan-Jewish couple, according to the Nazi myth). Between absolutely satiated sense and sense absolutely emptied out. Between desire (full of its lack) and truth (empty of its fullness). For this would no longer be a choice. In the final analysis, in both cases, it would be the same postulation of self-sufficiency.

As the double extreme of the political polarity, subjectivity and citizenship turn out to be two interpretations or configurations of a single scheme of self-sufficiency. This scheme itself would correspond, on the side of the concept, to sovereignty, and on the side of intuition, to community. In one way or the other, all the possible combinations and modalizations of these four terms gravitate around the index or ideal of self-sufficiency, to the point where the *political* as such seems to have therein its very Idea, and where in particular this "very Idea" does not allow any distinction between "left" and "right" politics. There are left- and right-wing versions of this Idea. "Left" and "right"—this singular empirico-transcendental orientation ought to mean something else. Its sense has not yet been sufficiently determined.

There is no possibility of choosing between the two poles of self-sufficiency, nor is there any possibility of choosing the hypothetical happy medium: the latter always amounts to renouncing, more or less visibly, now identity and now law, according to different versions of a more juridical or more "socializing" humanism. Both alternatives are henceforth naked, and with them "man" is naked as the final figure of self-sufficiency by default or renunciation. The (no doubt necessary) guardrails of democracy understood as more or less "Christian" or more or less "social" can no longer propose a politics. For the rest, the epithets "Christian" and "social" can no longer be distinguished from each other. They posit their common difference only by default, in a merely negative relation to the Other of democracy. Social democracy has no "figure" except in "values," whose place remains invincibly a Christian heaven. But on the earth, there is only the sufficiency of capital, its indefinite "self-preservation" and "self-valorization."[118]

Can one think through a politics of nonselfsufficiency? That is, as one will want to say, a politics of dependence or interdependence, of heteronomy or heterology? In the different figures of self-sufficiency, sometimes it is the social tie itself that is self-sufficient, sometimes it is the terms or units between which the social tie passes. In both cases, ultimately the tie no longer makes up a tie, it comes undone, sometimes by fusion, sometimes by atomization. All of our politics are politics of the undoing into self-sufficiency.

It is therefore a matter of going toward a thought (that means indiscernibly toward a *praxis*) of the (k)not as such. It is the *tying* of the (k)not that must come to the crucial point, the place of democracy's empty truth and subjectivity's excessive sense.[119]

The (k)not: that which involves neither interiority nor exteriority but which, in being tied, ceaselessly makes the inside pass outside, each into (or by way of) the other, the outside inside, turning endlessly back on itself without returning *to* itself—the link of mêlée and intrigue, confrontation and arrangement, need and desire, constraint and obligation, subjection and love, glory and pity, interest and disinterest. The tying of the (k)not is nothing, no *res,* nothing but the placing-into-relation that presupposes at once proximity and distance, attachment and detachment, intricacy, intrigue, and ambivalence. In truth, it is this heterogeneous *realitas,* this disjunctive conjunction, that the motif of the *contract* at once alludes to and dissimulates. The whole question is whether or not we can finally manage to think the "contract"—the tying of the (k)not—according to a model other than the juridicocommercial model (which in fact supposes the bond to have been already established, *already presupposed as its own subject:* this is the founding abyss or decisive aporia of the *Social Contract*). To think the social bond according to another model or perhaps without a model. To think its act, establishment, and binding.

One would thus demand a politics without dénouement—which perhaps also implies a politics without theatrical model, or a theater that would be neither tragic nor comic nor a dramatization of foundation—a politics of the incessant tying up of singularities with each other, over each other, and through each other, without any *end* other than the enchainment of (k)nots, without any structure other than their interconnection or interdependence, and without any possibility of calling any single (k)not or the totality of (k)nots self-sufficient (for there would be "totality" only in the enchainment itself).

Such a politics consists, first of all, in testifying that there is singularity only where a singularity ties itself up with other singularities, but that there is no tie except where the tie is taken up again, recast, and retied without end, nowhere purely tied or untied. Nowhere founded and nowhere destined, always older than the law and younger than sense. Politics would henceforth be neither a substance nor a form but, first of all, a gesture: the very gesture of the tying and enchainment of each to each, tying each time unicities (individuals, groups, nations, or peoples) that have no unity other than the unity of the (k)not, unity enchained to the other, the enchainment always worldwide and the world having no unity other than that of its enchainment. This politics requires an entire ontology of being as tying, that is, precisely perhaps this extremity where all ontology, as such, gets tied up with something other than itself. As long as we do not arrive at this extremity, we will not have displaced the theologicopolitical sphere. Which comes down to saying that everything remains to be thought about what Rousseau indicates in the most decisive, most un-"Rousseauist," and least analyzed point of the *Social Contract*: the point that the "civil state" is the only proper and original state of humanity.[120]

Still, it is not that one must simply abandon the quadruple instance "subject/citizen/sovereignty/community." Rather, one must displace its play by making apparent another determination that would play across the combinations of the others, not suppressing their tensions but changing the stakes—to those we have become accustomed to designating with the opposition between "right" and "left." (To be sure, if this opposition does not put into play a decisive excess beyond the theologicopolitical, it is introduced in vain. It is the tension of its lateral displacement that ought to be substituted for theological verticality. For the latter prevents the former from opening itself up.)

This supplementary determination does not arise from a demand for sense or from the postulation of a signification. It does not make of sense a political production, as does, in contrast, the polarity subject/citizen.

Consequently, it does not institute the political as another world charged with the task of presenting—now sense itself, now a pure space. It is merely, along the surface of this world—along the surface of our world that it is no longer a matter of either interpreting or transforming, if to transform still means to interpret, to engender a sense and an end—the specific determination of the link, the in-common *through which there is sense* that circulates and that ties and enchains itself, *perhaps without having any global or final signification* (not knowing, moreover, any global or final state), and without having any "sense" other than tying itself, which is not a signification.

Politics of (k)nots, of singular interlacings, of every *one* as the interlacing, relaying, and recasting of a (k)not, and of every (k)not as a *one* (one people, country, person, and so on), but as a *one* that is *one* only by virtue of concatenation: neither the "one" of a substance nor the "one" of a pure distributive count. But what is a (k)not? What sort of unicity does it possess, and what sort of unity? What is the mode of its ipseity? Or in what sense is all ipseity a (k)not, a node? What would happen if, in the Platonic comparison of the art of politics with the art of the weaver, one no longer considered weaving to be the second and as arriving after a given material, but as primary and as itself comprising the *res*? Or again, and in order to take up again a term I have already used, what if one considered that our coappearing [*comparution*] precedes all "appearing"?[121]

Not politics as a desire and quest for sense, but as an infinite tying up of sense from the one to the one, or as a tying up of this infinity that sense *is*—abandoning consequently all self-sufficiency of subject or city, allowing neither subject nor city to appropriate a sovereignty and a community that can only be those of this infinite tying.

This politics has sought itself obscurely, from Rousseau to Marx and from barricades to counsels, in the diverse figures of the "left," although it has always been obscurely mixed up with the scheme of self-sufficiency. It has always been mixed up with this scheme because it has never been sufficiently disengaged from the expectations and demands of the theologicopolitical. Nonetheless, it has also always clearly distinguished itself from this scheme, insofar as the "leftist" exigency has been that exigency that arises neither out of a foundation (or archi-subjectivity) nor out of a legitimacy (or archi-citizenship) but, rather, without foundation and without right, incommensurable, unassignable, as the exigency to grant its "rightful place," in the in-common, to every singular tying, to the singularity of all ties. Every time, the "law" and "project" themselves, *insofar as they precede themselves.*

What we are seeking—or what, as one says, "is seeking us"—is thus a politics of the tie as such, rather than of its untying [*dénouement*] into a space or substance. And consequently, what we are looking for is a consideration of the tie that takes it to be incommensurable with the ligature of the fasces. It is less the tie that binds than the tie that reties, less the tie that encloses than the tie that makes up a network. And if it is necessary to use this word at least once: yes, it is a politics of communication, but taken in the opposite sense of all our communicative ideologies, where "each communication is, above all, communication not of something held in *common* but of a *communicability,*" according to the formula of Giorgio Agamben.[122] Where, consequently, sense is not what is communicated but *that* there is communication.

This politics requires the establishment of ties as the infinite and incommensurable dimension of *every* (finite) *one.* In this regard, it manifests two traits.

It *requires:* it does infinitely more or other than demand, call on, or desire. It is a summons. It has all the invasive violence of every one as such. Every *one* as such subverts in fact the virtual closure or totalization of the network (in the subjective or in the civic mode). Every *one* displaces or disarranges sovereignty and community. Thus, it is a matter here of an intransigent politics of *justice* defined, above all, by an absolute and unconditional "equaliberty" of "everyone" as tying of the (k)not of sense (that is, as *existence*). One could be tempted to see therein nothing more than a quite formal and conventional principle of justice, if what is at stake were not something completely different from an equal distribution of rights and freedoms: it consists, indeed, in the real equality of what, beyond "rights" and "freedoms," constitutes the unique and incommensurable emergence of a singularity, an absolute, singular sense that is not measurable in terms of any signification. That all of what can constitute a *oneness* should have the real power to do so, to tie itself into a (k)not of oneness: this is, to be sure, a matter of *human rights,* but, first of all, as the *rights of human beings to tie (k)nots of sense.*

This politics thus requires an additional element, beyond justice, liberty, and equality. One could perhaps call this additional element "fraternity" if it were possible to conceive of fraternity without father or mother, anterior rather than posterior to all law and common substance. Or if it were possible to conceive of "fraternity" *as* Law and *as* substance: incommensurable, nonderivable. And if it is necessary to put it in these terms: without "Father" (or "Mother"), yet not at the sacrificial price of a "murder of the Father"—but, rather, in the dissolution of the Figure of the Father-already-Dead and his Thanatocracy. This would be the law of the Law, its very coming.[123]

Be that as it may, this something more, that which would come into the place of pure space or pure sense as into the *very* place of sovereignty and community, would be nothing other than the act of the tying, the act of the enchainment of singular sense to every other singular sense, the act of apportioning and interweaving that, as such, has no sense but gives a place to every event of sense (once again, people, country, person, and so forth).

Thus, politics does not arise out of an Idea, if there is no Idea of the (k)not, of the tying of the (k)not, or of what one could call the idiomatic style or complex of a singularity of sense. Its event could be called the *seizure of speech* [*prise de parole*]: the emergence or passage of some *one* and every *one* into the enchainment of sense effects, statement and offering in phrase or outline, including the cry, the call, and the complaint as much as the theoretical discourse, the poem, and the song, along with the gesture and even silence. Idiosyncratic and common, such seizures of speech would include all of the "singular decipherings" that comprise the "wandering labor of sense,"[124] at once within language and beyond (or just short of) language, but always responding to something inherent in language, in that language itself is the insubstantial tie.

What one needs to think through, then, is a politics of the seizure of speech, not of multiple wills competing to define a Sense, but of each one who makes sense, that is, ties (k)nots, from birth to death, and nothing else, and for nothing: the *(k)not* itself is neither a sense nor a goal nor a subject, even and above all if one wants to call it "the law." It is thus quite the contrary of what one calls today, in the magazines, the "search for meaning" with which our time is driving itself crazy. It is the "wandering labor of sense." And, without complacency, one can read the sumptuous graphical singularities and fleeting semantics of *graffiti* as one mode of inscription of this "wandering labor"—a crude and desperate mode, no doubt, but one that is therefore all the more demanding.

(To speak of *graffiti* or to evoke the French phrase from 1968, "let the walls speak" [*les murs ont la parole*], is not meant to induce a romanticization of 1968. Rather, the point is to invite the reader to distinguish finally between, on the one hand, what in 1968 was the general repetition of the end of political romanticism, that is, of laicized theologicopolitics and, on the other hand, what was the first announcement, still opaque to itself, of another approach to the political.)

But the seizure of speech—which is also a being seized *by* speech—presupposes at least two kinds of conditions.

1. Its material means must be given, which cannot be measured merely in terms of subsistence, but of information, education, and culture. If, in the theologicopolitical, the sovereign had an obligation to allow his people to lead decent lives, and if, in the laicized theologicopolitics of the production of man by man, he had an obligation to allow the appropriation of the means of this production, in turn in the space of an atheological politics—or of the infinite (k)not—the obligation is to allow "the wandering labor of sense," that is, the labor of thought, insofar as it is the labor of all. Far from being mutually exclusive, these three obligations, today or in the very near future, apply or will apply cumulatively to two-thirds of the planet. Because for two-thirds of the planet, it is the very possibility of a (k)not of whatever sort that has been undone. And if the havoc continues, it is the (k)not of all that will be in question—indeed, it already is.

2. The seizure of (or by) speech must be freed from the theologicopolitical or romantic model of the intellectual or prophetic announcement of a "message" (a sense in the sense of a truth instead of the truth of sense in its wandering), but it must also be removed from that other

model, let us call it the psychosociological model, of the subjective determination and appropriation of significations: the model to which, unfortunately, the most visible effects and interpretations of psychoanalysis often refer, sometimes against the grain of its deep requirements (but are these not requirements ultimately those of another politics rather than those of a "private" therapy in the interior of an incurable "public" sickness of civilization?).

The tying up of singular events of sense does not arise from either of these two models, but from access to the concatenation of acts of speech, even if—or, rather, *because*—this concatenation is not completeable, is infinitely reticulated, infinitely interrupted and retied, and even if—or because—these acts of speech tend toward the most naked function of language, toward what one calls its phatic function: the maintenance of a relation that communicates no sense other than the relation itself.

Political Writing

The arrow touches a thing in the night
that becomes its target
we are a sense
hungry for signs.

MICHEL DEGUY, *Arrêts fréquents*[125]

We call *writing* that which does not respond to any model whatsoever of the appropriation of significations, that which opens at once relation and, along with relation, significance itself. If there is an insistent modern tradition of writing, it has this sense and only this sense: "writing" is what precedes signification, what succeeds on it and exceeds it, not as another, heightened and always deferred signification, but as the outline, the breaking of the path [*frayage*] of significance through which it becomes possible not only for significations to be signified but for them to *make sense in being passed on and shared among individuals.* Sense is consequently not the "signified" or the "message": it is *that something like the transmission of a "message" should be possible.* It is the relation as such, and nothing else. Thus, it is as relation that sense configures itself—it configures the *toward* that it is (whereas signification figures itself as identity). The tradition of writing is the tradition of relation itself insofar as it is to be opened and tied. In one of the inaugural texts of this tradition, Benjamin wrote: "But there is nothing subordinate about written script; it does not fall away from a reading, like dross. It enters into what is read, as its 'figure.'"[126] The political task is quite precisely to let the relation as sense "ground itself" in the signification of being-together "as its figure." Only on this condition—that the "relation" should be a "figure"—can the *together* of the group avoid the alternative between *all* or/and *nothing*.

Writing is thus political "in its essence," that is, it is political to the extent that it is the tracing out [*frayage*] of the essencelessness of relation. It is not political as the effect of an "engagement" in the service of a cause, and it is not political—qua "literature"—according to either the principle of the "aestheticization of politics" or its inversion into the "politicization of aesthetics." It is indeed necessary to ask in what way literature and, consequently, aesthetics and fiction become involved here, but only after one has affirmed the political nature of writing: *the in-finite resistance of sense in the configuration of the "together."*

Thus, we have to do with relations of force. It is not merely through freedom of thought and expression that all forms of "writing" find themselves regularly confronted with the powers that be. It is, first of all, and more fundamentally, through the resistance of significance to being captured or subsumed by signification. Which is nothing other than the resistance of the "community" to its hypostasis, whether this hypostasis takes on the substantial appearance of a "communion" or the reasonable appearance of a generalized "communication." This resistance has the dimensions of the world—that is, it touches ceaselessly on the confines of the world—or else it is not, forming itself into and founding itself in an exclusionary subjectivity (individual, corporate body, minority, majority, church, or people). In order to be of the dimensions of the world, writing resists the cutting-up of the world into exclusive worlds such as occurs in the

> new division—which divides the human condition into the conditions of the more mortal and the conditions of the less mortal.... For [the division] is no longer the division that put all humans on one side and all the immortals on the other. It divides them from North to South as from less mortal to more mortal and returns again within each of these regions to divide this new mortality into the notoriety of money and the insignificance of anonymity.[127]

The writing of the sense of the world, or better, the sense of the world as writing, does not reside, first of all, in a worldliness of cultural variegation and "hybridity" as new identity—no more than it can reside in the uniformity of a world "order." It resides in what maintains the world as *existentiale of worldliness:* resistance to the closure of worlds within the world as well as resistance to the closure of worlds-beyond-the-world: the tracing out [*frayage*], in each instant, of this world *here.*

. . . tracing out [*frayage*] of all these seizures of speech, of all these testimonies of existence in the world, each one singular and singularly exposed to its end, yet all taken together in their dispersion writing the world itself, "which is great and is situated beyond words," as this prose of a poet has it:

> In fact the bridges to each other, over which one comes with a beautiful and stately air, are not *in* us, but behind us. . . . When two or three people meet up, this does not yet mean that they are actually together. They are like marionettes whose wires lie in different hands. Only when *one* hand guides all of them does a commonality come over them that forces them to bow to one another or to strike out at one another. And even the forces of the human being are there, where his wires end in a dominating hand that holds them. . . . Only in the common hour, the common storm, the single room in which they meet do they find each other. Only once a background stands behind them do they begin to have something to do with one another. They must, indeed, make reference to the *one* homeland. They must, as it were, show each other the certifications they carry with them, which all contain the sense and the seal of the same prince.

[I add here merely, although you have understood: the "sovereign hand" and the "prince" of the "country of origin" are nothing other than the bond itself, or the world.]

> Whether it be the singing of a lamp or the voice of the storm, whether it be the breath of evening or the sighing of the sea that surrounds you—there is always a wide melody watching behind you, woven of a thousand voices, in which just here and there your solo has space. To know *when it is your turn to fall in,* this is the secret of your loneliness: as it is the art of true contact: to let oneself fall out of the high words into the one common melody. . . . Everything common presupposes, however, a series of different lonely beings. Before them, there was only a whole without any relation, living from

> one day to the next. . . . And it is precisely the loneliest who take the greatest part in the commonality. . . . The one who perceived the entire melody would be the most lonely and the most common at once. For he would hear what no one hears.[128]

If one says that this text is ambiguous, that its content, aesthetics, and epoch place it on the border of "fascist" (or at least "conservative-revolutionary") temptations, I will not deny it. Indeed, to the contrary, I will say that, to the degree that the thirties still stand before us, we must take from the twenties that which, although they did not know how to preserve it, exceeded the gray tones of Weimar without for all that necessarily leading to the flames of Nuremberg. Rainer Maria Rilke, indeed, *is not* Heidegger, I mean Heidegger the writer (or the Heidegger of "thinking poetry"). And I quote him precisely under the sign of this difference, which does not mean as a "model": for everything remains to be invented.

Writing—and thus also necessarily its *poetry,* which is to say, above all, its *praxis*—is the task of sense, on condition that it not be the assumption of a sense that has already been tied up, but the response—without resolution—to the absolute injunction of having to establish ties. And this nonprescribable injunction is also irreducible to all "poeticizing" or "literary" aestheticization. The languages are to be tied. Each language is to be indefinitely tied up into the (k)not of its proper infinity and into the (k)nots of the proper infini-ties of the others. They are to be tied up into the unattached (k)not and into the nonsubjective ipseity of the in-common that does not communicate or commune. "The languages," their writings, this does not mean, above all, "literature" as model, but the poetries of styles, modes of existence, modulations of relation and retreat, languages, peoples, that is, cultures and ethnic groups as well as social classes and nonidentified populations, the peoples' idioms and countries, their passages from land to land, landscapes, worlds that are the world, worlds that are a world.

In this sense, the political exigency cannot not be an exigency of configuration, even though it ought to resist the figuration/presentation of a sovereign body. Democracy cannot be content to be the place of exposition to an empty truth—and we cannot simply replace the gray tones of Weimar with the scintillations of a pure dispersion of singularities. Idioms must be possible that resist the bloody idiocies of identities indicated by blood, soil, and self. Identities must *write* themselves, that is, they must know and practice themselves as non-identifiable (k)nots of sense. (Together, Giorgio Agamben, Werner Hamacher, Philippe Lacoue-Labarthe point out that in speaking of *nouage* [tying] I sound as if I were speaking of *nuages* [clouds]. It is time to stop. It will be necessary to rewrite these considerations.)

Art, a Fragment

By this time, no doubt, fragmentation, spacing, exposition, piecework, and exhaustion have begun to arrive at their most extreme limit. We have done so much fracturing, fraying, wounding, crumpling, splintering, fragilizing, shattering, and exceeding that we would seem to have begun to exceed excess itself. This is why worldliness may appear to be the reverse, in tiny pieces, of a totalization madly in love with itself.

Today, there is a chagrined, reactive, and vengeful tone in which this is often said. It gives its auditor to understand that our art, thought, and text are in ruin, and that one must call for a renewal. As in all such cases, this is nothing but a flight from the event and its truth.

There is certainly no lack of reasons for judging that a cycle should be completed, an epoch suspended, as is the role of any epoch: interruption, fragmentation. And something of the sort is indeed in the process of taking place.

However, nothing repeats itself, nothing ever comes back, except coming itself, which is never the same—but, rather, the indefinitely altered return of the same. That which has been fragmented will not be either reconstituted or reengendered—except by those for whom "art" would consist in aping an absent *cosmos* out of contempt for the event of the world.

But, of course, that which has been fragmented—a certain configuration of art and of the work, a certain *cosmetics* of the "beautiful" and the "sublime"—has not simply disappeared in the process of being broken down. One must know first of all what remains in the fragments: where is the beautiful in the fragments of the beautiful? How does it come to be fragmented? In other words, and even if one supposes that nothing remains, if one supposes that fragmentation has properly dislocated the essence on which it supervened, one must ask oneself if this "essence" has not itself been delivered, thrown, projected, and offered like what one would have to call, twisting Benoit Mandelbrot's word, a "fractal essence." (In this sense, rather than the contour of the "fragment," already outlined, the "fractal" would designate the dynamics and the initiality of dif-fraction, the uneven tracing of "fractal curves.") In still other words: in what direction are we to take the step from a fragmented cosmetics to an aesthetics of sensible tracing [*frayage*], and beyond this to the fragile permanence of "art" in the drift of the "worldly"?

From One Fragment the Other

One must attempt to distinguish between two different kinds of fragmentation. On the one hand, there is the fragmentation that corresponds to the genre and art of the fragment, whose history is closing before our eyes, and on the other hand, there is the fragmentation that is happening to us, and to "art." (Further, one must be careful not to oversimplify this opposition but, rather, to bear in mind that, although the second fragmentation—the one I have rather heavily called "fractal essence"—is indeed *happening*, it is happening at a distance from us and happens to be coming toward us across the entire history of art, a history that this fragmentation has always worked on and on which it has always bestowed a *fractal sense*, as the diffraction and spacing of linear and cumulative histories.)

The fragmentation that will henceforth have to be regarded as classical, that is, romantic fragmentation, consists in a certain recognized, accepted, desired state of detachment and isolation of the fragments. Its *end* is situated where the fragment collects itself into itself, folds or retracts its frayed and fragile borders back onto its own consciousness of being a fragment, and onto a new type of autonomy. Disruption transforms itself here into the gathering of itself into itself of the broken piece. The latter converts its finitude—its interruption, noncompletion, and in-finitude—into finish. In this finish, dispersion and fracturing absolutize their erratic contingency: they *absolve themselves* of their fractal character.

When Friedrich Schlegel compares the fragment to a hedgehog, he confers on it all the autonomy, finish, and aura of the "little work of art." Ultimately, it is only the "little" size of the fragment that differentiates here between the art of the fragment and the art of the "great" work.

Why "little"? Behind the entire history of art since romanticism there has been an uneasiness about the great, the monumental, about all art of cosmological, cosmogonic, or theogonic dimensions, all "sovereign art" in the "grand style." This uneasiness is a desire that, one way or another, ends in disaster: either it is infinitely disappointed, as in Nietzsche faced with Richard Wagner—and perhaps even in Wagner himself—or it considers itself to be disastrous and tears itself apart, from Arthur Rimbaud to Bataille and beyond. To this disaster, the "little"—like a meteoric fragment detached from the sidereal fall—would have liked to provide an answer.

(The obscene sense of "little" in Bataille belongs also to this configuration, as, for example, the following lines show: "The 'little' one: radiance of agony, of death, radiance of a dead star, fragmentation of the sky announcing death—beauty of the day at twilight."[129] Even more than the loss of the "great," what occurs here is the contraction of anxiety before the emptiness of the heavens, the world precipitated into a state of worldlessness that leads to disgust [*le monde précipité dans l'immonde*].)

However, the little is coupled with the great in the sense that the little does not stop referring to the great. The extremity of the fragmentary is reached here as an exhaustion, an agony, that is, also as an exhausting struggle of the little against the great, and thus as a struggle of the little against its own anxiety, or as a struggle to affirm this anxiety as accomplishment and revelation. The fragment becomes at once an *end* (limit, fracture) and a *finish* (annulment of the fracture), the torn borders folded back into the sweetness of microcosmic self-enclosure. Exposition itself ends up as introjection, return to self.

The "fractality" with which we will have to do from this point on—and which fragmentation also announced—is quite different. Instead of the ambiguous end of the fragment, it is a matter of the fraying of the edges of its trace [*son frayage*]. It is a matter of the frayed access [*l'accès frayé*] to a presentation, to a coming into presence—and by way of this coming into presence. For what is at stake can no longer be measured or unmeasured as a cosmology, theogony, or anthropogony. What makes up "world" and "sense" can no longer be determined as a given, accomplished, "finished" presence but is intermingled with the coming, the in-finity of a coming into presence, or of an *e-venire*.

The event is not a "taking-place": it is the incommensurability of coming to all taking-place, the incommensurability of spacing and fraying [*frayage*] to all space disposed in the present of a presentation. It is the *praes-entia* of being-present.[130] One could also formulate it by saying that it is *presentation itself,* distinguished this time from what would be the "presentness" [*la présentité*] of a presence, as transitive being is distinguished from intransitive being. The event is presentation as gesture or motion, indeed, as emotion, and as fractal ex-position: presentation as fragmentation.

Thus, there are two different forms of extreme fragmentation: on the one hand, exhaustion and finish, and on the other hand, event and presentation. This does not mean that the fragments that are really produced, fragmentary works or documents, can be simply classified into one category or the other. Every fragment, and indeed every work in general, ever since there have been works (since Lascaux), can be seen as one or the other. But the question is this: once the cosmetics and aesthetics of totality and fragment have been left behind, once the little as well as the great have been exhausted, does something still remain of (or for) art in this *coming* that no presence could ever *finish?* "Happenings" and "performance art," and all of that which, within contemporary art, has revolved around the motif of the event (for example, Polaroid and video, the residual, the accidental, the aleatory, staining, interruption, and so on)—all of this seems to have either merely prolonged one posture or the other (the "great" or the "little") or merely continued to destroy, reduce, and shatter art. Moreover, the two gestures are not contradictory, and much seems to suggest that it is possible to say that art petrifies and fractures itself in the pose of its own end. Romantic irony, which Hegel saw as the element of this end, attained in this way its extreme of yawning subjectivity. It seems that one should no longer count on art for the "coming"—for the breaking of the path [*frayage*]—of another sense. And yet, differing from Hegel (perhaps only) in this, we will not find it possible to call "philosophy" the element responsible for the breaking of this path [*frayage*]. Nor, moreover, will we find it possible to give that element any other name.

But this circumstance itself traces out a path [*frayage*], indicates a coming, or indicates itself as coming. The exhaustion of *cosmos* and *mundus*, the end of the "presentable" world, opens onto the worldliness of being. Being itself—existence—announces itself or insists anew, in an unprecedented way, and even if this way is *epeikeina tēs ousias*. What is coming is a birth that is neither a cosmogony nor a theogony nor an anthropogony. It can neither be assumed nor subsumed in either the work, form, art (little or great), or any finish. Rather, its presentation is a fragmentation—and its "art" is apparently no longer distinguishable from the *ars* prior to the "fine arts," that is, from a *teknē* that is henceforth to be seen as infinitely finite, situated beyond all finished works. But how to present this "fractal" birth?

In other words, the question is the following, taken up again as we take our departure from "art" and its infinite end, but also as at least one aspect of the question of "technology": if something remains beyond an aesthetics of the fragment, beyond the repeated echoes of the disaster and desire of "great art," if something remains *or if there is something that is coming anew* that would be like a "more essential," "more primitive," "more original," and consequently "more unprecedented" and "more future" fragmentation (but also by virtue of this a fragmentation from which would proceed in their way works of art as such), and if this fragmentation must have to do with the event of being that one also calls existence, and within existence with this—that it comes and "essentially" does nothing but come (come-and-go, toward the world)—if then there is something like this, and if it has a proper place (but with what sort of "propriety"?), a place where it exposes itself as such, is this place still (or in a new way) art? "Art" in what sense?

Or, can one think of art not as an art *of* the fragment—remaining obedient to the work as finished totality—but as itself fragmentary and fractal, and of fragmentation as the presentation of being (of existence), tracing [*frayage*] of/in its totality?

"Aisthesis"

It is a matter, then, of the relations between art and sense.[131] If the "absence" of sense—to take up Blanchot's word once again—defines the very sense of sense, and not its position or its modality, if this "absence" is nothing other than the sense of being insofar as it is in play *as the existence that is its own sense,* in other words—the words that have in the history of art a singular echo—if sense is the nudity of existing, in what way can this *nudity* be or become the *subject* of art? (In what way, perhaps, has it already become the subject of art?)

What we are asking here is thus what makes art apt to disengage sense in this way, this sense of sense: that existence is (the surprise of) sense, without any other signification.

What we are asking here in the same movement is thus also if there is something in art that would be "essential," and how it might be "essential," to nude existence—and that would not come down to merely embellishing this existence. In other words, is art necessary to the articulation of sense in its "absence," in its "surprise"? Is it necessary to the thought of the sense of the world? And how does this involve fragmentation?

It is necessary to take as our renewed point of departure the sense of sense as *aisthesis,* insofar as it implies neither transcendence nor immanence. The heterogeneous entelechy of the sensing/sensed, in the spatializing unity of its contact, implies relationship, in the form of being-affected-by, and consequently in the form of being-affectable-by, being-liable-to (of which intellection and intelligible sense are, after all, only modulations or modalizations, even affections of affect itself). Affectability constitutes the pres-ence of sensible presence, not as a pure virtuality, but as a being-in-itself-always-already-touched,[132] touched by the possibility of being touched. For this, it is necessary for being-passible in itself to have already offered some part of itself—

but here, the part counts for the whole—to something outside of itself (or to some part of itself set apart from itself). Affect presupposes itself: in this, it behaves like a subject, but as the passive or passible actuality of a being-subject-*to*.

This originary act of passibility necessarily takes place as the cutting and opening of an access, the access through which it is possible for a sensing thing to sense something sensed, for a sensed thing to be sensed. Exteriority as intimacy of the aisthetic entelechy gives us the cut of the place: sensation is necessarily *local. A sensation without difference and without locality—a sensation without world—would not be a sensation* (and would not be "a," would not be this singular being that a sensation as "a" sensation always is). Thus, the erotic body is zoned or it is not. (And this is why, inversely, perfect intellection is represented as total sensation, the solar or nocturnal immanence of a mystical "spirit.") Not only is aisthesis the act of this intimate exteriority, but it is also immediately the plurality of the senses. There are different senses, *non-communicable* senses, not because of a partitioning in accordance with the rationality of diverse "moments of the concept" (as Hegel wished to establish), but, rather, and as Hegel himself also says, because the sensible is "synonymous with what is self-external."[133]

The sensible or the aisthetic is the outside-of-itself through which and *as* which there is the relation to itself of a sense in general, or through which there is the *toward* of sense. But there is no sense "in general," nor is there a generic sense. There is sense only in local difference and differing division. In-sensible diff*éra*nce is sensible: it is the insensible in the completely sensible, infinitesimally sensible sense we give to the word when we speak, for example, of an "insensible diminution of the light." The five senses are not the fragments of a transcendent or immanent sense. They are the fragmentation or the fractality of the sense that is sense *only as fragment.*

Even if one affirms, with Aristotle, that there is no region of the sensible other than those by which our senses are affected, one will still not be able to produce the reality of a sensible Totality: the whole of the sensible owes its being only to its division, its dis-sent. But this is how it makes up the whole of this world here: nontotalizable totality and still without remainder—or at least without remainder that would not be in turn traced out along the surface of this world here. One should not even say that the "sensible whole" is *partes extra partes,* if this risks giving the impression that it is a matter of parts of a unity. The exteriority of sensible things is all there is of sensible interiority. In the same way, the reciprocal exteriority of the arts is the only interiority of their order, and the internal affinities of this order, Charles Baudelaire's "correspondences," always have the paradoxical character of affinities by incompatibility. The arts communicate only through the impossibility of passing from one to the other. Each one is at the threshold of the others.[134]

This fractality of (the) sense(s), exposed in the very place of the truth of sense, would be what is at stake in art, henceforth and for a long time to come—and perhaps also for a long time since.

This is indeed why aesthetics and art appear in our history (I mean appear as irreducible places of thought that seem necessary to the determination or to the problematization *of* sense itself) when the intelligibility of sense, in its cosmocosmetology, vanishes. This is what happens between the eighteenth century and Hegel. And this is why, when Hegel announces that art "is henceforth for us a thing of the past," he is announcing nothing other than the end of the beautiful (re)presentation of intelligible Sense—that is, of what he also calls "the religion of art"—and the sublation of this presentation in its modern mode of truth, the mode of the concept, philosophical "gray," the achieved immanence (without sensible difference) of a transcendence that has wholly come back to itself.

But at the same time, with exactly the same gesture, Hegel *delivers* art for itself: he delivers it from service to transcendence in immanence, and he delivers it to detached, fragmentary truth. Hegel, *volens nolens,* registers and salutes in fact *the birth of art,* the detachment of this "concept" that will henceforth be autonomous, exposed as the very detachment, separation, and fragmentation of sense.[135] Without a doubt, for Hegel, "the specific modes of the sensuous being of art are themselves a totality of necessary differences in art—the *particular arts*"; but this totality realizes itself only in maintaining its differentiation:

> What the particular arts realize in individual works of art is, according to the Concept of art, only the universal forms of the self-unfolding Idea of beauty. It is as the external actualization of this Idea that the wide Pantheon

> of art is rising. Its architect and builder is the self-comprehending spirit of beauty, but to complete it will need the history of the world in its development through thousands of years.[136]

Thus, the same Hegel who had presented the end of ancient religion[137] as the end of art in the death of the divine life that animated art (the "death of the great Pan") here presents art itself as the temple of all the gods, the numerous gods who are no longer gods but art itself in all its scintillating fragments—and this temple is on the scale of the history of the world.

The multiplicity of the "Pantheon" renders God absent, and art comes where God absents himself: a banal proposition, no doubt, but a proposition the implications of which remain still to be explored (so true is it that at the same time, and since Hegel, some have unfolded a "secularized" theologicoaesthetics: some of Kazimir Malevitch's discourses, for example, are closer to Plotinus than they are to Malevitch's paintings, and it is not certain that any philosophy of art has yet sufficiently realized what is at stake in fragmentation; inversely, Plotinus is perhaps also closer to Malevitch's or Pablo Picasso's paintings than to Plotinian truth). The *sense* that can expose itself only along the edges of the fragment is not an *absent sense* that would be comparable to the absence—itself full of sense—of God, who, precisely as God, does not cease to absent himself: it is a sense the absence of which makes no sense, that is, does not convert itself into an absent presence but consists entirely, if one can say it this way, in absence as presentation, or in the fragmentation of pres-ence.

If one can say it this way, for precisely one cannot, and art is always the art *of not saying it, of exposing that which is not to be said* (not an unsayable, but the not-to-be-said of sense) *along the edges of all that is exposed,* as the sayable itself, and further, as saying itself, as all of saying in its fragmentation.[138]

There remains then—what remains in the self-deconstruction to which the Occident has stubbornly and rigorously applied itself, precisely by reason of (and in proportion to) that nonpresentation of its Self to which it was destined from the beginning (to which it was destined by its own demand for truth, which for this reason can always dialecticize itself into "nihilism" as also into "nihilist" art). And what remains thus, or what is *coming* and does not stop coming as what remains, is what we call *existence.* It is "the existence of being," not in the sense of a predicate distinct from its essence, but in the sense of being that *is transitively* existence, or that *ex-ists.* Being exists the existent: it does not give the existent its sense *as* presupposition and end, but, rather, it is sense given with existence, as existence, more than a gift, being *toward* the world, where the world is not construed as a surrounding space, but as the multiple tracing out [*frayage*] of the singularity of existence. The world is multiple in regions and regimens of the existent, multiple in individuals and in events within each individual, but, first of all (and all the way to the end), it is multiple in materials, in material fragmentations of sense: sensible existence, fractal existence.

Fragment: no longer the piece fallen from a broken set, but the explosive splintering of that which is neither immanent nor transcendent. The in-finite explosion of the finite. Not the piece that has fallen, and even less the piece that has fallen into decay, but the piece that has *befallen,* that is to say, that has come by devolution. Devolution is attribution, division, destination, passing of contracts, transfer by unrolling (*devolvere*), unfolding, and disintrication. World, fragment: being devolved.

Fallen pieces, waste, wreckage, jagged bits, remains, inner organs of slaughtered beasts, shreds, filth, and excrement, on which contemporary art—*trash art*—gorges itself (and of which it disgorges itself), are all posited, deposited, and exposed on the infinitely thin limit that separates falling-into-decay from befalling, loss from scintillating fragmentation, and abandon from abandon itself. Art vacillates here between its own decay and a future coming of its devolution. Between its failure and its chance, art begins once again. It was not really so naïve of Marx, after all, to be astonished at the effect and affect produced by the works of the Ancients, now that the myths that supported them have fallen into disuse; he understood this effect as the effect of a perpetual childhood freshness.[139] Perhaps art is the *infans* par excellence, the one who, instead of discoursing, fragments instead: fraying [*frayage*] and fracture of the access.

Art has hitherto been considered, in all possible ways, in terms of both "creation" (*poiesis,* genius, and so on) and "reception" (judgment, critique, and so on). But what has been left in the shadows is its befalling or devolving, that is to say, also its chance, event, birth, or encounter—which, in other terminologies, has been called the "shock," "touch," "emotion," or "pleasure," and which participates indissociably in both "creation" and "reception." Aesthetic pleasure (it is a pleonasm if one is indeed speaking of aisthetic pleasure, for "all pleasure is physical";[140] the sensing/sensed entelechy is always also that of a sentiment of pleasure or of pain) is still that with respect to which the discourse on art remains most discreet, distant, or distracted. At least, this is the case for the modern discourse on art. The classical discourse focused on how *to give pleasure* at least as much as on rules: but the aesthetics of rules and how to give pleasure (rules *for* and *of* giving pleasure) gave way to the aesthetics of *poiesis* and works. Nonetheless, the classical discourse generally contented itself with designating the giving of pleasure—being charming, touching, or graceful—as the goal, and barely touched on it, so to speak, any further.

No doubt, discourse, qua discourse, cannot avoid distance or distraction, as far as pleasure is concerned. Signification can *touch* on neither senses nor sense. One could also put it this way: *jouiscience is impossible.*[141] For pleasure—mixed up with displeasure in Edmund Burke's and Kant's versions of the "sublime," as also in Freud's "pleasure of tension," which is a subliminal or preliminary pleasure, a pleasure at the limit that is perhaps the essence of pleasure and that is for Freud the aesthetic "premium"[142]—pleasure does not take place except through *place,* touch, and zone. It is local, detached, discreet, fragmentary, absolute. A nonfractal pleasure, a pleasure without limits, fragmentation, arrival, or falling due, is not a pleasure at all: at most, it is satisfaction, approbation, contentment. Pleasure is not, for all that, "partial": the structure here is not the structure of a *pars pro toto,* but that of a singular totality.

Art is a fragment because it borders on pleasure: it *gives* pleasure [*il fait plaisir*]. It is made both out of and for the pleasure it gives, the pleasure thanks to which it touches—and with a *touch* that comprises its essence. What art does is to *please:* and so it is neither a *poiesis* nor a *praxis,* but another kind of "doing" altogether that mixes together with both of the other kinds an *aisthesis* and its double entelechy. By means of the touch of the senses, pleasure surprises and suspends the enchainment of signifying sense. Or, rather, what one calls in French the "*touche des sens*" (touch of the senses) consists precisely in this suspension and being-taken-by-surprise of signifying enchainment. A position similar to that of truth: the sensuous presentation of truth.[143]

Of the Symbolic as Singular

Coming [*jouir*] occurs—or opens up [*fraye*] an access—only when the signifying or symbolic order is suspended. When it is suspended by an interruption that produces no void of sense but, to the contrary, a fullness and indeed an overfullness: an "absent sense" or the eruptive coming of the sense that is older than all signification, as it were its truth *as sense.* This is what theoretical language has sometimes thought to translate by speaking of the "impossible." And yet the "impossibility" of *jouissance* is merely the impossibility of its "sensible" (re)presentation, whereas from another point of view this "impossibility" of *jouissance* is the most extreme, originary possibility of all (joyous or painful) coming into presence, and of the potential significations of the latter.[144]

Obviously, it is not a matter of substituting for the theoretical discourse of impossibility that other discourse, itself no less theoretical, which thinks one can call *jouissance* or pleasure (or suffering) "natural." It is a matter neither of the immanence of nature nor of the transcendence of an impossibility. It is a matter of the double topology of presence coming into sense and sense coming into presence. Presentation without presentness [*présentité*], or pres-ence, does not transcend any more than it immanates: it comes, it comes and goes, as an interruption of symbolic enchainments and of substantial continuities. Or more precisely, it comes and goes, as an interruption of symbolic enchainments qua concatenations that ensure, by means of signification, a communication of substances (substances that are thereby signified, supposed, and subjectified).

This interruption is fractal—and "art" is what takes place wherever this interruption is opened [*frayée*]. Or, at least there is some art that is tied in one way or another to these openings [*frayages*]. This is why art is considered indissociable from erotic *jouissance*, and reciprocally (it is the *Art of Loving*), and also from the *jouissance* of power and glory and/or from the *jouissance* of the communal (k)not. And this is also why there exist what one calls the "minor arts" (gastronomy, the arts of scent, clothing, gardening, and so on). Even more broadly, there is a trace or presumption of "art" every time the dialectical complicity of immanence and transcendence, of being-in-oneself and ecstasy, is broken, diverted, or suspended. That is, there is "art" every time a *sense* more "originary" than any assignation of a "Self" or "Other" comes to touch us: sense itself, "in a sense," in its "unique" and singular sense, insofar as it cannot but precede both itself and the being "of which" it is the sense, cannot but precede being in being itself, in the entrancement of *praes-entia.*

This can take place in gestures, postures, the "art of conversation," social convention and ceremony, rejoicing, and mourning. It is not dissociable from *ethos* and *praxis* in general, nor is it dissociable from the exercise of discourse and signification. This does not mean that "art" is everywhere without distinction: "art" is merely that which takes as its theme and place the opening [*frayage*] of sense as such along sensuous surfaces, a "presentation of presentation," the motion and emotion of a coming.

Semantic family of the fragment: anfractuosity, fringe, shipwreck, to break a path [*frayer*], fraction, breach, brick, blunder, to pulverize, splinter, to infringe, to chamfer, needy, refrain. The refrain suspends the course of the song: it interrupts the song, launches it—but launches it again for the sake of the return of the refrain. Art as refrain: a fragment always subtracted from the series of historical events, always more or less than history, and yet linking itself up with history. Since Lascaux, art has been the implicit refrain of humanity—explicit since the Greeks or Hegel. There is a history of art, but it is the history of that which does not stop erupting within or breaking in on history, of that which gives itself always to be finished there, always taken up again. Inasmuch as art has a history, it is a culture or cult of forms, taste, divine service, or monument of power. But inasmuch as it

> is this refrain—anfractuosity, shipwreck, breach—it is "art," the fragment, ever anew a mere fragment of "itself."

But there is more. In a paradoxical way, it is precisely when the symbolic order is interrupted that it arrives at its own essence. The *symbolon* is breakage as much as reunion: it is breaking-for-reunion. It has its truth in its being-divided. There is never one *symbolon* alone. Like the *singulus,* it exists only in the plural—and the *singuli* are always as many *symbola.*

Symbola are the potsherds of recognition, fragments of pottery broken in the promise of assistance and hospitality. The fragment carries the promise that its fractal line will not disappear into a gathered whole but, rather, will rediscover itself elsewhere, lip against lip of the other piece. The symbolic fragment affirms that its fracture *is still itself elsewhere,* otherwise.[145]

The supreme law of the symbolic is not the constitution of a consistent link and a continuous circulation. It lies further back, in a more withdrawn place, in that which gives the condition of possibility of a link or exchange, an interlacing, a communication in general, by means of message or touch, *mimesis* or *methexis,* and that which always involves, and cannot but involve, the sharing out [*partage*] of the secret of communicability itself (a *symbolon* was also a secret).

Thus it is, for example, that we share the secret of language as something more remote than language itself—but nowhere else than exposed on the flowering surface of language. Or again, for another example, the secret, doubtless inseparable from the preceding one, of the communicability that one would have to call "pathic," communicability by means of "empathy," "sympathy," "pathetic," a secret more remote than all determinate *pathos,* the secret of pathic ambivalence (or what I have called *curiosity*), the secret of its simultaneity of touching and touched. The *phatic* and *pathic* double secret, in itself double and one, unidehiscent: condition, gift, or pres-ence of all being-in-common, the condition sharing out the world. *The secret of the symbolic consists exactly in its sharing.* The latter is thus evidently nothing that could be shared, and it is each time the *obvious obviation* of all sharing, both its patent ob-jectivity and the ob-stacle of its transitive dis-location. The secret is the obvious obviation of fragmentation.

On the one hand, the symbolic is shared in that it is common and communicated to everyone before any "communication" is established—in a secret communicability of all things in that they *are*, in the unprecedented fractal topography that makes up the noncohesive coherence of a world, of the absolutely empirical and absolutely transcendental *fact that there are* all things, this gift of all things, this coming of all things that have *between* them all of this coming itself, the *praesentia* of their being, of the being that is nothing but *theirs*, their being *toward* the world.

On the other hand, the symbolic is shared in that it is distributed, dispersed, disseminated into all the places—points, moments, subjects of truth—of its possible symbolization: thus, the symbolic is not (or does not consist) anywhere at any time. It is neither any part nor the nonexistence of the Whole, but the sharing that is the secret: an open secret, discovered, exposed as obvious on all sides and to all comers, like the dispersion of stars and worlds in the world, open secret of the openly offered—manifest existence without manifestation. The manifest of existence: nudity.

The fragment, or "art," is the symbolic itself in the place and instant of its interruption. It is the secret—pleasure and/or pain—that interrupts the symbolization of the symbolic and thereby delivers the (n)evermore-of-sense [*plus-de-sens*], the infinitely-(n)evermore-of-sense by means of which existence is related and exposed to itself. This relation does not close itself off into a circle of signification; it suspends all such circles, diffracts and renders fragile signified sense. It exposes sense as the secret of that which contains nothing hidden, no mysterious or mystical depth, as the secret of that which comprises nothing other than the multiple, discreet, discontinuous, heterogeneous, and singular touch of being itself.

Fragment: pleasure and pain in which being enjoys and suffers under existence. It is in this sense that art is a fragment: it is not the presentation of being, and thus it is not related to truth in the sense that philosophy would have liked. Whatever its various philosophical determinations may have been (mimesis, splendor, representation, unveiling, putting-to-work, poietization, and all of these at once), they have all left the following unperceived (which art doubtless cannot expose except in exposing itself all the way to the end): that being, before or beyond its truth, enjoys and suffers under existence. This enjoyment-and-suffering is the arrival into presence, presentation without presentness: this presentation does not possess a truth as does (the subject of) being. Rather, presentation itself *is* truth. But not truth on "the subject of": it is truth that is—or exists—as act. If art is the presentation of presentation and not of being, it is in this sense that it has a relation to truth: as truth's sense in action. As truth touches and cannot but touch.

This act is not an operation and does not culminate in a work—if a work is the production of an essence, an accomplishment, even if the essence or accomplishment of an infinite hermeneutics, as a certain tradition on art likes to think.

Which comes down to saying that the art-fragment is not a sacrifice (one of the senses of *operatio,* from which the Germanic *Opfer* comes): it neither operates nor ensures the continuity and homogeneity of being by mediating or sublimating the fractality of dispersed existence. The fragment in this sense is the opposite of sacrifice because it is the opposite of the continuity of essence that it was the task of occidental sacrifice to ensure: a eucharist that gathers and incorporates the fragments of its grace.

Art is the presentation of presentation insofar as presentation—the eternally intact touch of being—cannot be sacrificed. (*Eternally* means "in the instant," the "there" of the "here," "sea intermingled with sun.") This is indeed why, moreover, the entire tradition has stumbled over the sacrifice *of the senses* that it required in the name of truth and the good, a sacrifice, however, that art has not ceased to refuse to grant the tradition, withdrawing this sacrifice from the tradition in virtue of the breaking [*frayage*] of a completely different path.

This is indeed why "art" is also *ars* or *teknē:* which takes place whenever the essential and sacrificial—essentializing—operation that "metaphysics" projectively supposed to be the operation of a *phusis* is not taking place. *Phusis* would be the power [*puissance*] that of itself raises up its essence and carries it off to safety beyond the deadly contingencies of its manifestation. More precisely, its manifestation is certainly essential to it, but even more essential to it, even more pre-supposed is the power to be and/or to produce of itself its own manifestation, and in so doing to complete itself, to finish itself infinitely, in a finish without remainder, and in a finish where the power—supraessentially—does not stop preceding as well as succeeding on the act. (And it is this characteristic of "nature" that one has most frequently wanted to "imitate.") But *teknē* is *phusis* without this essence: the *meta-physics* of the act that precedes (itself) in pres-ence, the act that completes itself of itself, but that, in so doing, completes nothing other than itself, closing neither the circle of a proper self nor the circle of a proper sense, but, rather, ceaselessly opening the toward-itself as if onto the world. *Teknē* is that whose sense (or senses) is the sense (or are the senses) of an enjoyment and suffering rather than a completion and verification.

Teknē is fragmentary or fractal: the realm of essenceless existence. This realm lacks both domain and sovereignty. The power of technics may indeed go on and grow in an exponential manner. It does not produce the assumption of a sovereignty: it does not dispose over the instance of an End or a Sense. It is not astonishing, therefore, that the era of "technics" is also the era of the "end of art." The latter, in fact, has finished serving the finish of an end. It has finished being religious or philosophical art, as it has finished being (theologico)political art. Thus, art is open to this fragmentation of sense that existence *is*. It was always open to this. But today, the yawning of this opening distends and even tears it from one end to the other: on the scale of an in-finity of sense that we expect to respond *for* us. Not, first of all, as an "aesthetic" response but, rather, as an unprecedented art of being in the world, along the edgy surfaces of *aisthesis* and the intimate spacing of its double entelechy, a counterpoint without resolution.

"Coda: Orgia"

The fact that there is an (at least presumed) etymological relation between *ergon* and *orgia* indicates that the suffering of *jouissance*—its surprising suspension—is neither exogenous to nor merely externally attached to the work [*oeuvre*] but, rather, is intimately bound up with it. *Orgia* designates the orgiastic as a singularly sexual overflow only because it designates, first of all, a ritual or cultic operation that can give rise to this overflow. (In other words, *ta orgia* designates also the objects of this cult.)[146]

On the basis of this proximity and even contiguity—a contact of objects, a cult of touching—the orgy can designate the *jouissance*/suffering of the work (in both senses of the genitive), and thus its "inoperativity" [*désoeuvrement*],[147] if you will, but an "inoperativity" that is nothing other than the vibration, trembling, or touch of its very operation. Its e-motion and com-motion. (Thus, the etymological relation of *orgia* with orgasm, even though it has been proven inconsistent by etymological science, nonetheless persists in haunting its borders. Inoperativity: the orgasmic quality of the work.)

But I must immediately specify that by introducing the motif of the "orgy" here I do not intend to reintroduce the mystery cult into contemporary aesthetics. Moreover, one can (cautiously) distinguish between cults of "revelation" and orgiastic cults of "possession" in ancient Greek culture. It would therefore be possible to attempt to conceptualize a "possession"—an appropriation of the inappropriable, an appropriation of coming and of *intermediacy*—without revelation, and thus also without appropriation. But be that as it may, it is not a matter here of any cult whatsoever—no more than it is a matter here of the inverse and symmetrical preference for the orgy as a figure of the "decadence" reputed to be "Roman." (In a sense, of course, our own moment does resemble the end of Rome, and yet nothing repeats itself: it is not an empire that is currently becoming dislocated, but a world that is being articulated; the cracking of joints in each case sounds somewhat the same, but we are well aware that there is no cause for nostalgia, certainly not for empire, neither colonial empire nor the thousand-year Reich.) It is a matter of the *arrangement* of a *coming*, the contradiction-in-terms of the *framing* of an *overflow*. The fact that coming is always *overcoming* us, that presence precedes and prevents itself there, does not exclude a measure, frame, or arrangement: an exposition of ex-position. Indeed, on the contrary. *Because what precedes (itself) is not* (intransitive) *being, but is* transitively *what exists, precedence itself is already outline, contour, and local touch, and fragmentariness is originary.*

The entire logic of the world is concentrated here, and it is concentrated as the logic of art: the world is neither made nor to be made, but the aisthetic "making," the multiplicitous tracing [*frayage*] of places in accordance with which all things take place: the "making" of the "there is." It is the outline: incessantly multiple and suspended, incessantly tied and presenting. It is the *teknē* of the *stroke* [*touche*], as one speaks of a brush stroke in painting. In one sense, there is only one stroke; in another sense, which is nonetheless the same, there are an infinite number of strokes. The "essence" of art is not in a temple but in a trace, in the singular unicity of a naked trace on a naked canvas.[148] The trace is at once *orgion* and *ergon*, unbordering and border, the border unbordering itself in order to be the border it is. As *orgion*, the *ergon* is *toward-*: it is toward-the-world, it "makes up" a world, the whole of an exploding world. As *ergon*, the *orgion* is also *toward-*: it unborders in a measure, cadence, and rhythm that in turn make up a world, the very same exploding world.

The measure of unmeasure does not come to control or to bridle unmeasure: it is its very rhythm. The work, the trace itself, is also the propitious moment, the *kairos* of the rhythm tracing the trace.[149] The harmony of the orgiastic and the opportune rhythm of unbound time: this is the double value, the structurally and irreducibly double value of all opening, spacing, and taking place. *This is what makes up the sense of the trace and the trace as sense.*

That does not mean that we can simply turn the orgiastic quality of our world into a harmony. The unchaining is dreadful—and there is much of the dreadful also in our shattered art. But the gesture of art resists and repeats itself because the coming of sense resists. Perhaps nothing more, for the moment, than an art of the gesture—from which would be suspended, in a formidable and captivating challenge, everything at stake in "technics," "world," and "sense." A "rhythmic" art of the gesture—the gesture or style of thought, the gesture or style of establishing relationships, the gesture or style of *orgion* and *ergon,* the gesture or style of making sense, the gesture or style of being in the world: it is not a matter of forcing the world into a figure, but of displacing oneself into the world, onto all of its confines, without exiting from it and without relating it to anything other than itself, its event. It is a matter of transposing onto the world what Claude Lévi-Strauss puts like this, beginning by recalling that

> Benveniste demonstrated that in Greek the original sense of *rhuthmos* is "*a characteristic arrangement of the parts into a whole.*" ... in the decorative rhythm, it is the idea of "whole" that is dominant, for recurrence is perceptible only if the rhythmic cell includes a limited number of elements. In a finite collection of elements that are either procured by chance or selected by the bricoleur from his hoard, how will one establish an order? The notion of rhythm covers the series of permutations permitted in order for the set to form a system.[150]

The word *system* ought to be stripped here of its rigid, imperious, and hypostatizing connotations: it has no sense other than that of the rhythmic gesture of keeping together (in) coming.

Pain. Suffering. Unhappiness

Really these thoughts are quite meaningless. Things happen, and, like millions of people before me, I look for a meaning in them, because my vanity will not allow me to admit that the whole meaning of an event lies in the event itself. If I casually stand on a beetle, it will not see this event, tragic for the beetle, as a mysterious concatenation of universal significance. The beetle was beneath my foot at the moment when my foot fell; a sense of well-being in the daylight, a short, shrill pain and then nothing. But we're condemned to chase after a meaning that cannot exist.

MARLEN HAUSHOFER, *The Wall*[151]

Pain and suffering begin with existence and end when it ends, and this end gives pain and suffering to those who survive. Pain and suffering correspond to discounted sense ("discounted sense": this expression is to be taken here in an economic sense, as alluding to all calculations of sense, of which Pascal's wager is a kind of hyperbole, all drafts drawn, all capitalization and interest; the Reformation, the Counter-Reformation, Jansenism, Theodicy, Progress, History, Liberation, the Search for Times Past have all played themselves out either within or in the general vicinity of this economy, just as political economy has played itself out—and still plays itself—in a calculation of pain and suffering, of thresholds of toleration and profit). The sense of discounted sense is to remunerate pain. One must not forget that "redemption," that great word of the Occident, signifies "ransom" and "buying back": bills paid, having fallen due once and for all. But whether it takes the form of actual physical suffering or mourning, pain ruins this sense, and in death this pain does not disappear without taking sense away with it as it goes. Even in the very heart of Christianity, beginning with Christ's cry of abandonment, one can still find the trace—never quite effaced—of this pain: redeemed suffering will have been also aggravated suffering, simultaneously and indiscernibly.

Once sense is no longer discounted but disappears in full settlement—and this happens when theoanthropodicy disappears—the world appears, insofar as it is the world and precisely *this* world, as an exposition of suffering. The tableau of this world, produced in 1818, hardly requires revision even today, almost two centuries later:

> If, finally, we should bring clearly to a man's sight the terrible sufferings and miseries to which his life is constantly exposed, he would be seized with horror; and if we were to conduct the confirmed optimist through the hospitals, infirmaries, and surgical operating-rooms, through the prisons, torture-chambers, and slave-kennels, over battle-fields and places of execution; if we were to open him to all the dark abodes of misery, where it hides itself from the glance of cold curiosity, and finally, allow him to glance into the starving dungeon of Ugolino, he, too, would understand at last the nature of this "best of possible worlds."[152]

The notion of the "unjustifiable" character of suffering is of a piece with the hope for its possible justification or elimination, and consequently for a sense oriented by this justification or elimination. It matters little, from this point of view, whether evil is taken in its moral sense, as originating in freedom, or in its material sense, as originating in necessity. God himself can even play, in either case, the double role of origin and assumption. Whether it arises out of *evil* as such (the possibility of freedom) or out of *malady* (the possibility of necessity) or out of some sort of combination of the two in which neither can be distinguished from the other, which is tending to become the case in our *world* (in the painfulness of labor, in the increasing mutual entanglement of technical and natural causalities), suffering is ineluctably *un-*

happiness. Sense has been paired with unhappiness, sometimes positively, as tragic sense, sometimes negatively, under the sign of happiness.

There is nothing to be said of happiness, as the idyllic version of sense, the immanence of sense bought at a discount, the simple denegation of unhappiness. Nor is there anything to be said of its symmetrical reversal, which is, moreover, also its intimate threat: boredom. It suffices to say, with Ernst Jünger, that "nihilism is over. Action has become so strong that there remains no time for nihilism. It is a state of mind that one adopts when one is bored.... Nihilism is a matter of boredom, a good thing for rich people."[153]

I will not attempt to follow out the impressive destiny of tragic meaning that unfolds up to our own times, or up to the border of our world. Philippe Lacoue-Labarthe summarizes it this way: "To imitate the divine means two things: to want to be God (this is the tragic experience of the Greeks); to regulate oneself 'in all humility' in terms of God's withdrawal (this is the 'occidental' experience, again a tragic one, but in a different way)."[154]

He goes on to specify that the difference between the two "ways" resides in what separates "the figure of death" from the "face of the dead—the exterminated." That is to say, we have moved from a *plastics* of death to *nudity,* and to an extremity of both the "pathic" and the "phatic." The oppressive silence of our entry into the world, a world marked by pain without the least redemption. Here, "genocide" (as murder of a people and murder of the plural singular) exemplifies—technically and materially, from Armenians to Jews, from Gypsies to Homosexuals, from Communists to the Asocial, from Refugees to the Marginal, from the Exploited to the Excluded, from the Mad to the Hungry and Controlled—the putting to death of the *world* in the name of the *earth,* the *planet,* or the *universe.* The world will have begun with its end: the death of God as creator of the world, the hatred of this world itself as the *remains* of a lost creation, the will to re-create the world, to fashion it in the image or imprint of a Sense. The hatred of the Jew qua "stateless" and "cosmopolitan" is exemplary, insofar as the "cosmopolitan" is, precisely and paradoxically, that which is without a cosmos.[155]

Occidental tragedy will have arrived at its most extreme limit in the heroic ambiguity of the twilights of the gods: either the (ecstatic?) exposition to the abyss or the appropriation of the divine in order to recreate, refashion a world (and the two hypotheses can be mixed, while each has its right- and left-wing versions, its explicitly or implicitly sacred and sacrificial versions, its version of the aestheticization of politics and of the politicization of aesthetics).[156] What opens up beyond this point—but also at this point of departure—is something else: the *world* that will point neither to an abyss without foundation or form nor to a plastic (re)creation.

If it is reasonable to situate the tragic in relation to the divine and its withdrawal, it seems thus also reasonable to discern the structural trait of the tragic in this: tragedy becomes sense at the moment when sense is felt to be tragic. (In the final analysis, this is the structure of sacrifice.) According to an invincible dialectics (or at least a dialectics that no one can be sure of outmaneuvering), pure tragedy, absolute abandon, the most rending farewell—all turn themselves into a fulfillment of sense. Dark sense, but sense nonetheless. Being all torn up inside, and yet consoled. Oedipus finds himself again at Colonnus, even when Colonnus is called Vienna. In this sublime wisdom or courage in anguish, there is the lightning bolt of meaning. Doubtless, this is infinitely close to the "fragmentation" of which I have been trying to speak. And doubtless also the *jouissance* or joy deserves mention beside the suffering—I will come back to this. But first of all—first of all and all the way to the end—unhappiness is unhappiness, *and there is nothing else to say.* And one ought, perhaps, to be able to say only this, and to think that this alone is to be said, for the sake of saving nothing at all. It is not because what is at stake here is unsayable that there is nothing else to say, but because what is at stake lies beyond signification. It is as in-significant as joy—at the very point where pain and joy mixed together compose the nonsignifying origin of significance itself.

If sense, indeed, turns into salvation, in one way or another, then it has lost the sense of sense, the sense of the world of existence that is and that is only toward this world. A world in which there is no saving oneself, a world that is not to be saved, without its being nonetheless delivered to perdition: decidedly neither *cosmos* (smile of the Immortals) nor *mundus* ("vale of tears"), but the very place of sense.

There are perhaps only three formal structures of sense: (1) the *observance* of an order or ritual of the world, where all unhappiness is a tragic omission opening onto truth (Oedipus); (2) *salvation,* where unhappiness is an illness, a worldly alienation that calls forth the tragedy of its infinite healing/expiation (Parsifal); (3) existence, as the exposition of being-*toward*-the-world or being-world—where evil seems coextensive with good, the "worst" with the "best," and where therefore the exposition has to be decided each time. In other words, sense as given, sense as mediated, sense as surprise. Or again, on another register, sense as set of signs, sense as signification, sense as origin of significance.

It is not possible to keep these senses of sense rigorously separate from each other any more than it is possible to seize their succession as the trial of a single history that would itself provide the sense of their distribution. It is also not possible, however, to confuse them, or to give up thinking that something is *happening,* that something here called "world" is happening to us, and that it is here and now that this is coming to pass and that the here and now takes place in accordance with what it transmits to itself of what it represents as being where it comes from. The set of these contradictory conditions entails that the desolation of the earth and sky, the *evil* spread across the world like its very skin of war, famine, frightful inequality, and madness of ecotechnical domination—beyond unhappiness and illness, outside of the resources of the tragicotheological—this evil is not merely opposed to sense: it is becoming the unhappiness of sense itself.

There remains, thus, bitter gaiety:

THE CLIENT: God made the world in six days, and you, you can't make me a fucking pair of pants in six months.

THE TAILOR: But sir, take a look at the world, and then take a look at your pants.[157]

In other words, does not the deconstruction of both tragedy and Christianity—of their combination, which dialectically culminates in the unhappiness of sense as an *end* in all senses—does this deconstruction not have to take the form of another turn, return, detour, or turning-back of this dialectical knot? Neither happiness nor unhappiness, but another *happenstance,* neither negative sense nor negation of sense, giving their due to both resistance and suffering (to that which, within each, is undue, duly undue, a significance of the due), and for this reason ceasing to sublate the evil in the good, taking a break from all theodicy or logodicy, and calling finally for another *stance* of sense, or for another *stance* in the face of sense. For the whole question can be summarized like this: what *attitude* to adopt before, or in, self-differing and self-deferring sense. For tragedy, for Christianity, for philosophy, and for art, as also perhaps for being-in-common in general, it is always a question at least of this: maintaining oneself in the face of the eclipse, fainting, syncopation, or collapse of sense. That is, in the face of truth. It is always a matter of this. But all modes of "deportment" have been altered, all poses, whether proud or humble, bold or timid. Once again, it is necessary to invent how to give some kind of deportment to existence—to nothing but existence.

And thus, no theologoanthropopoetodicy—no *dicy* (that is, no justificatory redemption) and also no *dikē* (no destiny as justice). What is sought would be beyond tragedy, beyond dialectics, and beyond salvation. Nor would it collapse into that other figure of unhappiness, the figure of Job's cry (which Christ's cry prolonged). For Job cries out in the face of his God. But Job—singularly and continuously since Auschwitz—cries out in the disfigured face of the world, and what he cries out is in this sense the world itself.

"Neither *dikē* nor *dicy*": this is a call neither for despair nor for hope, neither for a judgment of this world nor for a "just world"—but for justice *in* this world, for justice rendered *unto* the world: that is, for resistance, intervention, compassion, and struggle that would be tireless and oriented toward the incommensurability of the world, the incommensurability of the totality of the singular outline, without religious and tragic remuneration, without sublation, and thus without discourse. Without discourse: for discourse, all discourse, sublates everything. The least statement is or makes a *dikē:* it apportions a fate, assigns a fate, and provides it with a meaning. But suffering is not a portion in this sense. It is disproportionate, impenetrable hardness.

To say more of it would contravene the rule we just established. There is an archi-transcendental condition of suffering that touches on the nude exposition to sense, on unbearable decay as constitution of sense, and this archi-transcendental condition provides neither object nor Idea nor regulative horizon. It merely shows wounded, undone, undermined bodies, their broken or convulsed areality. The suffering body was up until our own day a "quivering" body: a pathos-laden body, rich with signs, clearly mixed up with an obscure *jouissance,* a tortured, sacrificed body. But our suffering body is broken, dislocated, or eaten away, without any meaning and for no reason. It is assisted, repaired, plugged in—and again, there is nothing else to say.[158] Benumbed by fragmentative explosions on the nuclear, chemical, genetic, surgical, computational, sonorous, and luminous levels.... There remains not necessarily an "unhappiness," and yet a kind of highly acute pain on the point of exploding, with neither dimension nor remission, a touch of existence that saves nothing and loses nothing but exposes everything.

In this sense, the "passion" of the "flesh," in the flesh, is finished—and this is why the word *body* ought to succeed on the word *flesh,* which was always overabundant, nourished by sense, and egological [*égologique*]. For what is coming is the world of bodies, and suffering is simply established there, if one can put it this way, without any depth of passion whatsoever. This could mean that it is tendentially "anesthetized" (but what would *tendentially* then mean?): not merely in the hospitals, but also, in another way, in wars that are no longer accompanied by the pathos-laden celebration of suffering, but the cold horror of ignoble stupidity.[159] It means for sure that suffering is no longer sacrificial. And thus, that it is in no way redemptive. Suffering without remission, and in this sense without passion. Disassemblage of the cross: we are frozen in the moment of neither the agony nor the tomb but the *deposition* of the body. It is not by chance if painting chose this moment long ago: the moment of silent pity.

To know what stance to take, when there is nothing left to say, in the face of a deposited body (and yet not to resort to anatomy lessons, another way of establishing significations): when we know this, then only will we be able to think through the belonging of suffering (or unhappiness) to the constitution of sense *without sublating* suffering in sense. That is, we will be able to posit this suffering as inassimilable, irreconcilable, and intolerable. For it is this suffering that exposes itself thus; it is this belonging itself that repels itself and never sublates itself. One must thus refuse this suffering with all of one's might, not heal, on the one hand, while starving out and killing, on the other—yet without projecting either its final redemption or its final anesthetization. Without distorting the explosive pain of *aisthesis,* that other double face of the sensible entelechy, pleasure and pain. Without renouncing for one instant the struggle against evil, this thought—which is the most difficult thought because it is the thought that must know itself as nonthinking—would touch on suffering as on that which belongs to sense as its constitutive decay. Such thought would thus touch on the possibility of sense qua originary passibility. How not to constitute here a new dialectics? And yet this is what one must refuse. To be before the obscurity of a sense that is neither unveiled nor produced nor conquered, but suffered. To suffer sense—without any kind of dolorousness whatsoever. To suffer, *suffere,* as a mode of supporting, of receiving, of somebody who would be "subject to suffering." To suffer sense: to suffer one's being-absent.

(Not to constitute a new dialectics, a new tragedy: yet this is impossible, given that our entire discourse is made out of dialectics and tragedy. With every step, discourse dialecticizes. But to struggle, step by step, against dialectics in the process of its operation and against intentionality in the process of its signification, to strip away the sense that has been made in order to allow its sense to come in turn, this is the labor, thought, writing, and exscription that stand before us, their happenstance, their happiness and unhappiness.)

Only in this way—ever further, ever more thoroughly beyond the grasp of discourse—can the originary passibility and suffering of sense find themselves infinitely close to *jouissance.* But what do we mean by *jouissance* here? In order to deliver *jouissance* neither to the dialectical sublimation of an appropriation of the impossible nor to the joy that Spinoza, as its greatest thinker, maintained, in spite of everything, draped in beatitude, one must posit before all else that, about *jouissance,* too, there is nothing left to say. Joy has no more sense than suffering. But their conjoined—conjoined *and* dissociated—insignificance is significance itself. Although there is nothing left to say about them, everything we see, and every interruption of our discourse, is exposed to their demand. But there is no symmetry: one does not accept pain, it is *evil* itself, either physical or moral, and indeed, in the final analysis, always both physical and moral, each in the other. It is thus injustice itself and, as pain, it calls of itself for the insistent refusal of this injustice. It is no longer a question, when one is beyond the *cosmos,* of keeping one's distance from this pain: in the world, pain traverses things. Joy, in turn, calls of itself for its own suspension: it completes itself and escapes into a fugitive eternity. It is not a question of establishing oneself there. In a sense, one would have to say: the first is in permanence, the second in passage. Symmetry without symmetry, two faces of rhythm.

Neither happiness nor unhappiness, there is the *happenstance,* the sense of the *happenstance* [*Ni bonheur, ni malheur, il y aurait* l'heur, *le sens de* l'heur], of the good or bad encounter or confrontation, of the possibility—incessantly renewed—that there could be a good or bad happenstance, that it could be necessary to choose one against the other, but, first of all, to choose to have this choice *and* not to have it, not to master the sense of the happenstance, the fractal combinatory of events that makes up the world.[160] Neither mastery nor servitude, but sovereignty liable to the happenstance, to its coming and going. Not destiny, the Fates, Providence, the drawing of lots. Not irresponsible chance. But, on the contrary, the sovereign possibility of responding to the happenstance of sense.

Unhappiness is nonetheless not to be appeased, nor is happiness appropriable. And both for the same reason: the in-significance of their sense, their sense itself as absenting of sense, the point of pain or of joy. To have a sense of what is happening is quite precisely to respond to, and to be responsible for, that which is unappeasable and inappropriable as such.

This response represents all that we lack, all of that whose lack is interpreted as the decay and failure of sense. But this lack itself is not a state of privation whose suppression it would be necessary to require and assure. This lack is a lack of nothing.[161] Of nothing: that is, of no thing whose absence would be, first, to be deplored and, then, to be filled, in order to complete our being or our "humanity." Nothing is lacking in our being: the lack of given sense is, rather, precisely what completes our being. Nothing is lacking in the world: the world is the totality, and the totality completes itself as the open, as the nontotalization of the open or of the *happenstance.* In this sense, the being-existent of the world is infinite, with an *actual* and not a potential infinity. Being is the infinite actuality of the finite. Its act—existing—depends on nothing and does not have to progress in order to perfect itself. But its perfection is existing as unappeasable and inappropriable being-toward. The structure of existing is neither the in-itself nor the for-itself nor their dialectic, but the *toward*: neither toward oneself nor toward the other without being, first of all, toward the world, the *toward* of being-toward-the-world as constitution of ipseity. Neither toward happiness nor toward unhappiness without being, first of all, toward the *happenstance* that the world *is.*

That which, for itself, depends on nothing is an *absolute.* That which nothing completes in itself is a *fragment.* Being or existence is an absolute fragment. To exist: the *happenstance* of an absolute fragment.

This says almost nothing—such is the insignificance of sense itself, the nudity of absolute and sovereign significance. To say this almost nothing is the sole task of a writing—but its insignificant task, immediately exscribed by its own rhythm and delivered thus unto the world: the *end* of philosophy. To repeat it once again, this does not appease or fulfill either unhappiness or happiness. But it is the reason for which there is not to be resignation or indifference. Everything is at stake there, all possible sense, and all of the impossible, too. And there is nothing left to say: not because it would be a matter of the ineffable, but because it is already there, coming to the world and to lips here and now.

Where's that bound-down, nailed-down moan,
where's Prometheus—helper of cliffs?
Where's the black-flying hawk—the yellow-eyed urge
of his claws, leaping from sullen eyebrows?

No, never again—tragedies don't come back—
but those approaching lips,
those lips lead me down into the essence
of Aeschylus the wood-loader, of Sophocles the wood-cutter.

He is echo . . . landmark—no, the plow . . .
Rock-air theatre of growing time
standing—everyone wants to see everyone else—
see the new-born, the death-spreaders, and see the living.[162]

World

The *toward* as constitution of ipseity does not, first of all, define either a toward-the-self or a toward-the-other. Neither the "self" nor the "other" would be respected in the absoluteness of its fragmentation (which is each time its own) if "self" and "other" were not seen as *coming* from a place infinitely more remote than the position (that is, the positioning) that these expressions would confer on them, expressions in which the "toward" is overdetermined either as adhesion, occupation, capture, and belonging, or, on the contrary, as projection, impulsion, and alienation. *Toward* must, first of all, define the *ipse* as *toward the world.* But "toward the world" is not a predicate of the subject "ipse"—which (and for this very reason) is not a "subject." "Toward the world" is the entire constitution, being, nature, essence, and identity of the absolute fragment of existence. And this entire constitution gives itself in one stroke, in being *toward the world,* as the arrival of being in advance of itself—differing/deferring—in advance in one stroke, each time, all the way to the confines of the world, "present already where it is headed, where it is not."[163]

Or, more exactly, the confines of the world are, in each instant, that on which every arrival of existence touches. We have to do here with a monadology, that is, a universal structure of *pars totalis.* But it is different from Leibniz's monadology in the following way. In Leibniz, universality is an index of the reflection and refraction of each of the monads in the others, the law of which is gathered in God, the monad of monads. Here, however, it is a matter, at the same time, of a diffraction in principle, and not merely between the monads, but within each monad, and within the monad of monads that is the world: the pars-totalitarian, nontotalizable totality, where each part has all the extension of the whole, but where the whole consists only in the mutual *extra* of the *partes.* In which the singularity of the plural singular consists.

The "world" is thus not that with which an *ipse* would have "to do," as with a vis-à-vis or a surround. The world is exactly coextensive with the taking-place of all existing, of existing in its singularity—and coextensive is to be understood here in the double sense of co-extended (co-spaced, co-opened) and co-tendered (co-arriving, co-expressing). The world is always the plurality of worlds: a constellation whose compossibility is identical with its fragmentation, the compactness of a powder of absolute fragments.

This is why the slightest inert mineral fragment in space belongs also to the constellation of the *ipse,* to the singularity of sense, without any implication of "animating" it with any *aseity* other than that of *singular matter,* that is, the world itself in its fact, in its innate birth, if one can put it like this, or, rather, in its innateness, whose structure is throughout the structure of birth and surprising arrival, where all birth pre-vents itself, and where this pre-vention makes up all the significance there is. That is, in a sense, nothing, and "singularity rests on nothing."[164]

Nothing: the fact of the world, a being-the-there that, first of all, is the *here* of this world *here,* without any creation at its origin. This factuality is also that of all birth: that which is born in birth is not, first of all, the product or the engendered term of an author or parents, but precisely *being* insofar as nothing posits it and insofar as all exposes it, always singular being.

The world is the infinite resolution of sense into fact and fact into sense: the infinite resolution of the finite. Resolution signifies at once dissolution, transformation, harmonization, and firm decision. The world is the finite opening of an infinite decision: the space of the responsibility of sense, and of a responsibility such that nothing precedes it—

neither call nor question. It pre-vents itself and over-takes itself—this is the fact of the world.

Which is why the "itself" of this responsibility, or the "itself" of sense—ipseity as existentiale of the world—precedes all ego-ity and all subjectivity. Without this precedence, without this coming toward the world that the world in turn spatializes, an "ego" purely present-there would not properly speaking be (this is what Descartes cannot see), or it would be immediately all of given sense (and this is what philosophy desires from Descartes to Husserl).[165]

If the world is not the work of a God, this is not because there is no God, as if this were an annoying circumstance, a privative condition to which one had to accommodate oneself as best one could. (As if, in the final analysis, the world were not complete, as if the causal or final part of the totality had been simply amputated. Often, atheism has not known how to communicate anything other than this.) But there is no God because there is the world, and because the world is neither a work nor an operation but the space of the "there is," its configuration without a face. There is no God because God does not belong to the "there is": his name names precisely the category of that which would be subtracted from the "there is." "God" (the only one, the God of the West, the Helleno-Judeo-Christiano-Islamic God: the others are gods in the *plural,* figures within the world and not the agent of the world), "God" was the name of the transformation of the world into a work. The "man-god" was the name of its transformation into an operation. The "world" is henceforth the name of that which neither operates nor is operated: the sense of the "there is."

"World" says the *there* of the "there is." One must understand "there is" as saying the same thing as "I know" in the lines, "I know a song for which I would give / All Rossini, all Mozart, and all Weber..."—where the "I know" points to the common, anonymously singular character of the song in question.[166]

But "there is" localizes being. More exactly, the transitivity of being is, first of all, localization. Being entrances the existent in giving way to it, giving it a *place.* The *there* is thereby marked by dis-location, diffraction, and atomism.[167]

There [*y*] is the whole of the world. There is that there is. It is through this, or in this—there, here, down there, at the center, which is everywhere, at the confines, which are nowhere—that the world qualifies its being-a-world, or the making-up-a-world of all that there is: not, above all, as the gathering of all things (*what* there is, whose totalization takes place nowhere: for the *pars totalis* excludes that there should be any "total part" or any part "more total" than the others), but as their being-together in the "signifiable whole" of the fact *that* there are these things.

But—these *things:* there are things. All these things, all these bodies, their areas, their *arealities.* One cannot too strongly insist on it: the sense of the world cannot except a single atom, insofar as the fact-world is the resolution of sense. I have already said that a "philosophy of nature" is becoming again today a necessity for thought. Of course, such a "philosophy of nature" would have to involve a complete transformation of both "philosophy" and "nature." Neither a metaphysical ecologism nor a romantic symbolization (immanence or transcendence) would suffice. For the place of the "there is" is not a mysterious quality, a "spiritual dimension" that would add itself to material spatialization. Spatialization—space and time—first of all makes up, or entrances, existence qua liability to meaning.

Only when one has recognized the transcendental or existential condition comprised by the taking-place-there of all things, only then is one in a "position" to articulate with rigor that, as Heidegger wishes, humanity, or *Dasein* within humanity—within humanity without humanity—has to "be the there" (in German the *da* or in French the *y*), that is, that the human being articulates the opening as such of the there,[168] and that this articulation forms the very ipseity of the human being, his/her *humanitas.* Without this existential condition, the human being would be "human" only in the sense suggested by its *etymon,* the sense of "the terrestrial," either as immanent to the *humus* (already inhumed), or as facing the celestial (exhumed, and haunted by its dead gaze). But the human being is the terrestrial insofar as the earth is or becomes worldly: simultaneously, it is cast into the "void" of a space-time whose finite measure (since there is nothing else) *is* the infinite,[169] and it becomes worldly in the sense that it blurs the boundaries of the various territories and home soils that lie within it. In both ways, the worldliness of the earth—of the human being—means: the renewed putting into play of taking-place in general. The *there* is neither the heavens nor the humus, but that there is, and that there is a place for reconceiving sense on the basis of this point of departure.

In accordance with this existential condition, the primary theme of all existence, including the existence of the rock itself, is never who knows what inertia, pure inherence, inclusion, or juxtaposition, and still less a disposition of the "environment" or a texture of the "milieu":[170] this theme is, first of all, the spacing/spaced taking-place-there. This existential condition is *the worldly* [le mondial]. As long as we do not take into account, without reserve, the worldly as such, we have not gotten rid of demiurges and creators. In other words, we are not yet atheists. Being an atheist is no longer a matter of denying a divine instance that has reabsorbed itself into itself (and this can perhaps therefore no longer be called "atheism"). It is a matter of opening the sense of the world.

(For example, by laying bare the overdetermined identities of the "continents"—Asia, America, Africa, Australia, and Europe—to give oneself over to another "continental drift," not in order to disqualify their differences but, on the contrary, in order to multiply them, not in order to give them once again a taste for earth and roots, but in order to watch their fractal contours play. And along with these, the "races": colors and traits, bodies with neither model nor assumption. In which language(s) are the phrases "to be black" or "to have slanted eyes" uttered? What do these phrases say? What is denied, denegated, or repressed when one affirms simply that all of this has no pertinence with regard to universal man, his rights and obligations? Meanwhile, one black is not black in the same way as another is black, nor is one white white as another white. Racism is always the flip side of what one calls an "abstract universality," and its ignoble stupidity is on the—immense—scale of this universality. But what is not universal in this sense is that the equality of all has for its very condition the nonsameness of "humanity." And along with this equality, the curiosity of each about the other, and along with this *curiosity*, the *spacing*—figures and colors—that is its cause and consequence: the world. This world ought to give us countries back—neither earth nor nation nor people, but all these things together, the countryside of the country of the world.)

The mundaneness of the world, its being-world in the sense of its being-nothing-*but*-the-world, is indissociable from worldliness in this sense. (One could also say that *cosmos* and *mundus* together reexpose their values as worldliness.) The *there* of the "there is" is nothing but spacing as such—if it is possible to say the "as such" of spacing supervening on nothing (to say "the Big Bang" as such). As such, then, the *there* is nothing other than the Wittgensteinian "That" of the world, while at the same time being the world's original "how." In the *there,* the "that" and the "how" of the world coincide. It is not a place of places, or a *sensorium Dei,* or an a priori form. More likely, it would be a priori matter—but here the a priori, in its *act of birth,* would be the sensible entelechy itself: the unity, opened within itself, of the touched/touching.

In a sense, nothing: a process of arrival offered from the outside that itself has neither outside nor inside. A coming, consequently, that comes of nothing, not coming, coming absolutely, as you wish—and yet here is not the place for wishing, but for taking the *thing as it is.* As Gérard Granel says of the "world *as such:* not, to be sure, a 'nothing at all,' but the 'nothing' of the 'All.'"[171]

Nothing—*res,* the thing-in-itself, this thing whose appearing (presence) exceeds phenomenality in all senses because it is the *phainein* itself, the appearing we must dissociate, finally and radically, from all placing-in-view, illumination, and even projection, in order to take it up again in its essence, an essence that is at once much more and much less than phenomenal: the touch of *sense* itself, the coming offered from the inside/to the outside that has neither outside nor inside. To demand nothing else, but nothing less.[172] But not to "demand" it, for we are there.[173]

A noncreated coming that itself has not yet come, a nonregressive coming toward a proper anteriority always pre-supposed, and yet a coming that pre-vents itself, a pre-cedence of presence in itself, the surprise of a coming without necessity. Suddenly befalling, preceding, and proceeding on itself, the coming of the world that is also the coming to the world—the world as being pres-ent of being—escapes from the start all dialectics of transcendental cosmology. We do not have to ask if there is an infinite causal chain or inaugural spontaneity: there is one as the other, one in the other, it is necessary to stop trying to put it like this. *There is:* sense is there. We can no longer concern ourselves with antinomies of the origin, or with an assumption of the origin into truth—even if into the truth of an original division—although none of this is without validity. But the sense of all of this, the meaning of philosophy at its end, is that the world is the origin, and that the worldliness of the world, qua absolute existential condition, exhausts its finite sense—exhausts it, that is, opens it infinitely. *Mundus patet.*

So there we have it. This would seem to be the final word (that is, the first). The very excess of sense, its absolute fragment(ation), which cuts off all discourse. But for this very reason—that the first and last word are the same—there is neither first nor last word. If there were "first" and "last," it would be the exscription of all words: the taking-place-there of their sense, of all their senses, "outside," here.

But even this would not constitute an end any more than it constitutes an origin. "The world is the origin" means that the origin is *there* where it [*ça*] opens itself. Everywhere, then, from one end to the other of a world that has no ends. From birth to death, all the way across the spacing—that is to say, across the time[174]—of existence. But not everywhere indifferently: for existence spaces itself, singularizes itself in accordance with an infinity of rhythms of arrival, rhythms of decision to exist.

Sense That Senses Itself

There is a negation of sense that is as heavy with sense as the most fulfilled Sense—that is, a negation of sense that, to the precise degree to which it is a negation of sense, is also a confinement to Truth qua pure abyss of sense: an exposing Death, and not an exposition to death. Paradoxically, it is a negation of sense that makes an appeal to life, a living sense of life. Life becomes the true sense of sense, which as a result no longer has any sense other than the sense of life. The "living" represents the intimate palpitation that is immediately felt as sense. This is why it was possible to say: "Dada is for that which is without sense without being nonsense. dada is without sense like nature and life. dada is for nature and against art. dada wants to give to each thing its essential place."[175] (This was a moment of our history, with a necessity of its own, but once again we are led back to the turning point of the 1930s: the point at which it is most necessary to draw a firm distinction between nonsense and a lack of sense that would no longer be a symmetrical exacerbation of the desire of sense. Dada, along with many other movements, represented the entire ambiguity of this point, which depends on whether one distinguishes or desires . . .)

Whether as Death or as Life, it is the same expressive density that is at play here: the humanism of the *humus,* earth-tomb or germinative earth, subterranean sense or native soil, "if the grain does not die."[176]

Always sacrifice and dialectics. Sense wants to be felt, it wants to *sense* itself: it wants to sense itself and it wants to be sensed. To sense oneself making up sense would be properly to make sense. Desire is thus the desire to abolish aisthetic exteriority, to enclose within oneself the double entelechy of the sensing/sensed, to confer on it a unity that would not be simply numerical, and finally to *force the touch* to be more than a touch: to make itself into an invasive inherence of the self unto infinity. Sense as a leech [*sangsue*] of the self.

To sense oneself making sense, and even more, to sense *oneself as the engenderment of sense*—this is without a doubt the ultimate stake of philosophy, of which the first form deployed was the "hidden art" of the Kantian schematism (the first schema goes like this: "Number is therefore simply the unity of the synthesis of the manifold of a homogeneous intuition in general, a unity due to my generating time itself in the apprehension of the intuition").[177] Philosophy has not so much closed the circle of metaphysical significations as it has wanted, as its absolute intention, to appropriate the generativity of sense. The two operations are the same, but the first is only the exterior face of the second. "God" dies there in reengendering himself as philosophical presentation. The latter in turn reengenders itself as sensible presentation—as *literature* in the (romantic) sense in which this word means writing that figures and feels itself as the very *poiesis* of sense. That figures itself thus in order to feel itself thus, that feels itself to be thus in figuring itself thus. It is not by chance if the work that was Gustave Flaubert's obsession, *The Temptation of Saint Antony*, finishes with the complete tableau of the self-engenderment of sense in all senses:

> O happiness! happiness! I have seen the birth of life, I have seen the beginning of movement. The blood in my veins is beating so hard that it will burst them. I feel like flying, swimming, yelping, bellowing, howling. I'd like to have wings, a carapace, a rind, to breathe out smoke, wave my trunk, twist my body, divide myself up, to be inside everything, to drift away with odours, develop as plants do, flow like water, vibrate like sound, gleam like light, to curl myself up into every shape, to penetrate each atom, to get down to the depth of matter—to be matter![178]

Of course, the scene must be read in all directions at once: it bespeaks the heights of the desire to write, and it denounces these heights as the heights of temptation. It celebrates them and parodies them. It shouts out its despair along with its demand, both of which are infinite. The end of philosophy, the end of literature.

Beyond this point, it is the world that opens—and the world is the spacing that offers to let go of both despair and demand. Hence, to let go of philosophy along with literature. And to change styles to the point of no longer being tempted by the inscription of birth itself (be it the birth of the world, the birth of style, or the birth of the subject). But the temptation is here more than a seduction. It participates in that which, first of all, cannot fail to take the form of necessity: if sense is no longer given, how can one avoid wanting to reengender oneself as the gift of sense? How can one avoid getting caught up in an interminable autophagy of discourse? How can all significations not become reversible, and how can I not be at every moment vacillating between extreme destitution—saying, "so there we have it"—and the infinite circularity of the senses—the all-too-tempting game: "all senses are sense," "the sense of the world is the world of sense." This is why, with each step one must gain distance—the distance of the world. One must set oneself apart from "sensing oneself," without ceasing to be affected along one's "self" by the spacing of the world. To know, without knowing, that the sense is also that *one has not felt it passing.*

Consequently, one must not give up writing—with an attention disengaged from temptation, but attentive, rather, to this, that sense gives itself only when one no longer demands it, while remaining watchful. "The writer is himself like a new idiom in the process of constructing for itself, inventing for itself the means of expression and diversifying itself in accordance with its own sense."[179]

But writing *as an "idiom"* is also the fact of the voices, silences, and gestures that do not appear as or in the work. The words, their concepts and images, provide for this *praxis* its relays of signification and communication. In the end, each one is a "new idiom" in the process of being born, and the world is the common space of idiomatic significances.

Dialogue I

—But what if "worldliness" were in fact nothing but the indefinite extension of appearances, wherein the universal, displayed without depth, gives itself the spectacle of itself, so ubiquitously diffused that you take it to be "sense," whereas it is nothing but the general simulation of a circulation of sense?

—In saying this, your only mistake is to believe that the general representation that the worldly indeed gives (itself) of itself is still a representation, but a dissimulating rather than an expressive one, and one that dissimulates its own lack. You still expect the world to be a sign of something other than itself. Moreover, you are missing the point of worldliness: for the very idea of a spectacle of the world can only be an occidental idea. It is not only the case that there is no spectacle for all those whom famine and misery do not grant the leisure to be spectators. Further, of those who *are* watching, at the other end of the world, the *world show*[180] of multiplied screens, you do not have the right to presuppose that they are lost in the stupefied alienation you imply by your use of the word *spectacle*. You have neither the right nor the means to presuppose the sense that they are perhaps in the process of giving to practices of which you have only a nihilistic interpretation. At a given site, the world spectacle can constitute a breach in a system of interdictions, at another site, it can provide an opportunity for speaking together; at another, it can give rise to the kinds of unprecedented things that nourish invention. You are tetanized by "images"—an old occidental reflex—and you are unaware of all the *praxis* that has already laid hold of them . . .

—But finally, the spectacle signifies only itself: is this the whole "absent sense" in which you take so much pleasure?

—Yes, the spectacle signifies nothing but itself, and this is indeed the end of all the senses of the world that we have been able to signify up to now. But this very end addresses us anew to sense and situates it very clearly: no longer in the outside of signification, but along the surface of the world and its significance.

—But it is still a matter of *sense:* and sense must always, in one way or another, be signified, or else you are just playing with words.

—Certainly. I would even say that sense must be signified in all possible ways, by each and every one of us, by all "individual" or "collective" singulars.

—By all subjectivities?

—You can choose whatever words you wish, along with the sense you give them. As for me, I would say: by all that can make someone somewhere expose him/herself to sense, to making sense, to receiving sense, to leaving sense open.

—What you are describing, then, is "dialogue," the quintessence of good intentions, so-called "openness," "mutual enrichment": the lowest form of spectacle.

—You are not wrong. But I am talking about something else. Dialogue is the rhythmic interruption of the logos, the space between the replies, each reply apart from itself retaining for itself an access to sense that is only its own, an access of sense that is only itself . . .

—But that belongs to none . . .

—Yes. And to all.

Dialogue II

The in-significant is not that which is mean, without importance. It is the most important: the place where sense still detaches itself, disconnects itself from any signification. At times brutally, at times lightly. But sometimes also in an insignificant way? Sometimes this, too, it is true, we see it everyday. But everydayness is not even a quality. True, it is that for which one is always overqualified. One must not, then, requalify it or overqualify it. Thus, sense escapes in all ways. This escape is not insignificant, it is properly speaking out of its senses [*insensée*]. And yet, if I say that it is "out of its senses," I imply that it is marked by madness, fits of passion. The excess of sense of which I am speaking is not, however, madness. It is close to madness, true. (Indeed, it is perhaps this proximity that will have marked truth itself.) But finally, what is insanity is the attainment of truth, its possession, immediately lost, come undone, and yawning, and the frenzy and panic that ensue. Insanity is banging one's head against a wall, against the void. And of course this does occur. It cannot fail to occur. But it is still the exasperation of a desire of sense, still an ecstatic exasperation. Bataille wrote: "We attain to truth; we attain suddenly the point we needed to attain and then we spend the rest of our days in search of a lost moment."[181] No one is spared this struggle. However, it still bears the mark of demand, and it is precisely this mark that sense demands we efface. Along

with this mark, bitterness, rage, exasperation. Should one therefore speak of self-abandonment? This, too, is superfluous. This, too, should be effaced. One must give up abandon itself. When the undertaking has failed, neither rage nor self-abandon makes sense anymore. Neither madness nor anesthesia. Can one seize the moment to say: which undertaking has failed? The attempt at entering into sense. If I had entered into it, there would no longer be a question of sense. And in a sense, it should, from now on, no longer be a question of sense. The tact is to turn away from sense: not in order to protect oneself from its truth, but because this detour, this turning away is still sense, is sense even more than its truth would be. One will not protect oneself. But along the path of the detour, there are some fragments of existence that are absolutely valid as such, and nothing else. Absolutes that dissolve instantly—that dissolve into their absoluteness. The most fragile of all is the absolute of saying just this. The absolute knowledge of the absolute absolution of sense. The absolute that must let go of itself. But not in order to descend into the abyss. Gently, singularly, to let go of one's hold and to be unto ....
....
....
....
....

> And so he would go on, and she would listen to every word; interpreting them rightly, so as to see, that is to say, without his having to tell her, the phosphorescence on the waves; the icicles clanking in the shrouds; how he went to the top of the mast in a gale; there reflected on the destiny of man; came down again; had a whisky and soda; went on shore; was trapped by a black woman; repented; reasoned it out; read Pascal; determined to write philosophy; bought a monkey; debated on the true end of life; decided in favor of Cape Horn, and so on. All this and a thousand other things she understood him to say.[182]

Notes

Translator's Foreword. Between Nihilism and Myth: Value, Aesthetics, and Politics in *The Sense of the World*

Thanks to David Williams for help preparing the notes to the translation, to Bruce King for assistance on questions of Greek transliteration, and to Gilbert Pestureau for suggestions concerning a number of difficult idioms and wordplays in Nancy's French.

1. One very strong contribution to such an account, however, is to be found in Barbara Herrnstein Smith, *Contingencies of Value: Alternative Perspectives for Critical Theory* (Cambridge, Mass.: Harvard University Press, 1988). Smith's analysis tends to erode the distinction between absolute and relative values in a way that is close to that implied by what I will characterize below as Nancy's affirmation of "absolute relativization."

2. The crucial definition of *nihilism* here is of course Friedrich Nietzsche's: "That the highest values devaluate themselves," *The Will to Power,* trans. Walter Kaufmann and R. J. Hollingdale (New York: Vintage Books, 1968), 9. On nihilism generally, 9–84. For readings of Nietzsche that are particularly important for Nancy's reading of the question of "values," see Martin Heidegger, "Nietzsches Wort 'Gott ist tot' (1943)," in *Holzwege* (Frankfurt am Main: Vittorio Klostermann, 1980), 205–64; and Maurice Blanchot, "Reflections on Nihilism," in *The Infinite Conversation,* trans. Susan Hanson (Minneapolis: University of Minnesota Press, 1993), 136–70. For Nancy's own work on Nietzsche, where he argues that Nietzsche's negation of value is closer to an affirmation of value in a Kantian mode than Nietzsche might have suspected, see " 'Notre probité!' " in *L'impératif catégorique* (Paris: Flammarion, 1983), 61–86.

3. On the question of "history" that intersects with the question of reality here, see below the chapter titled (in allusion to Nietzsche) "How the Desert Is Growing."

4. For an explication of this logic to which Nancy alludes repeatedly in this work, see Jacques Derrida, "Différance," in *Margins of Philosophy,* trans. Alan Bass (Chicago: University of Chicago Press, 1982).

5. On the indeterminacy of the border between *muthos* and *logos,* see "The End of the World" below. On myth, poetry, and science, with respect to style, see the final section of "Philosophical Style." For Nancy's earlier work on myth, see especially the chapter on "Myth Interrupted," in *The Inoperative Community,* ed. Peter Connor, trans. Peter Connor, Lisa Barbus, Michael Holland, and Simona Sawhney (Minneapolis: University of Minnesota Press, 1991), 43–70; and (with Philippe Lacoue-Labarthe) "The Nazi Myth," trans. Brian Holmes, *Critical Inquiry* 16:2 (1990). On the way in which nihilism remains (marginally) one aspect of the sense of the world insofar as sense comes "before all significations" and thus takes place in the absence of signification, see Nancy's chapter "Suspended Step" below.

6. For the contemporary discussions of negative theology that comprise the background for Nancy's utterances here on the Good beyond being, see Harold Coward and Toby Foshay, eds., *Derrida and Negative Theology,* with a conclusion by Jacques Derrida (Albany: State University of New York Press, 1992). For the Derridian characterization of the impossible structure of the "gift" that is crucial here, see Jacques Derrida, *Given Time: I. Counterfeit Money,* trans. Peggy Kamuf (Chicago: University of Chicago Press, 1992).

7. For a reading of the way in which, in *The Sense of the World,* Nancy articulates and plays off against each other Lévinasian and Lacanian notions of desire, see Jeffrey S. Librett, "The Practice of the World: Jean-Luc Nancy's Liminal Cosmology between Theory and History," *International Studies in Philosophy* 28 (Spring 1996), 41–56.

8. For example: "Aesthetics and art appear in our history... when the intelligibility of sense... vanishes... between the eighteenth century and Hegel. And this is why, when Hegel announces that art is 'henceforth for us a thing of the past,' he is announcing nothing other than the end of the beautiful (re)presentation of intelligible Sense—that is, of what he also calls 'the religion of art.'... But at the same time, with exactly the same gesture, Hegel *delivers* art for itself: he delivers it from service to transcendence in immanence, and he delivers it to detached, fragmentary truth.... art comes where God absents himself.... since Hegel, some have unfolded a 'secularized' theologicoaesthetics... and it is not certain that any philosophy of art has yet sufficiently realized what is at stake in fragmentation."

9. An analogue of the autonomous artwork in contemporary America would be the given cultural identity seen as product of the given, collective cultural subject. Where multiculturalism imposes itself as an absolute value, it demands relativization of values (and their subjects), but in identity politics this relativization stops at the level of given cultural groups, whose values are then supposed to count as absolute. This phenomenon of partial relativization is analogous to the partial fragmentation that autonomous art carries out, and it is marked by the same lack of consistency or rigor that characterizes the thought of autonomous art.

10. Cf. the passage below in "Art, a Fragment" where Nancy refers to the ever-present possibility of the dialectical reversal of the occidental demand for truth into "nihilism" and "nihilist art."

11. "The whole of the sensible owes its being only to its division, its dis-sent [*dis-sentiment*].... One should not even say that the 'sensible whole' is *partes extra partes,* if this risks giving the impression that it is a matter of parts of a unity. The exteriority

of sensible things is all there is of sensible interiority. In the same way, the reciprocal exteriority of the arts is the only interiority of their order.... The arts communicate only through the impossibility of passing from one to the other. Each one is at the threshold of the others." Cf. also Nancy's *Les muses* (Paris: Galilée, 1994), published since *The Sense of the World*, in which this thought of the constitutive plurality and exteriority of the arts each to the other is developed at some length.

12. For a recent study of extraordinary subtlety on the topic of the avant-garde in general, with a specific focus on avant-garde theater, see David Graver, *The Aesthetics of Disturbance: Anti-art in Avant-garde Drama* (Ann Arbor: University of Michigan Press, 1995). For a wide-ranging critical response to the debates on the theory of the avant-garde in general, see especially chap. 1, "Defining the Avant-garde" (1–43).

13. Paul de Man has formulated this movement beyond demystification with particular explicitness in "Criticism and Crisis," in *Blindness and Insight*, 2nd ed. (Minneapolis: University of Minnesota Press, 1983), 3–19, in which he attempts to show why it is necessary to consider "the conception of literature (or literary criticism) as demystification the most dangerous myth of all, while granting that it forces us, in Mallarmé's terms, to scrutinize the act of writing 'jusqu'en l'origine' " (14).

14. See also Nancy's explicit rejection of both the aestheticization of politics and the politicization of aesthetics in the chapter titled "Pain. Suffering. Unhappiness" below.

15. Of course, it is quite possible that by *aestheticization* Benjamin means something very much like what Nancy means by *myth*, while by *politicization* Benjamin means approximately what Nancy means by *nihilism*, especially since Benjamin posits, in the "Theologisch-politisches Fragment," that the method of world politics should be called "Nihilismus" (*Gesammelte Schriften*, Band II, 1, ed. Rolf Tiedemann and Hermann Schweppenhäuser [Frankfurt am Main: Suhrkamp, 1980], 204). In this case, Benjamin's preference for politicization over aestheticization would be quasi-identical with Nancy's preference for relativization in the forms of both the fragmentation of the aesthetic and the politics of (un)tying. Both, however, would differ rather starkly—by an infinite nuance—from most of what goes under the name of politicization today, which tends to mean the *finite* rather than *infinite* work of the reduction of meaning to the interests of relative perspectives.

The Sense of the World

1. Granel, "Le monde et son expression," *La part de l'oeil* 8 (1992): 49–58.

2. Nietzsche, *The Will to Power*, ed. Walter Kaufmann, trans. Walter Kaufmann and R. J. Hollingdale (New York: Vintage, 1968), 327.

3. Blanchot, *The Writing of the Disaster*, trans. Ann Smock (Lincoln: University of Nebraska Press, 1986), 41.

4. Bénézet, *Ode à la poésie* (Bordeaux: William Blake, 1992), 26.

5. Claude Lévi-Strauss, Didier Eribon, *De près et de loin* (Paris: Odile Jacob, 1988), 225.

6. The expectation, demand, exigency, or disquietude of sense do not cease to insist today in the most current and quotidian manner: one could easily put together

an anthology of phrases on this theme, simply gathered in the course of the reading of journals, and in highly diverse contexts, political, religious, economic, and so on. Let one example suffice here, from this day on which I am writing, in an article on the last book of Ernst Jünger, *Die Schere,* 3d ed. (Stuttgart: Klein-Cotta, 1990), which is precisely a book about the expected return of a "spiritual" sense of the world: "Jünger makes use of his knowledge of mythology, his gift of poetic perception, his attention to irrational phenomena . . . in order to bring forth from this fin de siècle a sense that seems absent to many" (Michka Assayas, "Le temps des Titans," *Libération,* 22 April 1993, 22).

7. Like Jean Baudrillard, for example, in *The Illusion of the End,* trans. Chris Turner (Cambridge: Polity Press, 1994). For the rest, and if one takes a close look, Baudrillard, being more subtle than most of the others who disdain the "end," speaks of nothing but the end of a regime of sense. But he does not grasp the extent to which this regime is the entire regime of significant sense for us.

8. [I am translating the preposition "à" here and in what follows generally as "to," "unto," or "toward," in the latter case especially where Nancy seems to be making allusion to the Heidegger expression "Sein zum Tode," which translates into French as "l'être à la mort" and into English (in the translation by John Macquarrie and Edward Robinson [Oxford: Basil Blackwell, 1962]) as "being-toward-death." Since the preposition "à" can also translate roughly as the English words *at, in, into, on, by, for,* or *with,* these translations, too, should be considered to be virtually present in conjunction with the *to, toward,* and *unto* explicitly used to represent "à" in what follows. Trans.]

9. [The French title of this section, "Pas suspendu," signifies not only "suspended step" but also "not suspended," the two significations evidently meant to overdetermine and qualify each other. The play on the two meanings of "pas" as "step" and as "not" is also loosely an allusion to the "pas" in Maurice Blanchot's text, "Le pas au-delà" (*The Step Not Beyond,* trans. Lycette Nelson [Albany: State University of New York Press, 1992]), and to Jacques Derrida's essay "Pas I," *Gramma* 3–4 (1976): 111–215. Trans.]

10. [I shall translate *signifiance* below simply as "significance." See the following note. Trans.]

11. *Signifiance* [significance/signifyingness] is a term that diverse linguists have employed in various senses. These various senses have in common, however, the indication of an order or register anterior to the order of signification and forming its condition. For example, "*La signifiance* is . . . the endlessness of the possible operations in a given field of language. And it is no more one of the combinations that may form a given discourse than it is any of the others" (Oswald Ducrot and Tzvetan Todorov, *Encyclopedic Dictionary of the Sciences of Language,* trans. Catherine Porter [Baltimore and London: Johns Hopkins University Press, 1979], 358). Sense is the infinity of the occurrences of sense—that is, also of nonsense and absurdity—that are possible in the world and as world. Or else, to use Derrida's word, sense is its own *dissemination,* insofar as the latter sows originally each place of the world, no matter which one, and without privilege, as the possible taking-place of a sense, of a being-*toward.* On this account, the world is also an *earth.* But the earth is not a soil prepared before being

sown, a soil that would hold the secret of the germination of sense, no more than this secret would be hidden in the transcendence of a heaven. The earth is contemporary with the dissemination of sense. *Signifiance* [signifyingness] is also the word used by Emmanuel Lévinas to designate the excess of sense over significations, in his study of 1964, "Signification and Sense" ["La signification et le sens"] (republished in *Humanisme de l'autre homme* [Montpellier: Fata Morgana, 1972], and published in English as "Meaning and Sense" in *Collected Philosophical Papers,* trans. Alphonso Lingis [Dordrecht: Nijhoff, 1987]). I cite some sentences from this essay, whose preoccupation I share, although I interpret as "dissemination" the assignation of what Lévinas names "the unique sense": "Is it not necessary... to distinguish, on the one hand, significations, in their cultural pluralism, and, on the other hand, the sense, orientation, and unity of being, the primordial event in which all the procedures of thought and all historical life of being are situated?... Do not the significations require a unique sense from which they take their very significance?... This significance would reside, to take the example of a letter, in the writing and the style of this letter, in all that makes it the case that someone passes purely and simply in the very emission of the message that we capture through the language of this letter and of its sincerity" ("La signification et le sens," 37, 61). [My translations. Trans.] Or again, to "define" *signifiance*: "The unlimited, but in all the limits that give access to it despite everything, and that coincide with the arrival of sense, with the fact that there is sense" (Jean-Christophe Bailly, *Le paradis du sens* [Paris: Christian Bourgois, 1988], 113).

12. In this respect, one must undertake again and again, always in a new way, the movement toward the "concrete," the tension or impulse of being-toward-concretion, which begins in G. W. F. Hegel, and then again in Karl Marx, Friedrich Nietzsche, Martin Heidegger, Walter Benjamin, and Theodor Adorno (consider, for example, the preface to *Negative Dialectics,* trans. E. B. Ashton [New York: Seabury Press, 1973]: "Most of the time, in contemporary philosophy, concretion has not been introduced except in a surreptitious manner" [xix]), and which has been pursued, in spite of all their differences, in the thought of those who inaugurated our contemporary moment, in particular the thought of Lévinas, Gilles Deleuze, and Derrida. *But* this "concrete" is not opposed to the "abstract" if the "abstract" is nothing other than the concretion or the concreteness of the *concept* itself (and one can understand here the "concept" at once with Hegel, with Georges Canguilhem, and with Deleuze), which is the material and final cause of philosophical labor. The concreteness in question is indissociably that of the two senses of "sense of the world": its "sensed" being-there and its "sensing" concept, the apodictic character of the former and the problematic character of the latter, the in/exscription of the one on the other. It is necessary, therefore, also to recall several decisive stages of the obstinate insistence of the world in thinking since Edmund Husserl and Heidegger: at least, Benjamin's *Das Passagen-Werk,* ed. Rolf Tiedemann, 2 vols. (Frankfurt am Main: Suhrkamp Verlag, 1983), whose main theme is indeed worldwideness or worldliness as modernity; the great book of Alexandre Koyré, *Du monde clos à l'univers infini,* trans. R. Tarr (Paris: PUF, 1961) (*From the Closed World to the Infinite Universe* [Baltimore: Johns Hopkins Press, 1957]), which speaks of the "deeper and more fundamental process as the result of which man... lost his place in the world, or, more correctly perhaps, lost the

very world in which he was living" (2); Hannah Arendt, *Vita Activa oder Vom tätigen Leben* (Munich: Piper, 1981), where one reads this, for example: "The absence of world [*Weltlosigkeit*] that institutes itself with the modern epoch is in fact without equivalent" (312); Hans Blumenberg, *The Legitimacy of the Modern World,* trans. Robert M. Wallace (Cambridge, Mass.: MIT Press, 1983), which is a major interrogation of the "worldwideness" and "worldliness" (*Weltlichkeit*) of the modern world (it will be necessary to speak of this again with respect to the "secularization" of the political); Ernst Bloch, *Experimentum Mundi: Frage, Kategorien des Herausbringens, Praxis,* vol. 15 of *Gesamtausgabe* (Frankfurt am Main: Suhrkamp, 1975), who wanted to envision "this here and this now that would complete our sense" (15). The *sense of the world* already comprises the modern *tradition*—that no postmodernism will have truly interrupted. It remains for us, therefore, as with any tradition, to make it our *own,* that is, to take it further, further into the world.

13. Winfried Weier, *Sinn und Teilhabe: Das Grundthema der abendländischen Geistesentwicklung, Salzburger Studien zur Philosophie 8* (Munich: n.p., 1970), 21. Cf. also the references in Gerhard Sauter, *Was heißt: nach Sinn fragen?* (Munich: Kaiser, 1982), 12.

14. It is with this void of the truth of being and of the being of truth (or of the truth of truth) that both the Hegelian dialectic (where being *becomes*) and the Heideggerian *Ereignis* (where being opens itself up in its withdrawal) engage. Cf., for example, the preface to the *Science of Logic,* trans. A. V. Miller (London: Allen & Unwin, 1969), and the *Beiträge zur Philosophie (Vom Ereignis),* vol. 65 of *Gesamtausgabe,* ed. Friedrich-Wilhelm von Herrmann (Frankfurt am Main: Vittorio Klostermann, 1989), nos. 204 and 214. In both cases, but in two different ways, it is *sense* that is put into play or put in gear.

15. Heidegger declares that we need this impossible transitivity of "being": "being *is* Being. In this instance 'is' speaks transitively and means approximately 'gathered together,' 'collected.' Being gathers being together insofar as it is being. Being is the gathering together—Logos" (*What Is Philosophy?,* trans. William Kluback and Jean T. Wilde [London: Vision, 1956], 49). But it is clear that the equivalence with "gather" is no more tenable than any other equivalence: we still do not know what *Logos* means. In the lecture "Logos," Heidegger determines logos as "the name for the Being of beings" inasmuch as "the Greeks would have thought the essence of language from the essence of Being" (*Early Greek Thinking,* trans. David Farrell Krell and Frank A. Capuzzi [New York: Harper & Row, 1975], 77). Consequently, the transitive sense of "being" is determined only as a vicious circle and/or as the absolute limit of signification in general. (Heidegger comes at times very close to such a formulation, but his poeticoetymologizing will to appropriate significations makes him resistant.)

16. Heidegger, "Sein zum Seienden," for example, in *Sein und Zeit* (Tübingen: Max Niemeyer, 1972), sect. 44, 222; (*Being and Time,* trans. John Macquarrie and Edward Robinson [Oxford: Basil Blackwell, 1962], sect. 44, 264).

17. Derrida, "Différance," 3. Let us recall at least this passage: "It is because of *différance* that the movement of signification is possible only if each so-called "present" element, each element appearing on the scheme of presence, is related to something other than itself, thereby keeping within itself the mark of the past element, and already letting itself be vitiated by the mark of its relation to the future element. . . .

An interval must separate the present from what it is not in order for the present to be itself, but this interval that constitutes it as a present must, by the same token, divide the present in and of itself" (13). In terms of this passage, the distinction I am drawing between truth and sense is the distinction between the presentation of a present or the scene of presence and its division within itself. (Which is not in accord, moreover, with the equivalence of sense and truth that Derrida admits further on in his text, but in passing and without elaboration: "The thought of the *meaning* or *truth* of Being" [22].)

18. "That the being of the world 'transcends' consciousness in this fashion (even with respect to the evidence in which the world presents itself), and that it necessarily remains transcendent, in no wise alters the fact that it is conscious life alone, wherein everything transcendent becomes constituted, as something inseparable from consciousnesss, and which specifically, as world-consciousness, bears within itself inseparably the sense: world—and indeed: 'this actually existing' world" (Edmund Husserl, *Cartesian Meditations: An Introduction to Phenomenology,* trans. Dorion Cairns [The Hague: Martinus Nijhoff, 1973], 62).

19. Even if, for example, in the rarefied and aleatory form of the "finite place of a subject who is deciding," which definitively constitutes the instance of sense for Alain Badiou (cf. *L'être et l'événement* [Paris: Seuil, 1988], 475). The latter rejects, nevertheless, the category of "sense": his subject decides, concerning the "event," only in the face of the void of truth. One is, at bottom, on a Heideggerian register, that of "*Das Ereignis trägt die Wahrheit* = die Wahrheit durchragt das Ereignis" (the event carries truth = truth juts out through the event), where the verb *durchragen* would call for a long gloss. It is "jutting across," and thus also "piercing" and almost "tearing" ("incising" in Badiou's vocabulary). Any thought that privileges truth, that takes on *the style of truth,* dedicates itself to the tension of an internal tornness, whether it does so in a more pathos-laden mode (Heidegger) or in a cooler mode (Badiou). Again, it is not a matter of rejecting this truth of truth: but of establishing that it occurs only on the level of punctuation, not on the level of enchainment. Thus, the original point of sense can present itself either in the form of a constitutive self-evidence or in the form of an inaugural *decision.* In the first case, sense is always appropriated by truth in advance, and in the second case, it never takes place, but, rather, only the incisive, empty truth. (The question of decision does not by chance form the crucial bridge of the political, even when one has taken one's distance from the "political theology" with which Carl Schmitt surrounds it, and to which I will return below.) The two possibilities are mixed and intermingled in Heidegger without excluding a third resource, which I designate as sense without origin and without end, or without subject, the *coming* of sense and to sense. This third path is not without analogy, in spite of considerable differences, with the path opened [*frayée*] by Jean-Luc Marion in *Réduction et donation* (Paris: PUF, 1989). They have perhaps, above all, in common the trait of "surprise" (cf. ibid., 300 ff.), the pre-venient and super-venient trait of sense, which is also, for me, the determining trait of freedom (cf. Jean-Luc Nancy, *The Experience of Freedom,* trans. Bridget McDonald [Stanford, Calif.: Stanford University Press, 1993], 113 ff). I would not say, however, that the surprise is the surprise of a "call," as Marion wishes. Even if there is no recognition of the one who calls, the "pure form of the call" that

"is found at the origin" (ibid., 302) is by itself also the pure form of signifying sense, whose signified is always only provisionally hidden from the one who is called. But if *the world is sense,* or if it is itself "the origin," as will be maintained below, it is this no more in the mode of a transcendent call than in the mode of a pure exposed immanence. Rather, the world is sense or "origin" in a mode that precisely no longer can be indicated in the style of a categorization of "modes" in general, that is, of a punctuation of concepts, but that produces itself, that produces its sense, only as the enchainment, the entailment, and, indeed, the transport, of another style, writing, and exscription of philosophy. Anticipating what will follow, I might say here also: the call is still a beyond-phenomenality (or a phenomenality of the "beyond"), whereas the *world* invites us to think no longer on the level of the phenomenon, however it may be understood (as surging forth, appearing, becoming visible, brilliance, occurrence, event), but on the level—let us say, for the moment—of the dis-position (spacing, touching, contact, crossing). Attempting these distinctions and these statements, I would like to say, however, that if I oppose, in a sense, a "thesis" to other theses, in another sense I underscore, across the oppositions that divide also my own work, a community of epoch. *Something* is imposing itself on thought today, as occurs in every epoch (this is indeed what makes an epoch, and what makes it the case that "epochs" are as such attestations of sense). Each form of thought recognizes this thing in its own way, but it recognizes this thing to the degree that it does not run away from what is imposing itself (as occurs for all those forms of thought that attempt today to repair or to reconstitute the old world). This "something" has for us *at least* the very general (and quasi-formless) form of a worldwide ending of the world.

20. Cf., for example, and to prolong the preceding note, the manner in which Marion retains as far as possible the Heideggerian and Lévinasian motif of the "wonder" (Marion, *Réduction et donation,* 295), or these words of Badiou: "The break in being that the suddenness of the event crystallizes, the brilliance of that which is held in poor esteem" (*Conditions* [Paris: Seuil, 1992], 351). Or going back quite a bit further, to Jean-Paul Sartre as to the decisive moment, in the aftermath of Heidegger, when phenomenology was tied to Marxism, *that is to say,* in fact, when sense took on the sense of *praxis,* one will note the pregnancy maintained there of the motif of "luminous" being, if being is here History qua "totalization without a totalizer" (*Critique of Dialectical Reason,* trans. Alan Sheridan-Smith, ed. Jonathan Rée [London: Verso, 1976], 817: "Comprehension—as the living movement of the practical organism—can take place only within a concrete situation, insofar as theoretical Knowledge illuminates and interprets this situation" [in the preface to the original French publication of *Critique of Dialectical Reason,* published separately in English under the title of *Search for a Method,* trans. Hazel E. Barnes (New York: Knopf, 1963), 180–81]). Life, light, deciphering: such would be at bottom the triple assignation of which it would be necessary to undo the sense—but in no way by passing to the contraries, death, darkness, and hermeticism.

21. One could show how that occurs in Friedrich W. J. Schelling and Hegel, and then again in Nietzsche, and again in Henri Bergson. But in truth, it is the entire history of philosophy since Immanuel Kant at least that it will be necessary one day to rewrite from the point of view of styles of truth or of sense, from the point of view of

their extraordinarily complex and twisted distributions and interlacings where the most lively and the most intimate matter of thought is in play. And, indeed, it is a philosopher who poses the question today: "What is the operation of a style? Answer: in the flux that derives from the possibilities of language, which passes under the reed, to wet the latter—sudden, alive—so as to modify the currents and provoke this or that collision. The effect of which, anticipated in a lightning bolt before being produced, is to make the waves of thought be born and to pursue these waves of thought across a more or less great distance with more or less strength" (Gérard Granel, *Écrits logiques et politiques* [Paris: Galilée, 1990], 227). And to vary the style, we will take from another philosopher the necessity of recognizing: "In the generativity of expression a 'source of knowledge,' ... the grammatical contour of our synoptical intelligences" (Claude Imbert, *Phénoménologies et langues formulaires* [Paris: PUF, 1992], 14).

22. Heidegger, *Beiträge zur Philosophie,* 3. "Stil" is not a frequent word in Heidegger and was never, it seems to me, worked on by him as a concept. It is all the more remarkable that this word is here so charged—in a broad, indeterminate sense—with all that ought to distinguish in fundamental ways two allures, two engagements, two responsibilities of thought. [Nancy's word for "process" in his translation of Heidegger here is "pas"—as "step" and as "not"—which both serves as an adequate translation of Heidegger's "Gang" and links this passage to the "pas" of thought alluded to in the section above titled "Suspended Step." Trans.]

23. "Driven into the / terrain / with / the unmistakable / track: / Grass. / Grass, / written asunder," "Engführung" / "The Straightening," from *Sprachgitter* (1959), in *Poems of Paul Celan,* trans. Michael Hamburger (New York: Persea Books, 1988), 149. "Written asunder" corresponds here to *auseinandergeschrieben. Auseinander* means literally "out of each other," but in accordance with an exteriority that implies a primary mutual entanglement. If I take a poem as index here, it is not in order to privilege poetry: it is in order to locate a point in poetry where it is destabilized, disentangled from itself.

24. Jean-François Courtine, "Phénoménologie et métaphysique," *Le débat* 72 (November/December 1992), 88.

25. Michel de Montaigne, "Apology for Raymond Sebond," in *The Complete Works of Montaigne,* trans. Donald M. Frame (Stanford, Calif.: Stanford Unversity Press, 1957), 405; Baruch Spinoza, *The Ethics. Treatise on the Emendation of the Intellect: Selected Letters,* trans. Samuel Shirley, ed. Seymour Feldman (Indianapolis: Hackett, 1992), pt. 1, appendix, 59–60; F. W. J. Schelling, *Philosophie de la révélation,* trans. Jean-François Marquet and Jean-François Courtine, vol. 2 (Paris: PUF, 1991), leçon 17, 215.

26. [Nancy is playing on the overlap on the level of the signifier between "transir" and "transitivité" in order to characterize the relationship between Being and beings as a "transitivity" while suspending the sense of subject acting on object that the notion of "transitivity" invokes. The entry in *The New Cassell's French Dictionary* (New York: Funk and Wagnall's, 1971) for the (both transitive and intransitive) verb "transir" that overdetermines and displaces "transitivité" here is: "*v.t.* To chill, to benumb; to overcome with fear etc., to paralyse.—*v.i.* To be chilled; to be paralysed with fear, etc." (730). Trans.]

27. Cf. Aristotle *De Anima* 418a23 and 425b25. The same is the case for the act of science as knowledge and as thing known, as one can at least infer from 417a21 ff. For

an echo closer to us: "If it is true that gesture is sense, it must be so in opposition to linguistic signification. The latter constitutes itself only as a network of discontinuities. It gives rise to an immobile dialectics where the thinking and the thought are never confused, where the elements of the thought do not encroach upon one another. The gesture, on the contrary, as [Maurice] Merleau-Ponty understood it, is the experience of a sense where the sensed and the sensing constitute themselves in a common rhythm like the two edges of a single wake" (Jean-François Lyotard, *Discours, figure* [Paris: Klincksieck, 1971], 20). Lyotard writes also: "Sense is present as absence of signification; however, the latter gets hold of the former (and it can, one can say everything), it exiles itself along the border of the new speech-act. . . . To construct sense is never anything other than deconstructing signification. There is no assignable model for this evasive configuration" (19). One could prolong this thought in the following manner: there is no model because it is there, quite exactly, that it is a matter of modeling oneself or allowing oneself to be modeled, or in other words, of giving oneself a rhythm or letting oneself be given a rhythm (which does not mean letting oneself be "lulled" . . .) "by" sense or, rather, "in sense": a matter of "style" and/or of existence.

28. "The endeavor [*conatus*] wherewith everything endeavors to persist in its own being is nothing else but the actual essence of the thing in question" (Spinoza, *Ethics,* pt. 3, proposition 7, 117).

29. This provides us with the principle of the discussion one ought to have with the strong analyses of Michel Henry in *L'essence de la manifestation* (Paris: PUF, 1963). In a sense, phenomenology has advanced there as far as possible in the direction of the ecstasy in truth. But it remains there a thought of sense in the "sentiment" as "unique appearance of the absolute and its real being, Parousia" (vol. 2, 833). The task is to defer/differ Parousia. Not to cast it ever further but, on the contrary, to approach it in the most intimate manner: to defer the *para* (the near, proximity, presence) of the *ousia* (or *essentia*).

30. "Psyche is extended. Don't know anything about it" (Freud, posthumous note). Cf. Jean-Luc Nancy, *Corpus* (Paris: A.-M. Métailié, 1992), an excerpt of which appears in English in Jean-Luc Nancy, *The Birth to Presence* (Stanford, Calif.: Stanford University Press, 1993), 189–207, and of which this is the sole theme. One finds an exemplary confirmation of the *spatial* stake in general in the analysis that Jean-Louis Cherlonneix has done of the indecent "tumor" or "bloatedness" that space as such is for Saint Augustine: "Space, of which the tumor is the image, *is itself the image* of being that has begun to be: the image of this 'possibility of changing' [*mutabilitas*] that is for Saint Augustine the uneffaceable mark of being 'created.' Indecency is found again, in the final analysis, at the heart of the sense of the being of what is both as body and as spirit. In the end, all that is, in such a way that it could become other than it is, is of space or in space" (*Saint Augustin,* ed. Patrick Ranson (Lausanne: L'Âge d'Homme, 1988), 167.

31. *Kosmotheoros* ("the one who embraces the world with the gaze") was the title of a book by Christian Huygens, who perhaps himself picked up this word from an earlier tradition. Kant uses it in at least two passages of the *Opus Postumum,* ed. Eckart Förster, trans. Eckart Förster and Michael Rosen (Cambridge: Cambridge

University Press, 1993), fascicle 5, sheet 7, page 4 (82), and fascicle 1, sheet 3, page 3 (235).

32. "There is a technological différance. Or rather: différance *is* technological"—this is the central thesis of Bernard Stiegler in *La faute d'épiméthée: La technique et le temps* (Paris: Gallimard, forthcoming). This thesis, the first no doubt since Simondon (whom Stiegler rereads) to take into account "technology" as a proper mode of "being-ness" in general, is thus in solidarity with a thesis on "sense as consistency of the lack of origin," which leads to certain remarkable statements: "Sense is the future of signification"; "sense is always, in fact, the fruit of a . . . work of mourning for the self on the threshold of an *other* self. Sense is the contestation of established significations for this future of the other."

33. Kant, conclusion to *Critique of Practical Reason*, 3rd ed., ed. and trans. Lewis White Beck (New York: Macmillan, 1993), 169. The passage continues as follows: "I do not merely conjecture them and seek them as thought obscured in darkness or in the transcendent region beyond my horizon: I see them before me, and I associate them directly with the consciousness of my existence" (169). Thus, the *ego sum, ego existo* has become consubstantial with the "law" and the "world." The text goes on: "The heavens begin at the place I occupy in the external world of sense, and broaden the connection in which I stand into an unbounded magnitude of worlds beyond worlds and systems of systems and into the limitless times of their periodic motion, their beginning and their duration. The latter begins at my invisible self, my personality, and exhibits me in a world which has true infinity but which is comprehensible only to the understanding—a world with which I recognize myself as existing in a universal and necessary (and not, as in the first case, merely contingent) connection, and thereby also in connection with all those visible worlds" (169). By "contingency" in the "unbounded magnitude," on the one hand, and, on the other hand, by the nonsensible character of the "necessity" of the law, sense is here already absented or in excess. The world of experience and the world of the law are the two instances of truth. Sense is lacking in each of these worlds. But it is necessary to deduce that sense is quite precisely *in this existence* in accordance with which I am "in connection with" both worlds at once.

34. Since "Occident" designates the sunset, already the disaster. One finds also in Cicero the expression *vita occidens* to designate the proximity of death (*Tusculan Disputations*, vol. 1, ed. and trans. A. E. Douglas [Warminster: Aris & Phillips; Chicago: Bolchazy-Carducci, 1985], sec. 109, 80). The Occident is the epoch that will have begun at its end, and that accomplishes that end rigorously. But also every end is, for the Occident, not a beginning but an opening.

35. I have desire in view here in accordance with its major philosophical determination, the determination that attaches it to privation, in conformity with the very sense of *desiderium*, and the determination that consequently forbids itself access to finitude as being-in-act of existence. But I am not unaware that one can give a different value to the name of "desire," and precisely the value of finitude, as do, for example, in widely divergent ways, Francis Guibal in *L'homme de désir* (Paris: Cerf, 1990) and Bernard Baas in *Le désir pur* (Louvain: Peeters, 1992). At stake here, in the polymorphy and polysemy—and perhaps in the dissemination—of desire is something

of a necessity of the epoch. Gilles Deleuze and Félix Guattari had placed "desire" at the crossroads between its "accursed" interpretation according to the rule "Desire is lack. . . . *Jouissance* is impossible, but impossible *jouissance* is inscribed in desire," and desire given to an "immanent joy" wherein "pleasure is the flux of desire itself" (*A Thousand Plateaus,* vol. 2 of *Capitalism and Schizophrenia,* trans. Brian Massumi [Minneapolis: University of Minnesota Press, 1987], 154–56). But in the end, this latter desire seems as if it would be better called sense: being-toward of being itself. In which case, this sense of sense would not be so far from its Deleuzian concept: "As attribute of the states of things, sense is outside of being, it is not of being, but an *aliquid* that is appropriate to nonbeing. As expressed by the proposition, sense does not exist, but insists or subsists in the proposition. . . . Sense is what forms and deploys itself on the surface. Even the border [between bodies and propositions] is not a separation but the element of an articulation such that sense presents itself at once as what happens to bodies and as what insists in propositions. We should maintain as well that *sense is a lining.* . . . And yet, lining no longer signifies in the least an evanescent and disincarnated resemblance. . . . It is now defined by the production of surfaces, their multiplication, and their consolidation. The lining is the continuity of the inside with the outside, the art of installing this continuity, in such a way that the sense at the surface distributes itself from both sides at once: as expressed, it subsists in the propositions, and as event, it occurs to the states of bodies" (*The Logic of Sense,* ed. Constantin V. Boundas, trans. Mark Lester and Charles Stivale [New York: Columbia University Press, 1990], 31, 125). The *desiderium* is precisely the discontinuity of the inside and the outside, and the melancholy of not finding on the surface anything other than the loss or the lack of what one was asking for in the depths. Being-toward of being would form, on the contrary, the *conatus* of the *insistence of its différance,* opening and multiplying the space of sense, the spacing of sense. This connection of Deleuze with Derrida, itself like a continuity of the inside and the outside, seems to me to correspond to a knot of the epoch, to the necessity that makes sense under the cover of the most diverse names. But that this necessity is also that of the entire epoch of the Occident or of philosophy, and that it began therefore with Plato's Eros, is what Danièle Montet shows very well, writing with respect to Plato's *Symposium*: "What is at stake in desire is not exhausted in the quest for what is lacking, in the restoration of a primordial unity as Aristophanes believes, but, much more fundamentally, it consists in revealing the lack and limit from which the human being suffers, in order to make a work out of it, in accordance with Diotima's proposal. . . . Thus, the question of the object of desire is in error, but the question of what desire knows how to do, of what it gives birth to, is always open" (quoted in Danièle Montet, *Les traits de l'être: Essai sur l'ontologie platonicienne* [Grenoble: Jérôme Millon, 1990], 232).

36. Jacques Lacan had understood this, even if he prevented himself from understanding (or from saying?) that he had understood it.

37. According to the terms of Moustapha Safouan, *La parole ou la mort* (Paris: Seuil, 1993, 40), in whose work, however, the word *sense* takes the sense of "signification." From Freud's *Civilization and Its Discontents,* trans. James Strachey (New York: Norton, 1961), let us recall these lines: "In an individual neurosis we take as our starting-point the contrast that distinguishes the patient from his environment, which is

assumed to be 'normal.' For a group all of whose members are affected by one and the same disorder no such background could exist; it would have to be found elsewhere. And as regards the therapeutic application of our knowledge, what would be the use of the most correct analysis of social neuroses, since no one possesses authority to impose such a therapy upon the group? But in spite of all these difficulties, we may expect that one day someone will venture to embark upon a pathology of cultural communities" (91).

38. Claude Rabant, *Inventer le réel* (Paris: Denoël, 1992), 251.

39. I will draw a witness to this from the very interior of psychoanalysis (without necessarily committing myself to all aspects of the position cited) in these lines by Serge Leclaire: "To stake a claim to social practice implies, to be sure, firm and constant recognition of what the subject-function consists in, and sufficient familiarity with the practice of the subject of the unconscious. The training of the analyst could predispose one to such recognition; he would have to be doing his work properly in order to bear witness to this recognition. Nonetheless, one must observe that he does not always succeed in escaping from a very common trajectory of thought, which consists in believing that, under any circumstances, the virtue (*virtus*) of the symbolic is to protect, to defend, and to comfort. However, the void onto which the name of nothing opens [Serge Leclaire has said above that 'the symbol is a name of nothing'] is in no danger whatsoever of being filled up or exhausted in its emptiness. It is only by a perverse artifice of the denegation of difference that one can make the praise of the symbolic order into the motif of a crusade, a pretext in defense of a cause: the symbolic order is coextensive with 'human nature,' and the claim to protect it from some catastrophic ruin can only come from an exalted sublimation of murderous impulses quite commonly shared. Apocalypse, let us recall, is unveiling. It is not a matter of revealing the symbolic function but of putting it to work" ("De l'objet d'une formation social: Note sur le nom de rien," *IO: Revue internationale de psychanalyse* 1 [1992], 13. *Ergo*: praxis).

40. Freud to Marie Bonaparte, 13 August 1937, *Letters of Sigmund Freud 1873–1939*, ed. Ernst L. Freud, trans. Tania Stern and James Stern (London: Hogarth Press, 1961), 432.

41. "But as for knowledge and truth, even as in our illustration it is right to deem light and vision sunlike, but never to think that they are the sun, so here it is right to consider these two their counterparts, as being like the good or boniform, but to think that either of them is the good is not right. Still higher honor belongs to the possession and habit [*hexis:* state, disposition, manner of being] of the good. . . . the objects of knowledge not only receive from the presence of the good their being known, but their very existence and essence is derived to them from it, though the good itself is not essence but still transcends essence in dignity and surpassing power" (Plato, "The Republic," 509a-b, trans. Paul Shorey, in *The Collected Dialogues of Plato, Including the Letters*, ed. E. Hamilton and H. Cairns [Princeton, N. J.: Princeton University Press, 1973], 744).

42. Which one could render by saying that for Plato the highest knowledge, under the sign of "assimilation" ("becoming like the divine—*homoiōsis theōi*," "Theaetetus," 176b, trans. F. M. Cornford, in *The Collected Dialogues*, 881), takes up again the

sensible model from which it has rigorously separated itself. The *sense* of, and *sense* as, that which cannot be *sensed,* the touch of the intangible, this is the program. In order to evoke the access to the "good" in these terms, I am basing myself in particular on the analyses of Danièle Montet: "*Agathon* joins together knowing with the knowable in the light of truth. It grants the tie truth is. As principle and origin of the tie, the good is *idea, idea tou agathou.* As *Phaedrus* and the *Sophist* put it, the *idea* adds to the *eidos* the connotation of a tie, opposing 'ideal' union to eidetic division, as exemplified by the expression '*mia idea*': it underlines less the unicity of the idea than the unity it creates. Where the *eidos* signifies 'what it is' in the dimension of use, the *idea* states the '*ho ti estin*' in the dimension of the tie." (I would propose the gloss: the *eidos* signifies, absolutely, and the *idea* makes sense.) . . . In all its behavior, the soul proceeds in accordance with a visual seizure that can be accented in two different ways: visual seizure (as *eidos,* that is, *khreia*); or visual seizure (as *idea*). . . . The soul envisions, seizes visually, because it is visual seizure, stared down and subjugated by light and truth. . . . Not only is *agathon* not *eidos* because it does not sustain the question '*ti estin,*' because it cannot be defined as such; but it is not '*idea*' either, if one understands '*tou agathou*' in the sense of an objective genitive. The good does not come to qualify, to specify *idea,* but the latter proceeds from the former. . . . The expression '*idea tou agathou*' states the operation of the good. . . . As the principle of the 'there is,' of the 'it is,' the *agathon* establishes ties such that its undoing would imply the annihilation of what it gives a consistency to, what it holds together. . . . The good establishes ties because it ob-liges. . . . The obligation implied by the tie arises out of the design and the project . . . *hou heneka,* 'that in view of which,'" in Montet, *Les traits de l'être,* 114–15, 121, 123.

43. Let it be said in passing that one would have to pause to consider this expression: "*that is* to say," "that is *to* say," "that is to *say.*" The formula that serves to enchain significations in order to draw them into an indefinite substitution and supplementarity of *sense* can also be read in three ways as the formula—or better, the rhythm—of the *to* of being.

44. As Derrida has analyzed it, in particular in *Given Time: I. Counterfeit Money.*

45. I am appropriating the gift of this sentence here from Philippe Lacoue-Labarthe, who writes, in the context of an analysis of the gift of genius from Kant to the romantics: "The woman is the genius—the gift of nature—and shamelessness is thus quite simply the appropriation of genius. A pure impossibility. How could one appropriate a gift?" Interestingly, the immediately following remarks take us back to *teknē*: "No erotics can suffice to this, and Schlegel knew it quite well: genius is innate, there is no technique for the acquisition of the innate. Awkwardness is irremediably the essence of *teknē*: at bottom it is a question of deficiency. The artist can never truly be the woman, in her infinite patience toward *jouissance* (I could say that in another way: there is no reserve in woman, but woman is reserve itself, that is to say, *phusis*)," "L'avortement de la littérature," in *Du féminin* (Sainte-Foy: Le Griffon d'Argile, 1992), 13.

46. It is quite remarkable that the articulation of desire and gift in terms of appropriation, after having been emblematized at one time by ancient *vertu,* at another time by Christian grace, and then by artistic (and/or political) genius, should today be emblematized by *drugs.* It is indeed a banal proposition to suggest that the con-

temporary fuss about drugs sends us back to a question of sense by way of the socio-economic distortions and exclusions that are themselves convulsions of what one could call the sense of the *eco-* in general (of all the driftings of the *oikos:* habitation, domesticity, domestication, economy, ecology, ecotechnics, ecopraxis . . .). But in this banality, nothing less than the commonality of sense is at stake.

47. Jean-Christophe Bailly, *Le paradis du sens* (Paris: Christian Bourgois, 1988), 31.

48. "6.41—The sense of the world must lie outside the world. In the world everything is as it is, and everything happens as it does happen: *in it* no value exists—and if it did exist, it would have no value. . . . 6.44—It is not *how* things are in the world that is mystical, but *that* it exists. . . . 6.521—The solution of the problem of life is seen in the vanishing of the problem. (Is not this the reason why those who have found after a long period of doubt that the sense of life became clear to them have then been unable to say what constituted that sense?)" (Wittgenstein, *Tractatus Logico-Philosophicus,* trans. D. F. Peras and B. F. McGuinness [London: Routledge & Kegan Paul; New York: Humanities Press, 1961], 145, 149–50). One will not fail to notice that these propositions are contemporaneous with those of Heidegger and Freud: the twenties were the years when the end of philosophy and the question of sense came to light. We are still, or anew, in the twenties, and this is indeed why it is a matter of preventing the thirties from being in front of us, as Gérard Granel announces ("Les années 30 sont devant nous," in *Les temps modernes,* February 1993), as the years of the "ontological blastoff beyond the attraction of finitude [which] is the very soul of the modern world . . . [and which] does not appear simply by virtue of the fact that the modern idealities are those of infinitude, but presupposes in addition the lure of their totalization" (74). I am not as convinced as Granel of the persistence of this lure, or at least I think that we are despite everything less lacking than a little while ago in means for dissipating it. But this presupposes precisely that we take up again propositions such as Wittgenstein's, but without the "mystical," that is, without the horizon (even if it were *absconditum*) of a revelation (even if it were the revelation of the void), and in consecrating all necessary forces to make without respite *that which is designated as the "beyond" of the world pass back into the world.* Not in immanentizing transcendence, but in inscribing the latter—or sense—*along the edge of* immanence (which signifies, ultimately, the insufficiency of these concepts themselves).

49. One could translate in such a way Heidegger's notion of *Bedeutsamkeit,* "capacity or property of making sense" (*Being and Time,* sec. 32, 193).

50. Which signifies, to be precise, something other than a critique or a demolition: the bringing to light of that which will have been the agent of Christianity as the very form of the West, much more deeply than all religion and even as the self-deconstruction of religion, that is, the accomplishment of philosophy by Judeo-Platonism and Latinity, ontotheology as its own end, the "death of God" and the birth of the sense of the world as the abandonment without return and without *Aufhebung* of all "christ," that is, of all hypostasis of sense. It will of course be necessary to come back to this.

51. Heidegger, *Being and Time,* sec. 32, 193.

52. This perspective, still a phenomenological one, remains that of *Being and Time,* which declares: "Only *Dasein* can be sane or insane." But this perspective is

what the later "turning" placed in question. Beyond phenomenology, however, it is doubtless Christianity that will have persisted in Heidegger, never really subjected to deconstruction, remaining perhaps indeed the secret resource of the deconstruction of ontotheology.

53. For example, Heidegger, *Beiträge,* 296: "*Dasein* is a mode of being that, insofar as it 'is' the there (in a way actively-transitively)..."

54. *Fort-sein, Weg-sein* (being gone, far, taken away, distanced), *ex-istere.* Cf. *Beiträge,* 301 ff. It would be necessary to go through this entire section of the *Beiträge,* which begins moreover with a passage wherein one can discern something like a displacement and a hesitation on Heidegger's part concerning the "remains" of the world: "Being does not come to truth except on the basis of *Da-sein.* / But there where plant, animal, stone and sea and sky become being [*seiend werden*], without falling into objectivity [*Gegenständlichkeit*], there reigns the retreat (refusal) of being [*der Entzug (Verweigerung) des Seyns*], being as retreat. But the retreat is that of *Da-sein*" (293). A bit further on, it is precisely a question of "The *being-in-the-world* of *Dasein.* 'World,' but not the Christian *saeculum* and the denial of God, Atheism! *World* through the essence of truth and of the *Da!*" (295). It is evidently *here,* where the path is broken toward the coming of a "last God," that I separate myself completely from Heidegger, for this name of "god," including and even above all including the name as nomination of the unnamed and unnameable, cannot decidedly do anything other than place a muzzle over the opening of the sense of the world. It will thus be a matter of "atheism," but of an atheism where everything remains to be done, as Jean-Christophe Bailly demands when he writes: "Atheism has remained this 'dry land' of which Plutarch spoke in *Of Superstition.* It has not known how to irrigate itself on its own or to invent its own shadows, transforming at one blow its brief solar explosion into a simple opaque day," *Adieu* (La Tour d'Aigues: Éditions de l'Aube, 1993), n.p.

55. Heidegger, *Being and Time.*

56. And even if it is "not merely" that. Cf. Heidegger, *The Fundamental Concepts of Metaphysics: World, Finitude, Solitude,* trans. William McNeill and Nicholas Walker (Bloomington: Indiana University Press, 1996), 177.

57. Might it not be possible to think through the relationship between the atomists' original thesis and the fact that the "atomic" bomb defines a capacity of annihilation of humanity, that is, of the earth, as a senseless or mad [*insensée*] extreme of the sense of technology, being-together, and being-in-the-world?

58. *Materia* comes from *mater* and designates first of all the maternal part of the tree, the trunk, and hence the hardest part. The mother is the consistency proper to difference. That is, the contrary of a "phallic mother," or perhaps, rather, the *différance* of a phallus.

59. Perhaps it is necessary now to consider also, concerning semantic sense, that signification completes itself in the last resort as reference, that language attains its end, in both senses of the term, in the monstration or showing of the singular thing. Such was William of Ockham's thesis as Pierre Alféri analyzes it: "What does 'having a sense' mean? For Ockham it means: playing a role in the reference to beings, saying something in the most earthbound sense of 'thing,'" *Guillaume d'Ockham le singulier* (Paris: Minuit, 1989), 295. Sense as designation, monstration, and description of the

existent, and finally as exscription *into* or *unto* existence. *Sense the sense of which, far from adding itself to existence, completes itself in existence.*

60. It is not "primary matter," *materia prima,* and here again we encounter the thought of Ockham: "There is no reason therefore to suppose that unformed and undifferentiated 'primary matter' is anything other than the 'secondary matter' that is encountered in the formed singularities. The singularity of matter resides above all, and this is sufficient, in its *locality.* . . . In order to enter into the singular as a part, matter must be a real and actual thing. As such, it has therefore at least one property: it is extended" (Pierre Alféri, *Guillaume d'Ockham,* 96–97). Ockham thus develops into its mature form a thought of singularity and of *materia signata* (signed, designated, determined matter) begun by Thomas Aquinas (see *De ente et essentia,* trans. C. Capelle [Paris: Vrin, 1982], 24, and the commentary by C. Capelle: "A portion of sensible matter, that which falls beneath the pointing of the finger, this matter here," 87), then accentuated by Duns Scotus: "The individual reality is material, for it is constitutive of a being insofar as it is a subject," *Le principe d'individuation,* trans. G. Sondag (Paris: Vrin, 1992), 174, and the commentary by G. Sondag: "Matter does not signify 'the other part of the composite,' as opposed to its form; it signifies the individual entity that reduces or individualizes the quiddity. . . . From which it will result . . . that beings deprived of material matter, such as the angel or the soul, will be able to be called 'material' " (173–74).

61. Cf. " . . . the present punctuality, always evident and always singular, of the form of signature. Therein lies the enigmatic originality of all paraphes" (Jacques Derrida, *Margins of Philosophy,* 328). Derrida underlines that the principle of signature demands the "retention," in each new execution of the signature, of "the absolute singularity of an event": an impossibility that governs here possibility itself. I would say: this is indeed the logic of signature *in truth.* But (and) this is precisely why the signature differentiates itself, alters itself, in a word, differs in each event of signature. By the same token, the *signed* material singularity has its truth in its pure unicity, but it has or is its sense in the multiplicity of its events and situations, in its *going-coming.*

62. [Jean-Luc Nancy is building a portmanteau word here by inserting "peau"—meaning "skin" in French—in place of the "po" in "exposition." Trans.]

63. Cf. Jean-Luc Nancy, *Corpus,* 31–33.

64. Heidegger, *Fundamental Concepts of Metaphysics,* 196–97. On "touching" in general, I have discovered too late to make use of it that I am following some paths parallel to those of Jean-Louis Chrétien, "Le corps et le toucher," in *L'appel et la réponse* (Paris: Minuit, 1992).

65. And that corresponds exactly—almost to the point of caricature—to what Derrida has indicated in "*Geschlecht* II: Heidegger's Hand," trans. John P. Leavey Jr., in *Deconstruction and Philosophy: The Texts of Jacques Derrida,* ed. John Sallis (Chicago: University of Chicago Press, 1987), 161–96.

66. Martin Heidegger, *The Basic Problems of Phenomenology,* rev. ed., trans. Albert Hofstadter (Bloomington: Indiana University Press, 1988), 264. (The first version of this part was written for *Contretemps* 1 [Winter 1995].)

67. Immanuel Kant, *Critique of Pure Reason,* trans. Norman Kemp Smith (New York: St. Martin's Press, 1965), Second Analogy of Experience, 218.

68. "*Aeternitas non est aliud quam ipse Deus*" (St. Thomas Aquinas, *Summa Theologiae,* vol. 2, *Existence and Nature of God,* trans. Timothy McDermott [Cambridge: Blackfriars; New York: McGraw-Hill, 1964]), Ia. X, 2, 140). Here it is clear that eternity was never an "eternal duration."

69. Georges Bataille, "Espace," *Oeuvres complètes,* vol. 1 (Paris: Gallimard, 1970), 227.

70. Jorge Luis Borges, "Luna de Enfrente," in *Obra Poética: 1923–1966* (Buenos Aires: Emecé Editores, 1964), 80, 93.

71. [Nancy is alluding here to the New Testament, Matt. 16:18, where Christ says that he will build his Church on the "rock" of "Peter," in a Greco-Latin pun that still works in French as the quasi identity of "pierre" (as signifier for "rock" or "stone") and "Pierre" (as a masculine proper name). Trans.]

72. As Gilles Deleuze rereads him: "*The world is the infinite curve that touches at an infinity of points an infinity of curves, the curve with a unique variable, the convergent series of all series.* ... As an individual unit each monad includes the whole series; hence it conveys the entire world, but does not express it *without expressing more clearly a small region of the world, a 'subdivision,' a borough of a city, a finite sequence.* ... if the world is in the subject, the subject is no less for the world. God produces the world 'before' creating souls since he creates them for this world that he invests in them.... because the monad is for the world, no one clearly contains the 'reason' of the series of which they are all a result, and which remains outside of them, just like the principle of their accord.... Closure is the condition of being for the world. The condition of closure holds for the infinite opening of the finite: it 'finitely represents infinity,'" Gilles Deleuze, *The Fold: Leibniz and the Baroque,* trans. Tom Conley (Minneapolis: University of Minnesota Press, 1993), 24–26. (In the meantime, with respect to Heidegger, Deleuze has pointed out the proximity between this opening and that of *Dasein.*)

73. The preceding is a summary of the first part of an exposé published with the title "Un sujet?" in *Homme et sujet,* a collection edited by Dominique Weil (Paris: L'Harmattan, 1992). What follows is a revision of the latter part of the exposé. Concerning the "one," it would no doubt be necessary to involve oneself in a confrontation with the "ontology of number" practiced by Alain Badiou (cf. *Le nombre et les nombres* [Paris: Seuil, 1990], 125 ff.). My mathematical incompetence makes this impossible. But it does not prevent me from recognizing certain formulations as being strictly equivalent to those to which a deconstruction of ontotheology leads. For example: "*The one* as such ... is not.... One must therefore distinguish between that which *counts-for-one, or structure,* which makes the one arise as the nominal seal of the multiple, and *the one as effect,* the fictive being of which resides in nothing other than the structural retroaction within which one considers it" (Badiou, *L'être et l'événement,* 104). Up to a certain point, I perceive nothing other than a transcription based on a regulated change of terms. Beyond this, I am tempted to perceive in Badiou a negative theology of this "one through which the presentation of an infinity of multiples is structured" (ibid., 107). One is thus in a problematic of "supposition" or "truth" in the senses of these terms I have been developing here. In the problematic of "sense," in turn, if one can put it this way, the *some* [*quelque*] comes before the *one as such:* it pre-vents it or it comes before it as the *existing* of a coming-to-the-world.

74. The film title that has become quasi-proverbial, "Is there a pilot in the plane?" is the comic version of the ontotheological question as question of signification, and more precisely of a (signifying/signified) subject of signification. As one may recall, Descartes had already responded "that I am not merely lodged in my body, like the pilot of a boat" ("Meditations on First Philosophy," in *The Philosophical Writings of Descartes,* vol. 2, trans. John Cottingham, Robert Stoothoff, and Dugald Murdoch [Cambridge: Cambridge University Press, 1984], Sixth Meditation, 56).

75. Cf. *sponsi,* those who are fiancés, *sponsor,* the guarantor, and the Greek *spendo,* to make a libation to consecrate an accord or a commitment.

76. On the quasi synonymy of *hekaston* and *eskhaton,* and on the "final matter" (*eskhatē hulē*) that constitutes the individual, cf. *Metaphysics,* Z 10, 1035b28–32 and Tricot's note in his edition. The history of this eschatology is that of the *res singularis* such as one would have to follow it in its development from Aristotle to Ockham and to Francisco Suárez. I would underline here the decisive trait, as traced by Duns Scotus and then by Ockham, which is that the singular singularizes itself through its mere singularity, or that singularity is, of itself, its own "reason" and "agent." (Cf. Alféri, *Guillaume d'Ockham,* 98 ff.) Thus, Alféri comments: "*The identity with itself,* the self-affirmation of being . . . is *naturally unassignable,* unassignable within the horizon of the existent such as it is given to us" (103).

77. Hegel develops the demonstration of this point in the *Science of Logic,* I, 1, chap. 3, "being-for-itself." But it is not sufficient to say that the One is "empty": for this emptiness is *identically* the "fullness" of existing.

78. On the theme of the "whatever," one will do well to reread all of Giorgio Agamben's *The Coming Community,* trans. Michael Hardt (Minneapolis: University of Minnesota Press, 1993).

79. It is evidently the Heideggerian analysis that it would be necessary to take up anew and extend here.

80. Here, too, Leibniz can provide the point of departure, in accordance with the reading Michel Serres gives him in terms of a "*pluralistic philosophy of the example*": "The individual is universally expressive—the monad is the world itself from a point of view: to read, if possible, the complete law engraved onto the monad, to open the universal according to one perspective; in other words, *the individual is the profile of the universal*" (*Le système de Leibniz et ses modèles mathématiques,* vol. 2 [Paris: PUF, 1968], 555).

81. Marc Froment-Meurice, *Tombeau de Trakl* (Paris: Belin, 1992), 133.

82. Cf. Gérard Granel's analysis in "La phénoménologie décapitée," in Dominique Janicaud, *L'intentionnalité: Actes du colloque*: "What we call 'the perceived world' (as if there were other worlds possible, or as if it were a matter of merely one 'level' of The Constitution—in the capitalized singular—'between' nature and spirit) is to the contrary the World *tout court* (*in eo nascimur, movemur et sumus*)."

83. Jorge Luis Borges, "Death and the Compass," in *A Personal Anthology,* ed. Anthony Kerrigan (New York: Grove Press, 1967), 12.

84. Norman Mailer, *The Executioner's Song* (New York: Warner Books, 1979), 328–29. The entire story of Gary Gilmore recounted novelistically by Mailer can be read as the story of a man distraught by sense who ends up plunging into the night of truth.

85. Philippe Lacoue-Labarthe, "Préface" to Jean-Marie Pontévia, *La peinture, masque et miroir,* 2nd ed., vol. 1 (Bordeaux: William Blake, 1993), ix. Further on, Lacoue-Labarthe notes that Pontévia "conceptualized refulgence as 'a sign of nothing particular, merely that there is being' " (xiii). On all of this, cf. also Jacques Derrida, *Memoirs of the Blind,* trans. Pascale-Anne Brault and Michael Naas (Chicago: University of Chicago Press, 1993).

86. Hegel, *Science of Logic,* I, 1, chap. 1, C, remark 2, 93.

87. Cf. Jean-Luc Nancy, "Sur le seuil," written with respect to "The Death of the Virgin" by Michelangelo da Caravaggio, in *Poésie* 64 (1993).

88. Jean-Louis Schefer, *La lumière et la proie* (Paris: Albatros, 1980), 120–21.

89. Cf. Philippe Lacoue-Labarthe, *Musica Ficta,* trans. Felicia McCarren (Stanford, Calif.: Stanford University Press, 1994), 144. In the context of an analysis of what still keeps Adorno within a "religious" apprehension of music, even if in a negative-sublime mode, that is, of what prevents him from taking into account the "end of art" as "end of religion," Lacoue-Labarthe, taking this end into account without reservations, demands finally that one pass from a "beyond of signification" that would still be (a)significant or (over)significant to what I would call a suspended access to sense, or, in a Blanchotian mode, a "step [not] of access" [pas *d'accès*]. I am doing nothing but extending his gesture a bit.

90. Cf. *aiō,* to hear, *aēmi, aisthō,* to breathe, exhale, and the Latin *audio.* In a sense, each sense is an elective site for the very division of senses. . . . Which does not prevent there from being a difference and disparity of elections—indeed, quite the contrary. It will be necessary one day to devote to this question the treatise it requires, and that this supplementary question also requires: how is the division of the senses circumscribed in our tradition, and how does it arise out of a "philosophy of nature"?

91. This is why the discourse of music criticism and aesthetics seems to be affected by an insurmountable internal division: one passes without mediation from the most asignificant technique to the interpretation most charged with sense (with ideas, sentiments, evocations). In the end, one never knows where one has spoken of *music.* But here, too, we are confronted with an elective site for the threshold between signified sense and aisthetic sense. Adorno expresses this by employing the specific category of "musical sense," writing, for example: "An interpretation which does not bother about the music's meaning on the assumption that it will reveal itself of its own accord will inevitably be false since it fails to see that the meaning is always constituting itself anew" ("Bach Defended against His Devotees," *Prisms,* trans. Samuel Weber and Shierry Weber [Cambridge, Mass.: MIT Press, 1981], 144).

92. Anton Chekhov, *Three Sisters,* in *Plays,* trans. Elisaveta Fen (Baltimore: Penguin Books, 1954), 329–30.

93. This invalidates any derivation/sublimation of the political on the basis of love, such as occurs exemplarily in Hegel, but also, to some extent, in Freud, although in the case of the latter this occurs only up to the point where he realizes that it is necessary to add, that is, to substitute, on the level of the political, the enigmatic "identifications" for sublimations of libido. Which doubtless also entails, ultimately, the necessity of understanding "love" quite differently from Freud himself and the Christians along with him, when it is a question of "love thy neighbor," a "commandment

impossible to fulfill" that bears witness for Freud to the "unpsychological proceedings" that the "cultural super-ego" commits (Freud, *Civilization and Its Discontents*, 90). It will be necessary to return to this.

94. Cf. Jean-Luc Nancy, "L'insacrifiable," in *Une pensée finie* (Paris: Galilée, 1990). [In English, "The Unsacrificeable," trans. Richard Livingston, *Yale French Studies* 79 (1991): 20–38. Trans.]

95. Cf. the discussion of the "figure" between Jean-Luc Nancy and Philippe Lacoue-Labarthe, "Scène," *Nouvelle revue de psychanalyse* 46 (1992). This discussion will be continued elsewhere.

96. From among one hundred others, here is a simple phrase, of a simple contemporary obviousness, whose vertiginous political naïveté and ambiguity one would do well to reflect on, without suspecting for a moment the good intentions of its author: "Through which slogans [*mot clés*] could one make a new collective dream come alive?" (*Le pas suspendu de la cigogne,* film by Théos Angelopoulos, 1991).

97. More exactly, this is indeed what has happened to us and is continuing to happen. One will have noted, in the France of 1993, the effect that Pierre Bérégovoy's suicide produced. Regardless of the meaning of this gesture in itself, it will have been understood (one can at least risk this interpretation) as a sacrifice coming in the place of another sacrifice that had become impossible through the loss of the Cause. Thus, it was merely a painful sacrifice, and meanwhile one said and thought that it gave "sense" back to the political. . . . (It was a matter here of the same sacrificial sense that, for America and Europe, surfaced anew during the "Gulf War," with Sovereignty quasi-intact, as I have attempted to show in "War, Law, Sovereignty—*Techné*," trans. Jeffrey S. Librett, in *Rethinking Technologies*, ed. Verena Andermatt Conley on behalf of the Miami Theory Collective [Minneapolis: University of Minnesota Press, 1993], 28–58.) But what is "truly" happening to us is already beyond mourning: unless the mourning is finally becoming effective, without melancholic incorporation and its phantoms.

98. Étienne Balibar uses the term *equaliberty*—while seeing the mutual dependence of equality and liberty as "the political problem par excellence"—to designate "the democratic unlimitation of the process of the extension of rights to all of humanity," and the "right of each to become the 'subject' and actor of politics," it being understood that "no one can be liberated or emancipated by others, from 'on high,' even if this 'on high' were the Law itself or the democratic State" (*Les frontières de la démocratie* [Paris: La Découverte, 1992], 247–48).

99. Carl Schmitt, *Political Theology: Four Chapters on the Concept of Sovereignty,* trans. George Schwab (Cambridge, Mass.: MIT Press, 1985), 36. One must recall that this text was written in 1922.

100. Ibid., 46.

101. On this account, Hans Blumenberg's critique of Carl Schmitt, the affirmation of a nontheological "legitimacy of modern times," of a world permanently in the process of inventing itself, regulated by progress and liberty, would doubtless merit close consideration—but it remains more indebted to a negative theology than it believes, which is this time an anthropology (doubtless in several respects like that of Marx). (See Blumenberg, *The Legitimacy of the Modern Age,* trans. Robert M. Wallace

[Cambridge, Mass.: MIT Press, 1983].) It does not yet touch on the "metaphysics" of the *existence* and of the *world.* Or in a more lapidary formulation, it does not yet arrive at the act and remains at the level of *power* (which forms the crucial point of a deconstruction of metaphysics that would be decisively something other than a new critique internal to its *Kampfplatz*). As a result, it is not certain that it would not be necessary to take up differently the Schmittian theme of the friend/enemy that Blumenberg thinks he can evacuate. But I would not know how to do this for the moment.

102. Schmitt, *Political Theology,* 46.

103. Just one example, from Lou Reed: "Down at his job his boss sits there screaming / if he loses his job, life loses its meaning / his son is in high school / there's nothing he's learning / he sits by the TV" ("Video violence," *Mistrial,* RCA, 1986). In an interview, Johnny Hallyday declared: "At the time, one had no choice. It was either the factory or rock 'n' roll." And as for the "world": "Where are we, Billy? / Nevada? Malakoff? / In the desert / —(The desert is everywhere) . . . ," Kat Onoma, *Billy the Kid,* Fnac Music, 1992.

104. To speak the language of Balibar. Cf. note 98 above.

105. Marx fragment for *Le Capital,* vol. 2 (Paris: Bibliotheque de la Pléiade), 1488.

106. Marx, *Critique of the Gotha Programme,* rev. trans. (New York: International Publishers, 1938), 10.

107. Marx, *Grundrisse: Foundations of the Critique of Political Economy,* trans. Martin Nicolaus (New York: Random House, 1973), 706.

108. Ibid., 611. The formulation of the following question is due to Denis Guénoun.

109. Ibid.

110. Walter Benjamin, "Theses on the Philosophy of History," in *Illuminations,* ed. Hannah Arendt, trans. Harry Zohn (New York: Schocken Books, 1969), 259.

111. Dominique Janicaud designates in this way one of the dimensions he discerns in rationality, the dimension of "Power," to distinguish it from another dimension that "reserves a possibility" and for which "no surprise is excluded." As he puts it, this "division" of rationality "comes to contest . . . all sovereignty of Sense, all exclusive diction" (*La puissance du rationnel* [Paris: Gallimard, 1985], 346–48). But is it not rather necessary to have a presentiment of sense and of the sovereignty of sense—undecidably powerful and null—in the very dehiscence of the "rational"? It does not suffice to arm oneself in advance against an "exclusive" domination: beyond this, it is necessary that that make sense: this is the general form of our problems.

112. *Oikos,* house, habitation, family, whose root refers also to "village" and "group." *Domus* was its familiar and habitable figure, a figure that is being ruined today by "the great megapolitan spatial monad" according to which "metaphysics is realized in the physics, broad sense, operating in the techno-science of today. . . . domestication, if you will, but with no *domus.* A physics with no god-nature. An economy in which everything is taken, nothing received," according to Jean-François Lyotard, "*Domus* and the Megalopolis," in *The Inhuman: Reflections on Time,* trans. Geoffrey Bennington and Rachel Bowlby (Cambridge: Polity Press, 1991), 199. Lyotard nonetheless specifies that the *domus* "probably never existed" and that consequently "thought today makes no appeal, cannot appeal, to the memory which is tradition" (201–2). He concludes

from this that there remains only to "bear witness, and again, and for no-one, to thinking as disaster, nomadism, difference and redundancy" (203). Each of these terms is thus understood as a form of the definitively ruined extreme of "metaphysics." Lyotard's gesture has all the rigor and gravity of the last—interminable—gesture of philosophy. I merely wish to raise two objections: (1) Each designation of the extreme has already silently and inevitably been returned or extravasated into itself and has exscribed itself qua sense. That is, it has not been taken up again or sublated into another signification, but reopened onto unlimited significance. And to be sure, neither exscription nor opening occurs without some suffering. This is the point where one must ask which suffering is torture and which is existential painfulness (itself not more tolerable, however, than torture). (2) Lyotard speaks here of the philosopher as a *laborer* in thought and writing, a worker who finds him-/herself "inoperative" in this sense, not so much in *thinking* itself, but, rather, in the thinking and thinking-itself of sense along the surface of the existence of everyone in the world. I myself have said that a certain philosophical work-production is obsolete (as one says of machines), and that it is necessary to make a change on the level of philosophical style (and Lyotard does this and has been doing it, along with a number of others, exemplarily since he began writing!)—and, moreover, this is not new, it is perhaps for this reason that there has been philosophy ever since the beginning of philosophy, assuming one can date such a thing. But that sense should be in books of philosophy—whatever their style—this is indeed a metaphysical-megapolitan trap. Sense is in the exscription of the book, sense is *that sense does not stop coming from elsewhere and going elsewhere,* indeed, all the way to the confines of the "great monad," exposing it in itself, and this is what the laborer-philosopher inscribes. But the other laborer (this other that the "philosopher" is *also* in his body, in the ecotechnics of his work) is otherwise *along the surface of* this coming of sense. I mean: praxis is not lacking in him, whether as reform or revolt, migration or habitation, pain or joy, invention or routine, or as decision endlessly replayed. A secular melancholy of the Occident should not blind itself on this point: that this melancholy itself is a descendant of the division between the two kinds of labor, and that the philosopher risks being melancholy because he *believed* himself already to be in the place of "free" labor, whereas he *believed* the other to be simply in the place of servitude. But it is not so simple, even though, in all evidence, it is also not the reverse. For the moment, it remains—and it seems to me urgent—to say the following: let us not decipher the world in terms of our philosophical melancholy—no more than in terms of a maniacal optimism that is another form of the same thing. But let us learn to think *toward* the world.

113. I am evoking here the conclusions drawn by Fernand Braudel in *La dynamique du capitalisme* (Paris: Arthaud, 1985).

114. At this point, one must above all avoid confusing the access to sense with "leisure," which is nothing, as one henceforth can see, but an economic notion within the economy (on which has been superimposed, of course, a nostalgic image of the *scholé,* the beautiful leisure of the free man and, more precisely, as if by chance, of the philosopher . . .). We are not at "leisure" to deliver ourselves up or not to the meditation of sense. Sense comes to us and traverses us urgently and necessarily. This is why it is a matter of making it possible for "the time of nonlabor . . . [to] cease to be *op-*

posed to labor time," thus making it possible for "the individuals [to be] much more demanding, concerning the nature, content, goals, and organization of labor [and no longer to accept] 'idiot work' or to be submitted to an oppressive surveillance and hierarchy," so that "the liberation *of* work will have led to liberation in work, without, however, transforming work (as Marx imagined) into a free personal activity.... Heteronomy cannot, in a complex society, be completely suppressed for the sake of autonomy" (André Gorz, *Métamorphoses du travail: Quête du sens* [Paris: Galilée, 1988], 119). These propositions may appear "idealist," and in fact, I am not certain that André Gorz, despite the precision and necessity of his proposals, is in a position to respond to all of the questions I have raised above. Nonetheless, it is no longer Fourier dreaming here. It is *ecotechnics* itself that develops, even in its contradictions, the possibility, that is, the necessity, of another "labor." It is thus that it can appear necessary to speak today of "the first crisis of postfordism" as of a crisis in which the new "productive valorization," insofar as it implies in many respects the initiative of the workers, "is radically opposed to [international] control" by "the instruments of monetary-financial control" (Toni Negri, "La première crise du postfordisme," *Futur antérieur* 16:2 [1993]). A first version of this part on labor was published in the same review, 18:4 (1993).

115. A first version of this part was written for the colloquium *Subject and Citizen*, organized by the review *Intersignes* (Fethi Ben Slama and Abdelwahab Meddeb) at Monastir, Tunesia, in May 1993. The review will be publishing the proceedings of the colloquium.

116. Hegel, *Philosophy of Right*, trans. T. M. Knox (London: Oxford University Press, 1967), sect. 258, 157.

117. Precisely, religion provides the knowledge of the origin (of the State) as appropriation of negativity and thus as violence, which knowledge appeases or places at a distance in a sacrificial or metasacrificial mode. But the politics of the Subject (let us say, even, of the State in this sense—but today's "State" turns away also from this schema) nonetheless remains marked, fascinated, by this foundational violence that it pre-supposes. But it is not a matter of presupposing the reverse, an original love: it is a matter of not presupposing that the tie is given.

118. Karl Marx, *Le capital*, 2nd ed., vol. 1, ed. Jean-Pierre Lefebvre (Paris: PUF, 1993), 680.

119. To avoid all ambiguity, it is necessary to point out that religion has nothing to do with the tie [*lien*], contrary to what a counterfeit etymology pretends. *Religio* is scrupulous observation, and consequently, it implies that the knot is already tied or given.

120. Jean-Jacques Rousseau, *On the Social Contract. Discourse on the Origin of Equality: Discourse on Political Economy*, trans. and ed. Donald A. Cress (Indianapolis: Hackett, 1983), bk. 1, chap. 8, 26–27.

121. [Cf. Jean-Luc Nancy and Jean-Christophe Bailly, *La comparution* (Paris: Christian Bourgois, 1991). Trans.]

122. Giorgio Agamben, "Forme-de-vie," *Futur antérieur* 15 (1993).

123. Although it may astonish a certain number of readers, this says nothing other than Lacan himself: "To be a subject is something other than to be a gaze before another gaze.... it is to have one's site in the great *A*, in the place of speech" (*Le sémi-

naire, bk. 8, *Le transfert* [Paris: Seuil, 1991], 299). To make this more precise, since it is a matter of vocabulary: in order to be the "place of speech," the "great *A*" would have to remove its excessive dimensions from the "great" and the excessive essentiality from the "*A*." Some consonance, at least, is necessary to the *a*: several speaking beings are necessary, as well as their interlacing. But a matter of vocabulary—of choice of words and therefore also of images and affects—*is* at once also a matter of politics. It is thus perhaps insufficient to distinguish between the empirical Father and the symbolic Father: it is necessary also to think about what the use of the word *Father will have already become tied up with,* on the levels of the imaginary and the symbolic. In this regard, it seems to me indispensable to formulate the originary instance of speaking in the direction opened up by Nicolas Abraham (who calls it "the source of significance of language"): "The very notion of the Father" has to appear in the first place, and it therefore cannot generate significance itself or be a signification anterior to the latter. Nicolas Abraham writes: "*Language draws its significance from the fact that it gives itself as a communion in the lie about the anasemic desire of Clinging,*" which can be translated—to avoid entering here into the details of the Abrahamian conceptuality—as "a lie about the desire of immanence at the origin." Thus, "*To speak is to render present a phantom with the requirement that it not take on a body,*" since it has already been rendered null by the fact of the speaking community" (*L'écorce et le noyau* [Paris: Aubier-Montaigne, 1978], 386). In other words, significance originates in the separation and relation that presents Presence as always already absented by the relation itself. (I will introduce, however, a reservation on the concept of "lie," which still maintains too much solidarity with a "truth" supposed to precede it, not without remarking that the "lie" introduces ipso facto, and more surely than truth, the dimension of community.)

124. Which Jacques Rancière determines as the proper activity of the "aleatory network of individuals" who are held, or have fallen, far away from given senses and identifications (cf. "Après quoi?" in *Après le sujet qui vient, Confrontations* 20 [1989]. In English, "After What?" trans. Christian Davis, in *Who Comes after the Subject?* [New York and London: Routledge, 1991], 246–52). To speak of "wandering" is not supposed to induce here a kind of generalized drift but, rather, a necessary dimension of the "democratic invention," to take up Claude Lefort's word: "The democracy we know instituted itself by savage paths, under the effect of claims that have turned out to be unmasterable" (*L'invention démocratique* [Paris: Fayard, 1981], 28). The democracy that is still coming, that is in coming itself and in the tying of (k)nots, passes and will pass by way of other savage paths.

125. Michel Deguy, *Arrêts fréquents* (Paris: A.-M. Métailié, 1990), 115.

126. Walter Benjamin, *The Origin of German Tragic Drama,* trans. John Osborne (London: NLB, 1977), 215.

127. Michel Deguy, *Aux heures d'affluence* (Paris: Seuil, 1993), 181.

128. Rainer Maria Rilke, *Notizen zur Melodie der Dinge,* in *Sämtliche Werke,* vol. 5 (Frankfurt am Main: Insel-Verlag, 1965), 416–25.

129. Bataille, "Le petit," *Oeuvres complètes,* vol. 3, 40. The Germans call a remote place "the ass of the world" (*Arsch der Welt*).

130. One could say, for example, the event is not the execution of Louis XVI, but

that the king becomes executable and the leader culpable.

131. I am keeping myself here in constant and problematic proximity to the stakes, or to the only stake, of the great modern philosophical statements on art, from Hegel (the sensible presentation of the Idea) passing by way of Nietzsche (the apotropaic access to the abyss of truth) to Heidegger (the *Dichtung* of truth).

132. Which would point to some, at least, of the analyses of affect that have been carried out by Nicolas Abraham, in particular to this definition: "A lived experience, already act, but not yet an act of transcendence—the *affect*" (*L'écorce et le noyau,* 80).

133. *Hegel's Philosophy of Subjective Spirit,* ed. and trans. M. J. Petry, vol. 2, *Anthropology* (Dordrecht: D. Reidel, 1979), addition to sec. 401, 167.

134. Two remarks: (1) What is said here must be understood as applying to all that we call "sensible," starting beyond the mere "sensorial" sphere, which is itself nothing but an already abstract division; it is a matter of the sensual and the sentimental, of affect and sense in all of their extensions. Finally, it is a matter of *sense* insofar as it would be: being touched by existing. (2) One can imagine the consequences to be drawn concerning the desire for a "great art" as "total art," whether in the mode of a sublime synthesis from Kant to Wagner, or in the mode of a subsumption of all the arts beneath the art of "poesy," from Kant again and Hegel to Heidegger. I point here again to Lacoue-Labarthe's analyses concerning Wagner, Heidegger, and Mallarmé in *Musica ficta.*

135. This reading of the end of the "religion of art" in Hegel's *Phenomenology* is carried out and justified in "Portrait de l'art en jeune fille" (in Jean-Luc Nancy, *Le poids d'une pensée* [Montréal and Grenoble: Le Griffon d'Argile, 1991], and in *L'art moderne et la question du sacré,* ed. Jean-Jacques Nillès [Paris: Cerf, 1993]). It goes without saying that a finer investigation would have to show precisely how art has not ceased to be born since Plato, Aristotle, and Plotinus, even when the subsumption of art beneath the intelligible is the organizing theme. Art appears as soon as sense makes itself atheistic: but this is no doubt as old as Lascaux. Art is more "primitive" than any schema of primitivity and progression, any schema of the advance of knowledge or the flight of the gods. And the same goes for the world.

136. Hegel, *Aesthetics,* vol. 1, trans. T. M. Knox (Oxford: Clarendon Press, 1975), 73, 90. To be precise, one must add that the side of the "concept" can conquer for itself, in terms (and according to the general economy) of the *Aesthetics,* neither its autonomy nor its interior unity: it remains as such deprived of sensible life, color, and taste. This is, in the final analysis, what is at stake in the impossible dialectical step from "poetry" to "thought," as also in the nonsublatable contradiction within poetry itself, for poetry does not stop coming back to the sensible in the very moment when it is about to dissolve the sensible. The infamous "end of art" is at the very least, to put it quickly, only half of Hegel's thought here. The other half is the "vast Pantheon" of different arts, art as difference of presentation. And this itself belongs to the necessity of thought, for the latter "in a relative sense is indeed abstract, but it must be concrete, not one-sided" (72). That concrete thought gives itself in a dialectical Christology does not prevent the latter from engendering "Christian art," which culminates, *never to finish,* in the intimate contradiction of poetry-thought (and/or poetry-prose), and consequently in the unachievable "Pantheon." I will show elsewhere how that can

be read right off the page of Hegel's text.

137. In the text of the *Phenomenology.* This remarkable turn in Hegel escaped, in particular, Heidegger's notice, although the latter knew quite well that Hegel was not affirming the end of the production of art, but the end of the necessity of its presentation. But it is also this necessity that Hegel not only maintains but installs philosophically despite himself. By this very fact, Heidegger's interpretation of art finds itself at once in advance of and lagging behind Hegel's own account. A long analysis would be necessary, but I will note the principle of such an analysis briefly here: Heidegger's understanding of art is "in advance of" Hegel, insofar as it is an understanding of art as "opening of a world," that is, of the set of "relations" and their "joints" where "this being-open of the There is the essence of *truth*" (and my own approach owes much to this understanding: it is indeed a matter of a presentation of presentation or of coming). But Heidegger's understanding of art "lags behind" Hegel's to the extent that the relationship to the "earth" as "depth and closedness of the abyss," itself in a relationship to the divine that is implied by the paradigm of the "temple," seems to me to reenclose art within another sacredness that is also the same (to which is then added the assignation of the "people"). It is not that one must object to Heidegger that the world is "pure" opening: in a sense, this world here is indeed "the earth." But it is the earth-world, and without gods, if not without places altogether. (Cf. Heidegger, "The Origin of the Work of Art," in *Poetry, Language, Thought,* trans. Albert Hofstadter [New York: Harper & Row, 1975].)

138. Or else it is the reverse: God absents himself when art arrives. And yet art is always arriving, ceaselessly renewed since Lascaux, whereas "God" (sense knotted into the dialectics of transcendence and immanence) will have merely signaled the occidental trajectory. In this sense, the divine figures of ancient art have nothing to do with the divinity of God. Hegel is thus right to see art there, but he is wrong to see there a moment of religion, destined to pass into revealed religion, then into thought. However, the Christian-philosophical (or Judeo-Christian-philosophical and also Islamic) God is also not determined as a pure exteriority to the pagan "divine," no more than the latter, in its other aspect, is simply identical to "art" (of which it has, in a sense, no concept). The mixture of these distinctions is, to the contrary, at the very origin of the Occident. This is indeed why the most extreme ambiguity of occidental art occurs in the superb effervescence of Christian art (the one that Hegel is silent about in the *Phenomenology* but celebrates, in the *Aesthetics,* with fascination, above all, in the form of painting). Christianity represents the undecidably aesthetic and theological exigency of a "sensible presentation of the Idea." The Idea incarnates itself here, but the incarnation dialecticizes itself, denies or sacrifices the fragmentation that the sensible is. The body of God may well be presented in a multitude of pieces of bread—this "bread and wine" that will have haunted Hegel, Hölderlin, Mallarmé...—in the end it is his *corpus mysticum* that is consumed. On this account, art appears as a eucharist (the "gift of a grace") that remains in broken fragments, that consists in their fragmentation. A eucharist without communion. A eucharist that would be the deconstruction of the eucharist. Still, if deconstruction must effectively set adrift the pieces of the assemblage and must dislocate it (fragment it) in order to break the path [*frayer la voie*] of another sense, then the disassembled "art" of "religion" can, no doubt, no more remain "art"

than "religion." The aestheticotheological has not finished causing us trouble.

139. Marx, *Grundrisse: Foundations of the Critique of Political Economy,* 111: "A man cannot become a child again or he becomes childish. But does he not find joy in the child's naïveté, and must he himself not strive to reproduce its truth at a higher stage?" Do this native truth of art and this return of sense-being-born have to do also with "emancipated labor"?

140. Immanuel Kant, *Critique of Judgment,* trans. Werner S. Pluhar (Indianapolis: Hackett, 1987), sec. 29, "General Comment on the Exposition of Aesthetic Reflective Judgments," 139. Kant picks up this point again with respect to Epicurus. Cf. sec. 54.

141. This is the reason why, when one speaks of such matters, the chances are that a poem rather than expository prose will be the result. Thus, to take an arbitrary example, Michel Butor writes (in 1973) about Pierre Alechinsky: "His soluble gaze surrounded / by the turban of exquisite odors / with the noise of his studio / and kisses on the windows" (*Pierre Alechinsky: Extraits pour traits,* ed. Michel Sicard [Paris: Galilée, 1989], 105). Still, it is too simple to deny *jouiscience.* Signification and discourse do not occur without pleasure or pain. But this is not my object here.

142. [Nancy examines this Freudian notion as it develops in *Jokes and Their Relation to the Unconscious* and in *Three Essays on the Theory of Sexuality* in "In Statu Nascendi," in *The Birth to Presence,* trans. Brian Holmes et al. (Stanford, Calif.: Stanford University Press, 1993), 211–33. Trans.]

143. Which does not mean that pleasure and art are distributed simply in accordance with the five senses of an abstract sensoriality. Sensuality fragments otherwise, up to a certain point. But it fragments nonetheless.

144. In order to follow the—obvious—thread of *jouissance* here, one would have to reread Jacques Derrida's "Pas I," *Gramma* 3–4 (1976): 111–215, a text dedicated to coming and to the command "Come" as its structure or law.

145. The things one throws into the urn, the suffrage of the citizens, belong also to the family of the fragment. *Suffrage* is a portmanteau word made of "symbol" and "fragment" . . .

146. Cf. *Kernos* 5 (1992), "L'élément orgiastique dans la religion grecque ancienne," Centre d'études de la religion grecque antique, Athens-Liège. See in particular the article by A. Motte and V. Pirenne-Delforge, "Le mot et les rites: Aperçu des significations de *orgia* et de quelques dérivés." Cf. also Pauly-Wissowa, who underlines the initially nonecstatic character of the word's signification.

147. [Cf. Jean-Luc Nancy, *La communauté désoeuvrée* (Paris: Christian Bourgois, 1986), and its English translation as *The Inoperative Community,* ed. Peter Connor, trans. Peter Connor, Lisa Garbus, Michael Holland, and Simona Sawhney (Minneapolis: University of Minnesota Press, 1991). Trans.]

148. "In the earliest Antiquity, there were no rules; the Supreme Simplicity had not yet divided itself. Once the Supreme Simplicity divides itself the rule establishes itself. On what is the rule founded? The rule is founded on the unique stroke of the brush" (Shitao, *Propos sur la peinture du moine Citrouille-amère,* trans. P. Ryckmans [Paris: Hermann, 1984], 9). The pictorial or technical metaphysics of a Chinese man in the seventeenth century comes before the ancient Occident. This is not a model, but a stroke, trace, or touch. For all that, I am not forgetting that the *templum* is, first

of all, a trace delimiting a sacred space. But the condition of the world is that nothing/all is sacred: the world is a temple, there is only one trace, and that which is to be thought is not its beyond but its unique/multiple fractal curve. (The dialectics of the temple and its destruction dissolves as world. Cf. Jean-Luc Nancy, "L'indestructible," *Intersignes* 2 [1992].)

149. On the proximity of the problematics of *metron* and *kairos,* cf. E. Moutsopoulos, "Musique et états orgiastiques chez Platon," in *Kernos* 5 (1992).

150. Claude Lévi-Strauss, *Regarder écouter lire* (Paris: Plon, 1993), 157.

151. Marlen Haushofer, *The Wall,* trans. Shaun Whiteside (Pittsburgh: Cleis Press, 1990), 209–10.

152. Arthur Schopenhauer, *The World as Will and Idea,* vol. 1, trans. R. B. Haldane and J. Kemp (London: Routledge & Kegan Paul, 1883), 419.

153. Interview published in *Le monde,* 7 May 1993, 30, taken and translated by Pierre Deshusses. That there is no longer time for boredom is confirmed by the henceforth anachronistic character of Heidegger's analysis of boredom from 1930: "The absence of oppressiveness is what fundamentally oppresses and leaves us most profoundly empty, i.e., the *fundamental emptiness that bores us.* . . . For in all the organizing and program-making and trial and error there is ultimately a universal smug contentment in not being endangered" (*Fundamental Concepts of Metaphysics,* 164). This brief quotation suffices to measure a historical distance that is also the distance between what Heidegger, in 1930, could call the task of "configuring" or "forming, fashioning" the world (*die, eine Welt bilden*)—a task he had several reasons for recognizing in certain aspects of the Nazi will—and the task we ought to recognize today. We do not begin with boredom, but with a disorientation that knows itself to be its only resource. We do not want to "*bilden*" the world, we want this world here.

154. Lacoue-Labarthe, *La poésie comme expérience* (Paris: Christian Bourgois, 1986), 165.

155. And this is also why to identify it with the figure of the "Jew" is already to condemn it: worldliness has come from the Occident *insofar* as the Occident is Greek-Jewish-Roman-German and none of these names taken by itself, along with several others, Arab, Slav, Etruscan . . . : in truth the enumeration and the distinction of Names is always a sacralizing (or sacrificial) operation. One needs names, but one needs them insofar as "what the name calls in discovering it and in dissimulating it . . . calls the name, as if the name called itself, but without closing itself again upon itself. . . . an opening that cannot be seized as such" (Alexander García Düttmann, *La parole donnée* [Paris: Galilée, 1989], 73). Names are necessity *to the world*: the world is the totality of names that call from each to each, and the fractal outline of these calls as all of sense.

156. This ambiguity, analyzed in the relationships a certain number of writers have had to literature itself, is the object of Denis Hollier's *Les dépossédés* (Paris: Minuit, 1993). Hollier speaks of an "aesthetic promotion of constraint" "that has broken with the principle of the agreeable, which requires the association of pleasure and freedom" and that has to do with "the properly aesthetic seduction exercised on men of letters by the evocation of a literal world, a world without metaphor, in which there would no longer be a place for art" (196). In more than one respect, I am in accord with this

sentiment, and also with this corollary, his plea "for the profane" (19) as opposed to sacrality or its "laicized" absence. Further, Hollier is right to implicate philosophy, which "will always prefer sadness because it has at least the advantage of always wanting to say something or, which comes down to the same, of suffering from not being able to do so. It addresses itself to the need of sense, respects it, satisfies it" (103). However, he seems to neglect this other side of the analysis: the intimate struggle of these writers against a facility of aesthetic pleasure constituted also the real, difficult, serious, and necessary experience—with which it is easier for us to begin to be finished because it was done before us—of what one could risk calling the "tragedy of the tragic": arriving at one's own limit in the face of what is indeed the question—or the coming—of the *world.* It is indeed certain that the matter at hand resides in a distance, let us say, on the level of "style," with respect to the tragic and the dialectical (or the philosophical). It is not certain, nonetheless, that gaiety and mixing, in a Bakhtinian and Joycean vein or, today, as "hybridity" [*métisse*], suffice simply, even if they are necessary, to what is at stake in the world. It is not certain that there is not a trap there, too. This is the point beyond which it is necessary for us to take the risk of styles and the expectant search for what is coming. In the meantime, it is not a matter of indifference that the "vein" of which I have spoken is that of Salman Rushdie in *The Satanic Verses* (New York: Viking, 1988), whose end I will cite here for what it says about a coming: "Childhood was over, and the view from this window was no more than an old and sentimental echo. To the devil with it! Let the bulldozers come. If the old refused to die, the new could be born. 'Come along,' Zeenat Vakil's voice said at his shoulder.... 'Let's get the hell out of here.' 'I'm coming,' he answered her, and turned away from the view" (547). The bulldozer is perhaps a style that is worthy of discussion, and the "new" may well be a category that remains imprisoned to "progress." But it is necessary also to know how to say, "I'm coming."

157. Samuel Beckett, *Le monde et le pantalon* (Paris: Minuit, 1989), 7.

158. As an example of the limits of our phrases: organ transplants are the object of a public discourse of the gift, communication, progress, and exploit of a "miraculous" survival to which there is nothing to object; a body that has received a transplant, however, is also in truth a body that has exploded, not by virtue of a phantasm of the "foreign body," but as a function of the multiple alterations and dependencies that the transplant introduced along with it in order to survive: the control through lowering of the immune system, control of secondary effects, inscription in a space that is no longer simply that of "life" or of "illness," chemical and hygienic training, *teknē* installed for good, the slow lesson of the inanity of *phusis.* And yet this type of condition concerns more and more other bodies, the sick, the aged, compromised, handicapped, assisted, pieced-together bodies. There is a "salvation" here that we do not know how to say because it is not a salvation. It is also not a "maintenance." It is another inscription, a narrower one, in the world.

159. Cf., closest to us, *Les Bosniaques* by Velibor Colic (Paris: Galilée, 1993).

160. The French word *heur* (which is still used in the expression "avoir l'heur de plaire," to have the good fortune to meet with someone's approval) comes from *augurium,* (good or bad) omen, and then designates (good or bad) chance or fate. By an effect of phonetic proximity, expressions such as "à la bonne heure" (right, very good)

and "à la mal heure" (wrong) used to bring together the values of chance and instant.

161. [Cf. Jean-Luc Nancy, "Manque de rien," in *Lacan avec les philosophes*, Natalia Avtonomova et al. (Paris: Albin Michel, 1991), 201–6. Trans.]

162. *Complete Poetry of Osip Emilevich Mandelstam*, trans. Burton Raffel and Alla Burago (Albany: State University of New York Press, 1973), 268. The poem is dated from 19 January to 4 February 1937. Mandelstam had been under arrest since 1934.

163. Jean-Louis Chrétien, in a very penetrating article on the "spatiality" of "being in advance of oneself:" "De l'espace au lieu dans la pensée de Heidegger" (From space to place in Heidegger's thought), *Revue de l'enseignement philosophique*, 32nd year, 3 (February-March 1982).

164. Emmanuel Lévinas, *Dieu, la mort et le temps* (Paris: Grasset, 1993), 152. In these courses from the 1970s more than anywhere else, perhaps, Lévinas's thought is close to the thought of the world. When he says, "Is sense always an event of being? Being—is this the significance of sense?" (69), and when he refuses to respond positively, in order to give sense a more advanced and exalted place, in "my responsibility for the death of the other," I am in accord with his refusal if what he is refusing is "that all that is at stake in being is being itself." But *being* means nothing other than the fact of the world, and the world is the fact of sense qua transitivity of existence: that it is exposed, to "itself" as much as to "the other." Without this infinite resolution of fact into sense and of sense into fact, the absenting of God that Lévinas ceaselessly indicates, moreover, cannot occur.

165. Claude Morali puts it this way: "*I*, even in the sense of transcendental ego, does not arise except at the issue of my birth, that is, of the edification of the sense of my coming into the world. A consciousness that would not posit its origin in the alienation of a birth could not be a first person. In this respect, the biblical text granting to an infinite being the utterances "I am that I am" (at least according to the traditional readings) might appear absurd. Heidegger's philosophy has accustomed us to linking the appearance of the *I* in a consciousness with the intimate conviction of its own death: it would seem more just to make it depend upon the nonknowledge implied by its birth" (*Qui est moi aujourd'hui?* [Paris: Fayard, 1984], 278).

166. [The passage is drawn from "Fantaisie," a poem by Gérard de Nerval, in *Oeuvres*, ed. A. Béguin and Jean Richir (Paris: Gallimard, 1952), 48. Trans.]

167. The French *y* (there) comes from *ibi*, "there, in this place," and from *hic*, "here" and "in this moment." Beyond its locative value, it can function as a pronoun, referring to a noun or an entire proposition, as in "y penser," "to think of it." For the lexicologist, it "does not have any analyzable meaning in diverse expressions such as *il y a* [there is], *il y va de* [it concerns there], *savoir y faire* [to know what to do there], *ça y est* [there we are], etc." (*Dictionnaire historique de la langue française*, ed. Alain Rey [Paris: Le Robert, 1992]). *Avoir* seems to retain here [in the *a* of *il y a*] a primary value of *habere*, "to take, occupy, inhabit." In old French, "il y a" could also be formulated as "y a," and even "a."

168. And with an articulation that is not simply linguistic: which means that language itself is not simply linguistic, precisely in that it is pre-vented by the significance of sense.

169. Cf. Albert Jacquard, *Voici le temps du monde fini* (Paris: Seuil, 1991), 28 ff. So

much for physics. As for the politics and morals of the earth, and as for the necessity of their becoming worldly, I will content myself with being lapidary with August Strindberg: "The upper class takes all that is on earth for itself and offers the heaven to the lower class" (*Petit catéchisme à l'usage de la classe inférieure* [Arles: Axtes Sud, 1982], 15).

170. Ecologism is always much too pusillanimous in philosophy: it limits itself either to the pragmatic argument of the preservation of the conditions of life or to the puerile enchantment of a vague animism.

171. Granel, "Le monde et son expression," 53.

172. This would be the condition of philosophical seriousness. Wittgenstein exposes it this way: "If someone who believes in God looks round and asks 'Where does everything I see come from?, 'Where does all this come from?', he is not craving for a (causal) explanation; and his question gets its point from being the expression of a certain craving. He is, namely, expressing an attitude to all explanations.—But how is this manifested in his life? / The attitude that's in question is that of taking a certain matter seriously and then, beyond a certain point, no longer regarding it as serious, but maintaining that something else is even more important" (*Culture and Value,* ed. Georg Henrik von Wright and Heikki Nyman, trans. Peter Winch [Chicago: University of Chicago Press, 1984], 85e).

173. "Being in the world does not mean being among the things that form the totality of what is, but, rather, being in a 'total' way among that which is. Because we are in the world in a 'total' way, we have never been, in relation to the world, in an outside by leaving which we would have penetrated into the interior of that world. Because we are there in a total way, we have, in a sense, never 'come into the world.' . . . the mystery to be elucidated is not to know *how* we have been able to enter into the world, but of constating that we have never entered into it, that we have always already been in the world" (Rémi Brague, *Aristote et la question du monde* [Paris: PUF, 1988], 44–45). It is on this basis that Brague's reflection becomes a reflection on the Aristotelian "act," which he goes on to characterize in this way: "'Acts' are situations such that we are 'in' them. But 'within' them to such a point that we cannot enter into them. We are in them or not." He proposes, as a consequence of this, that one seek the secret of the meaning of the words *energeia* and *entelechheia* "in the prefix, quite discreet, that they have in common: *en.* What does it mean, indeed, to be in something? With *energeia,* we are in the work, in its interior . . . we were never 'outside.' . . . *energeia* is the Aristotelian name for being-in-the-world" (492–93)—and further on: "The presence of perception or thinking is not that of a thing that would act on other things. Presence in the world and presence *of* the world, at the limit, coincide" (496): this coincidence takes place, indeed, as the internal limit of the sensible entelechy, the outline of the world.

174. Cf. *Spanne* above.

175. Jean Arp, *Jours effeuillés* (Paris: Gallimard, 1966), 76. The text is from 1931.

176. [The phrase is the title of a novel by André Gide, *Si le grain ne meurt* (Paris: Gallimard, 1955), originally published in 1921, in English as *If It Die,* trans. Dorothy Bussy (London: Secker and Warburg, 1950), which refers in turn to the New Testament, John 12:24, "Except a corn of wheat fall into the ground and die, it abideth

alone: but if it die, it bringeth forth much fruit." Trans.]

177. Kant, *Critique of Pure Reason,* "The Schematism of the Pure Concepts of Understanding," 184.

178. Flaubert, *The Temptation of Saint Antony,* trans. Kitty Mrosovsky (Ithaca, N. Y.: Cornell University Press, 1981), 232.

179. Maurice Merleau-Ponty, *The Prose of the World,* ed. Claude Lefort, trans. John O'Neill (Evanston, Ill.: Northwestern University Press, 1973), xiii.

180. [In English in the original. Trans.]

181. Bataille, *Oeuvres complètes,* vol. 3, 114.

182. Virginia Woolf, *Orlando: A Biography* (London: Hogarth Press, 1990), 167–68.

Index

Jean-Luc Nancy teaches at the University of Human Sciences in Strasbourg, France. Of his numerous books, those to appear thus far in English include *The Literary Absolute: The Theory of Literature in German Romanticism* (with Philippe Lacoue-Labarthe), *The Inoperative Community* (University of Minnesota Press, 1991), *The Title of the Letter: A Reading of Lacan* (with Philippe Lacoue-Labarthe), *The Birth to Presence, The Experience of Freedom,* and *The Muses.*

Jeffrey S. Librett is associate professor of modern languages and literatures at Loyola University Chicago. He is the author of numerous essays on various philosophical and literary authors, including Immanuel Kant, Friedrich Schiller, Friedrich Schlegel, Friedrich Nietzsche, Martin Heidegger, Martin Buber, Paul de Man, and Jean-Luc Nancy. Librett has widely translated criticism from German and French into English, including *Of the Sublime: Presence in Question.*